Chapter by Chapter

An easy to use summary of the entire Bible

Written by
Troy Schmidt

Chapter by Chapter
An Easy to Use Summary of the Entire Bible

ISBN-13: 978-1499610239
ISBN-10: 1499610238

Table of Contents

The Old Testament

The New Testament

Introduction by the Author

The Bible has 929 chapters in the Old Testament and 260 Chapters in the New Testament.

And all of them point to one thing – God.

They prove that He is real, that He loves his people and has a plan for them. Every chapter reveals that He'll stop at nothing to make sure His love reigns forever.

However, getting through 1189 chapters is not easy. From Genesis to Revelation, over 2,000 years of history is covered, not including creation or the eternity that lovers of God await.

That history is written by over 40 authors, from a variety of backgrounds. Their style and purpose for writing the books may be different, but all of them synchronize perfectly to communicate God's plan for salvation through Jesus Christ.

Every believer should read through the Bible at least once in their lifetime, but everyone needs some help. This book cannot be the Cliff Notes replacement for reading the Bible, though, like Cliff Notes it is meant to be a companion to be carried alongside the Bible.

CHAPTER-BY-CHAPTER gives a paragraph summary of every chapter of the Bible, allowing the reader to quickly understand what each chapter says. I have not injected my perspective into the chapter nor explained what it means, just given you a simple summary of what it says.

As a teacher, pastor and producer for "The American Bible Challenge" game show, I have been through the Bible many times, appreciating its beauty and hoping more and more would dig into its pages. I hope this book helps you know God better as you study His word more deeply.

Troy Schmidt, July 2014

THE OLD TESTAMENT

GENESIS

Number of Chapters: *50*
Most likely author: *Moses*
Approximate time span: The beginning of time to the 1800s BC

GENESIS 1

God created the heavens and the earth, from the stars in the universe to the seeds on the ground. The creation timeline was explained using a framework of six days.

- Day 1 – Light
- Day 2 – Sky
- Day 3 – Land and sea
- Day 4 – Sun, moon, stars
- Day 5 – Birds and fish
- Day 6 – Land animals and man

All of God's creation he called "Good." On the sixth day, God created man in the likeness of Himself. When God saw it all, he called it "Very good."

GENESIS 2

On the seventh day, God rested, or ceased from creating any longer. He made that day holy. The perspective shifts looking back at the sixth day and specifically the garden in Eden where God created man from the dust of the ground. God created tasty fruit trees, but two in particular – the tree of life and the tree of knowledge of good and evil. He commanded man to not eat from the tree of the knowledge of good and evil. Seeing that man was alone, God brought all the animals to him. After Adam named the animals, God saw it was not good that man was alone, so he allowed him to sleep and made a woman from the rib of man. The concept of marriage was started—a man left his father and mother and became one flesh with a woman. They were sinless and pure with nothing to hide (referenced by their nakedness with no shame).

GENESIS 3

The serpent – Satan – caused Eve to doubt God's commands about eating from the tree of the knowledge of good and evil. He tempted Eve, who ate the fruit, then gave some to Adam, who also ate the fruit. They realized, when their eyes are opened, that they were naked. They hid from God and blamed others for their sin. The serpent, Adam and Eve all received punishments that would change their lives, cause separation and made life more difficult, eventually leading to death. Adam and Eve were kicked out of Eden, away from the tree of life (or eternal life). Eden was closed, off limits to mankind.

GENESIS 4

Adam and Eve gave birth to Cain – a farmer – then Abel – a shepherd. Cain's offerings to God were rejected by Him while Abel's (fat portions) was accepted. Cain sulked. God questioned Cain about his attitude. Cain invited Abel into the field and murdered him. God banished Cain from farming and caused him to wander. He protected Cain by "marking" him. Cain had a son named Enoch. Adam and Eve had another son named Seth, who had a son named Enosh.

GENESIS 5

A genealogy from Adam to Noah, with the ages of their death. Adam had many sons and daughters. Enoch, an ancestor of Adam's, had a close relationship with God and God took him one day. Methuselah lived the longest, 969 years. Noah was born to Lamech and Noah had three sons, Shem, Ham and Japheth.

GENESIS 6

The world got so wicked that God limited the age of people to 120 years of life. Every thought people focused on was doing evil. God regretted he ever made man. So God wanted to wipe the human population out, but Noah, the only blameless man on earth, found favor with God. God decided to send a flood to wipe out all the people and animals, but he gave Noah the dimensions and directions on how to build an ark.

Pairs of each species of animal would come to him. Noah did what he was told.

GENESIS 7

God told Noah that the flood was coming, so get ready. Noah was 600 years old. Along with two pairs of every kind of animal, Noah took seven pairs of clean animals and seven pairs of each bird. Seven days later, the water burst from the underground streams and from the sky, lasting forty days and nights. The water covered the earth, above the highest peaks, for 150 days.

GENESIS 8

The water began to recede and the ark rested on Mount Ararat. Noah released a raven once and a dove three times to see if they would return, indicating the emergence of habitual land. The dove returned a second time with an olive branch, but finally, the third time, the dove did not return. So, over a year since the flood began, Noah and his family and all the animals, stepped off the ark. Noah built an altar and sacrificed to God. God promised never to destroy the earth like that again.

GENESIS 9

God encouraged Noah and his family to repopulate the earth and eat meat. God made a rainbow covenant with Noah, promising never to destroy the earth with a flood. Noah planted a vineyard and got drunk on its wine. Ham saw his father naked and passed out in his tent, then told his brothers what he saw. Shem and Japheth covered Noah up, turning their eyes from Noah's nakedness. Noah woke up, found out what Ham did and cursed Ham's descendants, his son Canaan, while blessing the other sons.

GENESIS 10

The genealogy of each of Noah's sons – Shem, Ham and Japheth – is detailed. From Ham, places and people such as Egypt, Cush, Babylon and Nineveh emerge. From Canaan, the future enemies of Israel began, such as the Hittites, Jebusites, Amorites, and Hivites. Also, the towns of Sodom and Gomorrah were established. From the line of Shem, Abraham's ancestry begins.

GENESIS 11

The whole world spoke one language, so they settled in Shinar/Babylonia where they began a construction project to build a city and a huge tower to honor their greatness and to keep them united in one place. God confused their speech, dividing them into many tongues, so the city was called Babel. They scattered all over the world. The genealogy from Shem led to Terah, the father of Abram, Nahor and Haran. Haran's son was Lot. Abram's wife was Sarai, who could not give birth. Terah wanted to travel to Canaan with Abram, Lot and Sarai from the Ur of the Chaldeans, but they stopped in Harran where Terah died.

GENESIS 12

God told Abram that he would give him the land of Canaan and make a great nation from his descendants. Abram saw the land and built an altar near Bethel. Because of a famine, they went to Egypt where he told Sarai that, because of her beauty, the Egyptians would desire her. Fearing for his life, Abram told the Egyptians Sarai was his sister. Pharaoh took her as his wife and gave Abram lots of sheep, cattle, donkeys, camels and servants. But after God sent a plague to Pharaoh's household, Pharaoh discovered why it happened and escorted Abram's family out of Egypt.

GENESIS 13

Because of their large herds of animals and quarreling between their herdsmen, Abram and Lot split. Lot took the land east of the Jordan (including Sodom and Gomorrah) and Abram took the area west, Canaan (Israel). God promised Abram again that his descendants, too numerous to count, would populate the land. Abram settled near the great trees of Mamre.

GENESIS 14

A war broke out among the kings of the area and Lot was taken hostage by one side. Abram took 318 men and defeated those armies and rescued Lot. A king and priest, Melchizedek of Salem (today Jerusalem), brought Abram bread and wine and Abram gave Melchizedek a tenth of his possessions. Abram took nothing from the king of Sodom for his services because didn't want him to think he made Abram rich.

GENESIS 15

God reiterated his promise to Abram but Abram wondered when he would get a son since his relative Eliezer would get possession of his property. God told Abram to count the stars and promised he would have just as many descendants. Abram believed God and it was credited to him as righteousness. Abram and God make a covenant through the sacrifice of animals. God told Abram in a dream that his descendants would one day be in Egypt and it would take them four hundred years to get out. They would eventually return to this land.

GENESIS 16

Unable to have children on her own, Sarai gave her servant Hagar to Abram to possibly create a family through her. Abram did what Sarai suggested and Hagar became pregnant. Hagar began to treat Sarai with contempt so Sarai treated her harshly. Hagar ran away and an angel told her to return, saying the baby would be called Ishmael, one who would be at odds with his brothers forever. Ishmael was born.

GENESIS 17

God revisited Abram, now at the age of 99, reminding him of the covenant to create a nation through him. God then changed Abram's name to Abraham, meaning the father of many nations. The acceptance of this covenant would be secured through many generations by the act of circumcision, so their bodies would bear the mark of agreement. Sarai's name was changed to Sarah, meaning the mother of many nations. God gave Abraham the name of his future child, Isaac, promising to bless him and Ishmael too. Abraham laughed, unable to believe he would be a father at the age of 100 and Sarah at 90. Every male in the household was then circumcised.

GENESIS 18
Three visitors arrived and met with Abraham. When told Sarah would have a baby next time the Lord visited, Sarah laughed, then denied laughing when confronted about her reaction. The Lord revealed his plan to wipe out Sodom. Abraham bargained hoping that the presence of righteous people in the cities would keep God from destroying them. But apparently there were not ten to fifty righteous people in those cities and no good reason to keep them around.

GENESIS 19
Two angels arrived in Sodom and Lot took them into his home. A mob of men showed up at the door and demanded to have sex with these two visitors. The angels struck them with blindness. Lot, his wife and two daughters ran out of the city as sulfur and fire leveled the cities. Lot's wife looked back at the destruction and turned into a pillar of salt. Hiding in a cave, Lot's daughters got Lot drunk and slept with him. They gave birth to the patriarchs of two future enemies of the Israelites, the Moabites and the Ammonites.

GENESIS 20
Abraham moved the family to Gerar and encountered King Abimelek. Afraid the king would kill him for his beautiful wife, Abraham told everyone Sarah was his sister. Abimelek took her then was warned in a dream by God not to touch her or his whole family would die. Abimelek returned Sarah to Abraham, along with compensation, including livestock and silver.

GENESIS 21
Isaac was born exactly as the Lord told them. When Sarah witnessed Hagar and Ishmael mocking Isaac, Sarah wanted them kicked out. God comforted Abraham, saying it would be okay, he'll take care of Hagar and Ishmael. God reassured Hagar and Ishmael in the desert, showing them water. Hagar found a wife for Ishmael in Egypt. Abraham agreed to a peace treaty with Abimelek.

GENESIS 22

Abraham was called by God to sacrifice his one and only son on the mountain in Moriah. Abraham trusted that God would provide a sacrifice. As they traveled up the mountain, Isaac carried the wood and Abraham carried the fire and knife. With the knife above his head, Abraham was stopped by an angel of the Lord. A ram appeared in the thicket as a substitute for Isaac. Since Abraham obeyed and did not withhold his son, God promised to bless his descendants like the stars and the sand. Abraham called the place God Will Provide.

GENESIS 23

Sarah died at the age of 127 in Hebron. Abraham went to the Hittite elders and asked to buy a piece of land to bury her. Ephron the Hittite wished to give him the land, but Abraham insisted on paying for it. Abraham bought the cave of Machpelah and buried Sarah in it.

GENESIS 24

Abraham sent his servant to the land of his people to find a wife for Isaac. He did not want Isaac to take a wife from the Canaanites. The servant arrived in Abraham's home land and prayed for a woman who would ask to water his camels. Rebekah walked up and did just that. The servant communicated to her family how God showed him the wife for Isaac. The family (including Rebekah's brother Laban) agreed that this was the Lord's will. Rebekah returned with the servant. Isaac loved her and she became his wife.

GENESIS 25

Abraham married a woman named Keturah who bore him more sons. Abraham died at 175 and Isaac and Ishmael buried him at Machpelah. Ishmael had twelve sons, the leaders of twelve tribes. Isaac prayed to God for a child and Rebekah conceived twins. God said there were two rival nations inside her struggling with each other. Esau, the hairy one, was born first, but the second, Jacob, came out grasping his heel. As the boys grew, Esau loved the outdoors and to hunt, making his dad proud. Jacob preferred to stay around the tents with his mom.

One day, famished from being outside, Esau sold his birthright to Jacob for red (lentil) stew.

GENESIS 26

Because of a famine, Isaac moved his family to Gerar. Afraid that the men there would find Rebekah attractive, he told them she was his sister. Abimelek, king of the Philistines, saw Isaac and her making out, so he knew they were much closer. Abimelek told everyone not to harm Isaac. Isaac's crops and livestock grew tremendously and caused disputes with locals over water/well rights. Abimelek showed up, asking for a peace treaty, which Isaac agreed to.

GENESIS 27

Isaac, now old, asked Esau to prepare a feast of wild game for him before he blessed him. Rebekah overheard and told Jacob that she would make a meal from two goats just as Isaac liked it. Jacob wrapped his arms in goatskin and pretended to be Esau. Isaac blessed him and put him in charge of everything. Esau showed up and learned that Jacob had stolen his blessing. Because of Esau's fury, Rebekah told Jacob to run to Haran and stay with her brother, Laban.

GENESIS 28

Isaac told Jacob to go to Paddan-Aram and find a wife from Laban's family. Esau heard that Isaac despised Canaanite women so he married someone from the Ishmael's line. On his way to Haran, Jacob slept in the area promised to Abraham. Jacob saw a dream of a stairway from earth to heaven with angels going up and down. He called the place Bethel, the "house of God."

GENESIS 29

Jacob arrived in Haran and met Rachel by a well. He instantly fell in love with her and offered Laban, her father, to work seven years for her hand in marriage. When the seven years were up, Jacob got married but woke up and discovered Laban had given her Leah, the older sister. He offered to work seven more years for Rachel, marrying her one week later. He loved Rachel more. God saw that Leah was unloved, so he gave her four children – Reuben, Simeon, Levi, Judah.

GENESIS 30

Jacob had two sons, Dan and Naphtali, with Bilhah – Gad and Asher with Zilpah – Issachar, Zebulun and Dinah with Leah – and Joseph with Rachel. Jacob told Laban that he needed to leave and offered to take all the speckled and spotted goats from Laban's flock. Then Jacob set out poplar and almond branches by the water where the goats drank and mated. The branches caused the goats to have speckled and spotted kids. This caused Jacob's flock to increase and be stronger.

GENESIS 31

Jacob, sensing Laban didn't like him, grabbed his family and left Laban without saying goodbye. Rachel took her father's idols. When Laban heard that they had left, he went after them. God warned Laban in a dream not to harm Jacob. Laban caught up with Jacob, asking for the idols. Rachel sat on them and hid them. Jacob made a peace treaty with Laban using a pile of stones and called it Galeed. Laban returned home.

GENESIS 32

Jacob sent greetings to his brother Esau, giving him an update to his status. When Jacob heard that Esau was coming with 400 men, Jacob split up his family to protect them. One night, Jacob wrestled with an angel and, when the match became a draw, the angel touched Jacob's hip socket, knocking it out of joint. The angel gave Jacob a new name Israel, which means "he struggles."

GENESIS 33

Jacob and Esau met face to face. Esau was happy to see his brother, much to the relief of Jacob. They finally split and went their separate ways. Jacob bought land from Hamor, father of Shechem and camped there.

GENESIS 34

Dinah was raped by Shechem, a Hivite, who then fell in love with her. Hamor, his father, tried to negotiate for Dinah's hand. Dinah's brother told the Hivites that if all the men got circumcised, then they could intermarry. The men did and while they recovered from the painful surgery, Levi and Simeon killed all the men and plundered the town. Jacob was mad, knowing his reputation among the Canaanites and Perizzites had been tarnished.

GENESIS 35

Jacob met God in Bethel. God reconfirmed with Jacob that he would be called Israel and that a great nation would come from him. Rachel, pregnant, suffered giving birth to Benjamin and died. Jacob buried her in Bethlehem. Jacob returned to his father Isaac, who also died.

GENESIS 36

Esau's genealogy detailed. The beginning of the Edomites, one of Israel's worst enemies.

GENESIS 37

Joseph was Jacob's favorite son because he was born to him in his old age. Joseph had dreams of sheaves of grain bowing to another sheaf and the sun, moon and stars bowing to one of the stars. This made his brothers mad. They understood the interpretation that one day they would bow to him. One day, while Joseph came to check on his brothers and their flocks, they threw him into a cistern and tore off his cloak, dipping it into goat's blood. They sold Joseph to Ishmaelite traders who sold him to Potiphar, the captain of the palace guard.

GENESIS 38

Judah married a woman and had two sons, Er and Onan. Er was wicked and God took him, so, according to the rules, Onan had to take his brother's wife, Tamar. Onan refused to put his seed in her, so he spilled it on the ground. God took Onan and later Judah's wife died. Judah's third son, Shelah, was too young to marry and Judah didn't pass Tamar to him. Hearing that Judah was coming to town, Tamar dressed as a prostitute, veiled her face, and slept with Judah. As payment, Judah offered a goat but Tamar wanted a guarantee that he would pay her – his seal, a cord and a staff. Tamar got pregnant and Judah wanted to have her killed for prostitution, but when she showed the three items, Judah understood he should have passed her to Shelah. Tamar gave birth to twins – Perez and Zerah. Zerah stuck his hand out first, having a scarlet cord tied to his hand, but Perez was born first.

GENESIS 39

After Joseph arrived at Potiphar's house, everything there began to prosper. Potiphar put Joseph in charge of everything. Since Joseph was handsome, Potiphar's wife made advances towards him that Joseph refused. When Potiphar's wife tried to grab Joseph, Joseph pushed away, leaving his cloak in her hand. Frustrated, Potiphar's wife cried "rape" and, with the torn shirt in her hand, had Joseph thrown into jail. In jail, Joseph found favor with the jailer and was put in charge of all affairs.

GENESIS 40

Joseph found himself in prison with the chief cupbearer and chief baker. The cupbearer had a dream of three grape vines which he used to squeeze wine into Pharaoh's cup. Joseph interpreted the dream and said in three days he would be restored to his position. Joseph asked the cupbearer to put in a good word for him to Pharaoh. The baker had a dream of three baskets of bread on his head and the birds taking the bread away. Joseph interpreted this to mean in three days the baker would die. Both dreams turned out as Joseph said, but the cupbearer forgot to mention Joseph to Pharaoh.

GENESIS 41

Two years later, Pharaoh had a dream about seven fat cows being eaten by seven skinny cows and seven healthy heads of grain being eaten by seven shriveled heads of grain. No one could interpret the dream until the cupbearer remembered Joseph in prison. Joseph gave glory to God to interpret dreams. He told

Pharaoh that the dreams meant the nation would have seven years of abundance followed by seven years of famine. Joseph told Pharaoh he must put someone in charge of storing away food during the abundance to prepare for the famine. Pharaoh promoted Joseph to the second in command of Egypt. The dreams came true and people came to Joseph for food during the famine.

GENESIS 42

Joseph's brothers went to Egypt to get food. They did not recognize Joseph when they bowed before him, but Joseph recognized them. He accused them of being spies and put them in jail. To see if they were honest, he held one brother (Simeon) and told them to return to their family and bring back the youngest brother, Benjamin. The brothers believed this was judgment for how they treated Joseph. When they got home, they found the money they had given in the sacks with the grain.

GENESIS 43

With the famine so bad, Joseph's brothers returned to Egypt with Benjamin and the money from the sacks. The household manager said the money was put there by God, since they collected the money. The brothers stood before Joseph and Joseph saw Benjamin. Overcome with emotion, Joseph allowed them to stay and treated them to dinner, releasing Simeon from prison.

GENESIS 44

Joseph had his personal silver cup put in the sack of Benjamin and allowed the brothers to return home. The household manager caught up with them and accused Benjamin of stealing the cup, threatening to detain him. The brothers pleaded with Joseph for a pardon, knowing this would kill their father.

GENESIS 45

Sobbing, Joseph revealed himself to his brothers, telling them what God did to bring him here to lead this land out of the famine. He did not blame them for what they did and instead told them it was God's will. Joseph told his brothers to go home and bring Jacob back to Egypt, where they would be given the finest land to live in Goshen. The brothers were stunned and Jacob was overjoyed.

GENESIS 46

God gave Jacob permission to go to Egypt, promising him that he would bring Jacob's descendants back to the land of Canaan. Sixty-six people (not including wives) travelled to Egypt. Joseph and Jacob tearfully reunited. Jacob felt he could die happy. Joseph told Jacob to say to Pharaoh when they meet that they were shepherds, since Egyptians found that occupation detestable, so Pharaoh would move them out to Goshen for both isolation and fertile land.

GENESIS 47

Joseph introduced his family to Pharaoh. Pharaoh confirmed that they had land in Goshen and put them in charge of his own livestock. The famine grew worse and worse until the people used up all their money. Joseph took livestock and land from them in exchange. Then he provided the people with seed but asked that one-fifth of all food be given back to Egypt. Jacob, dying, asked not to be buried in Egypt.

GENESIS 48

A dying Jacob blessed Joseph's sons, Manasseh and Ephraim, born in Egypt. He adopted them and promised them an inheritance just like his other sons. But, while blessing them, he crossed his arms, putting his right hand on the younger, Ephraim, and his left on Manasseh. Joseph tried to switch the arms, but Jacob knew what he was doing. The younger would receive the double portion.

GENESIS 49

Jacob blessed (and cursed) all his sons. Reuben got no blessing for sleeping with Jacob's concubine. Judah got the most meaningful blessing, calling him a lion, whose scepter would never depart. He gave a prophecy of a Messiah riding a donkey and a colt, a vine and the branches, and garments stained in blood. Jacob asked to be buried in the cave of Machpelah with his grandfather, father and family. Jacob died at the age of 147.

GENESIS 50

Jacob died and Egypt had a national mourning. A procession of family and Egyptian delegates buried Jacob in Canaan, near the Jordan River. Fearful that Joseph would retaliate now that their father was dead, the brothers requested mercy. Joseph reassured them that all was well and that what they intended for harm, God intended for good. Joseph lived for 110 years then asked for his bones to be carried to Canaan before he died.

EXODUS

Number of Chapters: *40*
Most likely author: *Moses*
Approximate time span: 1800s-1445 BC (over 480 years)

EXODUS 1

The Hebrews were being oppressed by the Egyptians after Joseph died four hundred years ago. A new regime had moved into power and felt threatened by the Israelites over time since they were growing in number. The king of Egypt told the midwives to kill all the newborn male babies. The midwives refused and God blessed them with their own families. Then Pharaoh asked that every male be thrown into the Nile.

EXODUS 2

Moses' mom gave birth to Moses and hid him for three months. Unable to hide him any longer, Moses' mom put him in a basket and sent him down the Nile only to be found by Pharaoh's daughter. She called him Moses because she drew him out of the water. Pharaoh's daughter asked Moses's sister to find a woman to nurse Moses and she found Moses' mom. When Moses grew older, Moses' mom returned him to Pharaoh's daughter. Moses grew up and saw an Egyptian beating an Israelite. Moses killed him. When Moses tried to break up a fight between Israelites, they asked if he was going to kill them too. Pharaoh wanted to kill Moses for the crime so Moses fled to Midian where he met a priest with seven daughters. Moses protected them from some shepherds by a well. They reported the information back to their father who invited Moses to stay with them and gave him his daughter Zipporah. God heard the prayers of his people in Egypt who were suffering under the oppression of the Egyptians.

EXODUS 3

God spoke to Moses through the burning bush on Mount Horeb. God commissioned Moses to free the Hebrews from the Egyptians. Moses asked for God's name and God replied, "I am who I am." Moses wondered "Who am I" to do such an incredible task, but God reassured him that he would be with him all the way. God told Moses his plan to free the Hebrews and lead them to a land of milk and honey. He warned Moses that Pharaoh would not comply, but God would strike back and reveal great wonders.

EXODUS 4

God showed Moses miraculous signs by changing a staff to a snake, a healthy hand to leprous hand and water to blood so people would see God's miraculous power. Moses balked at being God's mouthpiece, saying he wasn't eloquent of speech. This angered God so he allowed Aaron to step in and help. Moses told his father-in-law Jethro what God called him to do. Jethro permitted him to go. God warned Moses that Pharaoh's heart would harden. On the way back to Egypt, Moses did not circumcise his son so God almost killed him because of his disobedience. Zipporah stepped in and did it for him. Moses met with his brother Aaron and the Hebrew elders who were comforted to know God heard their cry.

EXODUS 5

Moses confronted Pharaoh about letting the Israelites go and Pharaoh responded by making the work harder for the Hebrews. The Egyptians forced the Israelites to gather the straw to make the brick and increased the quota. The people were not happy with Moses and Aaron.

EXODUS 6

Moses returned to God and wondered why God allowed this plan to fall apart now that Pharaoh had tightened the screws. God reassured Moses, saying he would take care of them. The family lines of Levi, Moses and Aaron are mentioned as Moses prepared to face off with Pharaoh once again.

EXODUS 7

God told Moses his plan, making him like a "God" in Pharaoh's eyes. God wanted Moses and Aaron to ask Pharaoh if the Israelites could leave to worship God in the wilderness. Moses was eighty years old at the time and Aaron was eighty-three. God displayed his first miracle by turning a staff into a snake but the magicians were able to copy it. Aaron's staff, though, ate the magician's staffs. God turned the Nile into blood. The magicians were able to do the same trick. The Egyptians could not find any drinking water around the Nile.

EXODUS 8

God caused frogs to infest the land. The magicians were able to copy the same trick. God caused two plagues of gnats to swarm around people everywhere. The magicians were unable to copy this trick. Then God sent flies to infest the land but the Israelites were protected from them. All along, Pharaoh's relented and said he would allow the Israelites to go out into the wilderness to make sacrifices to God. Then once the plague stopped, Pharaoh relented on his promise and his heart got harder.

EXODUS 9

God allowed two more plagues to strike the Egyptians – a disease on livestock and boils on humans. Even the magicians were infested with boils. Pharaoh's heart got harder and harder. God allowed a plague of hail to strike the Egyptian crops and anyone standing outside, but hail did not strike where the Israelites lived. Pharaoh repented briefly, admitting he had sinned, but his heart changed and he refused to allow the Israelites to go.

EXODUS 10

God allowed a plague of locusts to strike the land of Egypt. Pharaoh again repented, admitting his sin, but changed his mind and kept the Israelites from leaving. God struck Egypt with darkness for three days, yet the Israelites were in light. Pharaoh again told them to get out, then hardened his heart.

EXODUS 11

God communicated to Moses his plan to kill all the firstborns in Egypt, his last and most powerful act to free his people. As the Israelites left, God told them to ask their Egyptian neighbors for gold and silver.

EXODUS 12

God gave Moses instructions regarding the Passover lamb, that it must be a one-year old male without defect. The blood of the lamb needed to be applied to the doorframes of their homes so death would pass over their homes. Moses communicated the instructions about Passover to the people who followed the instructions. Death came to the Egyptian houses that did not follow instructions of putting the blood of the lamb on their doorposts. Pharaoh told the Israelites to go. So nearly 600,000 men (not counting women and children) quickly packed up their things after living in Egypt 430 years. The Egyptians gave them silver, gold and clothing as they left. The Israelites left so quickly, they didn't have time to wait for the yeast to rise in bread.

EXODUS 13

As the Israelites moved out of Egypt, God gave Moses instructions about the Passover, regarding the bread and meat that would be consumed. He also spoke about the consecration of the firstborn of every womb, sacrificing the animal and redeeming the firstborn son. The Israelites moved into the desert, through a longer route, so they wouldn't turn back. They took the bones of Joseph and God lead them by fire and smoke.

EXODUS 14

As the Israelites camped near the Red Sea, Pharaoh and his army decided to pursue them. The Israelites cried out in fear, wishing they had never left. Moses told the people not to panic. God would protect them. The angel of God moved behind the Israelites, between the people and the enemy. Moses lifted his hand and staff and the Red Sea parted. The Israelites walked through safely and God closed the sea as the Egyptians tried to cross behind them.

EXODUS 15

Moses and the Israelites sang a song of praise for God. Miriam led a song with the women also. The Israelites arrived in a desert and encountered a body of bitter water. Frustrated, the people grumbled, but God had Moses throw a piece of wood into the water to make the bitter waters drinkable.

EXODUS 16

The Israelites grumbled, wishing they had died in Egypt with food instead of the desert with nothing. God came to Moses and Aaron and told them he would rain down bread and quail on them. The people looked at the manna and said, "What is it?" The Israelites were given instructions for collecting the manna every morning, taking only enough for the day and trusting there would be more tomorrow. Any extra they gathered would spoil with maggots. Also, instructions were given for collecting twice as much on the sixth day, so they could have a day of rest on the seventh. The manna was white, like coriander seed and tasted like honey wafers. They were instructed to put a jar of it aside with the two stone tablets to show future generations. God provided this manna for forty years to come.

EXODUS 17

When the Israelites arrived at Rephidim and there was no water to drink, so they grumbled. God instructed Moses to strike a rock and water came out. The Amalekites attacked the Israelites. As long as Moses' hands were raised, Joshua and his army defeated the enemy in battle. As Moses grew tired, Aaron and Hur held his hands up until the Israelites won.

EXODUS 18

Jethro, Moses' father in law, traveled to see Moses and hear what God had done. Moses told him everything the Lord had done. Jethro, a priest of the Midianites, confirmed that God's hand was surely on Moses and his people. Jethro watched how Moses worked, taking all the responsibility on to himself. He told Moses to train responsible people to help him. Moses did, appointing judges for the smaller cases then Moses handled only the more difficult cases. Jethro returned home.

EXODUS 19

The Israelites arrived at Mount Sinai and Moses began his communication between the people and God. First order of business, the people must agree to do everything God told them to do. God told the Israelites not to approach the mountain when he was present. Only Moses and Aaron could come to the top. If anyone disobeyed, they would be put to death.

EXODUS 20

God gave Moses the Ten Commandments, starting with the first four that deal with our relationship to God and the last six that deal with the primary ways we should treat other people. God showed his power on the mountain through thunder and lightning and it scared the Israelites.

1. Do have any other gods.
2. Do not make an image of any god.
3. Do not misuse the name of God.
4. Keep the Sabbath day holy.
5. Honor your mother and father.
6. Do not murder.
7. Do not commit adultery.
8. Do not steal.
9. Do not lie about your neighbor.
10. Don't desire what your neighbor has.

EXODUS 21

God gave Moses instructions regarding servants and how they can become a servant for life after six years of service. God gave Moses instructions for finding justice in cases involving violence, death and personal injury – an eye for an eye, tooth for tooth, hand for hand, foot for foot.

EXODUS 22

God gave Moses rules for specific situations that involved stealing, destroyed property and what to do if a piece of property was stolen while in the possession of another person. God gave Moses rules that involved being good to widows and foreigners, not sacrificing to other gods but giving God his tithe and lending money interest-free to fellow Israelites.

EXODUS 23

God gave Moses various instructions about fairly treating the poor, foreigners and enemies. Plus the rules for following the Sabbath and three major festivals. God told Moses that he would go ahead of the Israelites and defeat the enemies for them. He would cause terror in the hearts of the enemies and, little by little, establish the borders of this new nation.

EXODUS 24

God asked Moses and others to come up the mountain. They read the book of the covenant and promised to do everything it said. God showed himself to the leaders then called Moses up to get the tablets of stone. Moses stayed there for forty days and forty nights.

EXODUS 25

Moses began a forty day period with God all alone. God told Moses to have the Israelites bring an offering that their heart prompts them to give. Various items were suggested, to go towards making the tabernacle. God gave Moses instructions on how to build the ark, the table and the lampstands.

EXODUS 26

God gave Moses instructions on how to construct the curtains and frames that surround the Tabernacle and separate the Holy Places.

EXODUS 27

God gave Moses instructions on how to construct the altar of the burnt offering, the courtyard and the oil for the lampstand.

EXODUS 28

God gave Moses instructions on how to construct the priestly garments – the breastpiece, an ephod, a robe, a woven tunic, a turban and a sash. The breastplate contained the Urim and Thummin for decision making and twelve stones with the tribes' names written on them. God gave Moses instructions on how to construct the priestly garments, which needed to be worn by Aaron and his sons or they would die when they entered the Holy Place. Written across the front of the turban on a plate of pure gold were the words "Holy to the Lord."

EXODUS 29

God gave Moses instructions on how to consecrate the priests, making them holy through sacrifices and the sprinkling of blood. God gave Moses instructions on sacrifices for the priestly ordination and regular sacrificial offerings so the generations to come would know who God was.

EXODUS 30

God gave Moses instructions for the altar of incense and the atonement money paid according to the census. God gave Moses instructions for the wash basin and the ingredients for the anointing oil (including frankincense and myrrh) that covered the tabernacle. This perfume was only meant to be used for the sacrifices and nothing else.

EXODUS 31

God chose Bezalel, Oholiab and other workers and filled them with the creative ability to accomplish the artistic design of the tabernacle. God gave Moses instructions regarding the Sabbath, then gave him two tablets of stone inscribed by God.

EXODUS 32

When the people thought that Moses wasn't coming down from the mountain, Aaron collected earrings from the people and fashioned a golden calf. They sacrificed offerings and prepared for a festival. God's anger burned against the Israelites and he was ready to destroy them. Moses pleaded for the people and God relented. God gave Moses two tablets, inscribed on both sides. Moses went down the mountain. Joshua also heard the commotion going on. Moses saw the people worshipping the golden calf. He smashed the stone tablets. Aaron lied and said the people forced him to make the calf. He said he threw the gold into the fire and this calf came out. Moses called for anyone who was on his side to join him. The Levites joined him and slaughtered 3,000 Israelites. Moses went up to the mountain to see if could intercede for the people. God struck the people with a plague.

EXODUS 33

God called the people stiff-necked and told them to go to the Promised Land; however, he made it clear that he would not go with them. God would send an angel to help them. God met Moses at the Tent of Meeting, as the cloud descended over it. When Moses entered it, the people stood. God spoke to Moses there, face-to-face. Moses asked to be taught so he could lead these people. God promised his presence at all times. Moses asked to see God's glory, but God refused saying no one saw him and lived. He promised to put Moses in the cleft of a rock and pass by.

EXODUS 34

God told Moses to make two new stone tablets. Moses chiseled them out and presented them to God, praising him. God told Moses not to make treaties with other nations and to destroy their altars. He went over the sacrificial and festival requirements. Moses stayed with God for another forty days and nights, writing down everything. When Moses came down from the mountain after being with God, his face glowed. Every time after that, when Moses was in the presence of God, he had to put a veil over his face because people were afraid of him.

EXODUS 35

Moses commanded the people to give offerings. Many brought valuables while others used their talents to make items for the tabernacle. God chose Bezalel and Oholiab and gave them the talent needed to design the articles in the tabernacle and to teach others.

EXODUS 36

Bezalel and Oholiab got to work but people brought more than enough. They had to be told to stop giving. The workers designed and made the curtains, clasps, crossbars and posts.

EXODUS 37
Bezalel and all the workers constructed the ark, the table, the lampstand and the altar of incense with incredible detail.

EXODUS 38
Bezalel and all the workers constructed the altar, the basin for washing and the courtyard. The amount of materials used included great quantities of gold, silver and bronze.

EXODUS 39
Bezalel and all the workers made the priestly garments, including the ephod, the breastplate, the tunic, the turban and the sash. The people completed all the work that God had outlined for them. Moses inspected the work and saw that it had been done precisely as God asked.

EXODUS 40
Moses set up the tabernacle with the all items that had been made. When the cloud set over the tabernacle, the glory of the Lord filled the temple. Moses couldn't go inside because it was so powerful. When the cloud lifted, they packed up and followed it. When it stopped, they stopped.

LEVITICUS

Number of Chapters: 27
Most likely author: Moses
Approximate time span: Around 1445 BC (One month)

LEVITICUS 1
God gave instructions to Moses for the sacrifices, detailing how the procedure would go. The burnt offerings (bull, sheep, goat) must be without defect and the blood must spill. Birds (doves and pigeons) also have specific procedures.

LEVITICUS 2
The procedure for the grain offering.

LEVITICUS 3
The procedure for the peace offering, using a bull/cow, sheep or goat. The blood or fat must never be eaten.

LEVITICUS 4
The procedure for the offering of a sin committed unintentionally by the high priest, a leader, the entire community or an individual.

LEVITICUS 5
The procedure for the sin offering, which included confession and bringing a sacrifice to a priest for atonement.

LEVITICUS 6
Instructions were given for the burnt offering, the grain offering, the priestly anointing and general instructions for the sin offering.

LEVITICUS 7
Instructions were given for the guilt and peace offering. It was forbidden to eat blood or fat from an animal. Priests received a portion of the peace offerings.

LEVITICUS 8

Detailed instructions were given about the process of ordaining priests. The high priest, Aaron, received special clothing, including the Urim and Thummin. The priests were anointed for the first time and ready to carry out their duties in the Tabernacle.

LEVITICUS 9

The priests performed the first offering in the Tabernacle. Fire blazed from the Lord's presence and consumed the burnt offering. The people fell to their faces.

LEVITICUS 10

Aaron's sons, Nadab and Abihu, tried to burn the wrong kind of fire and were consumed by it. Moses told Aaron and his two remaining sons not to mourn. The priests were told not to drink wine or any fermented drink before going into the Tabernacle.

LEVITICUS 11

Detailed instructions regarding which animals were clean and which were unclean, including land animals, sea creatures and insects.

LEVITICUS 12

Instructions regarding a woman and her cleanliness after birth.

LEVITICUS 13

Ceremonial cleanliness instructions regarding skin diseases, rashes, boils, burns, sores, baldness and clothing.

LEVITICUS 14

Instructions for cleansing a person of skin diseases, plus how to treat a house that had been contaminated.

LEVITCUS 15

Instructions for cleansing a person contaminated by bodily discharges, semen, menstrual bleeding and what to do after sex.

LEVITICUS 16

Instructions for the Day of Atonement, including the release of the scapegoat, who carried the sins of the people into the wilderness.

LEVITICUS 17

The Lord prohibited people from eating or drinking blood, cutting off people who did.

LEVITICUS 18

Very detailed instructions about who NOT to have sex with, including relatives, same sex partners and animals.

LEVITICUS 19

A variety of rules required for holiness, including sacrifices, harvests, business practices, slander, revenge, sexual relations, witchcraft, mediums and personal grooming. These rules affect the way the blind, deaf, poor, workers, family and foreigners were treated.

LEVITICUS 20

The punishment of death was given for people who worshipped Molech, cursed their mother and father, adultery, homosexuality, bestiality, incest. God desired for these people to be separate and holy, not like the other nations around them who God was going to drive out.

LEVITICUS 21

Strict rules for the priests were given, who must try to avoid touching dead relatives, never shave their beards and abstain from contact with prostitutes and divorced women. It's the same for the high priest, except all contact with the dead was forbidden and he must marry a virgin. No priest can have a physical defect.

LEVITICUS 22

More rules for priests, who must stay holy by staying away from dead things, bodily emissions and defiled people. Also rules for proper offerings, mostly that the sacrifices not have a physical blemish.

LEVITICUS 23

The rules for all the holidays and festivals, including Passover (one day), Feast of the Unleavened Bread (seven days), Festival of Firstfruits (one day), Pentecost (one day), Trumpets (one day), Day of Atonement (one day) and the Festival of Booths/Shelters (seven days).

LEVITICUS 24

Instructions for the holy bread of God's presence, which were twelve loaves baked and set on the gold table of bread. A story of blasphemer who used God's name in vain and had to be stoned outside the camp.

LEVITICUS 25

Rules for the Year of Jubilee, which happened every fiftieth year, when crops were not planted for a whole year, land debts forgiven and Israelite slaves were set free.

LEVITICUS 26

If the country was obedient to God, he would bless them. If they were disobedient and followed other gods, he would punish them with the full fury of his wrath, creating fear and turmoil in their land.

LEVITICUS 27

A list of instructions for special vows of dedication for people, animals, houses and land.

NUMBERS

Number of Chapters: 36
Most likely author: Moses
Approximate time span: 1444-1405 BC (39 years)

NUMBERS 1

Two years after they left Egypt, God asked the Israelites to take a census of all men twenty years and older who could serve in the army. The tribes were counted for a total of 603,550. The tribes camped around the Tabernacle and the Levites were put in charge of setting up and taking down.

NUMBERS 2

The tribes were organized around the Tabernacle, three tribes in every direction (north, sound, east, west). The Levities camped in the middle next to the Tabernacle.

NUMBERS 3

The three Levite clans – the Gershonites, Kohathites, Merarites – were given responsibilities to set up and take down the Tabernacle. God instructed Moses to collect redemption money for every first born son. The money was given to Aaron and his sons.

NUMBERS 4

God gave specific duties to each of the three divisions of Levites. The Kohathites were responsible for the sacred articles in the Tabernacle. The Gershonites carried the curtains. The Merarites carried the poles, frames, pillars.

NUMBERS 5

God gave instructions to remove those defiled by contagious skin diseases or who touched a dead body. If a man accused his wife of unfaithfulness, the priest mixed a bitter water drink that would cause her to be infertile if she drank it. This would answer the man's jealous accusations and prove one of them right.

NUMBERS 6

Instructions were given for the special vow of the Nazirites, who abstained from any food or drink from the vine, did not cut their hair and stayed away from dead bodies. When the vow ended, they were to go to the Tabernacle and make offerings.

NUMBERS 7

The leaders of each tribe presented gifts of dedication for the altar when it was anointed. These gifts included silver platters, silver basins, gold incense containers, grain offerings and animal sacrifices.

NUMBERS 8

Instructions for dedicating the Levites, who began work at the age of 25 and retired at 50.

NUMBERS 9

The Passover was celebrated for the second time and some had questions about what to do if they had to miss the Passover because they were ceremonially unclean. God told them to celebrate one month later. The Israelites moved when the cloud moved over the tabernacle, then camped when it stopped. Sometimes it stayed for a day, week or a whole year. The cloud changed into fire at night.

NUMBERS 10

God gave instructions regarding the silver trumpets which were used to call everyone together or just the leaders, to announce the start of a festival or to call the nation to war. During their second year in Sinai, the Israelites packed up when the cloud moved and left Sinai, entering the wilderness of Paran. They marched for three days.

NUMBERS 11

The people began to complain, so a fire of anger killed people on the outskirts of the camp. Then foreigners longed for Egypt and the food. Moses got angry and asked God, "why do I have to put up with these people?" Moses, frustrated with being a leader, brought 70 elders before God who told them that he would feed the people meat. Quail blew in, three feet deep. God saw the way they ate and caused a plague to break out.

NUMBERS 12

Miriam and Aaron criticized Moses for marrying a Cushite woman. God called Moses, Miriam and Aaron to the Tent of Meeting and after the cloud moved off them, Miriam was infected with leprosy. Moses pleaded for her life and God sent her outside the camp for seven days to get clean.

NUMBERS 13

God told Moses to send one person from each tribe to spy on the Promised Land. They returned forty days later with a huge cluster of grapes and reported sightings of large warriors, whom they called descendants of Anak. Caleb wanted to attack, but the others felt like grasshoppers next to them.

NUMBERS 14

The people felt defeated and wondered why they traveled so far only to die at their destination. Joshua and Caleb tried to encourage the people, but were almost stoned by them. God wanted to kill all the people, but, after Moses defended them, God decided only to bar one generation from entering the Promised Land. For forty years – one year for every day the spies were gone – the Israelites would wander the wilderness. The ten negative spies were killed and only Joshua and Caleb remained.

NUMBERS 15

The Lord passed on more regulations for offerings, some of which would take effect when they entered the Promised Land. The people stoned a Sabbath breaker collecting wood. God told the people to put tassels on their clothing to remind them of God's commands.

NUMBERS 16

Korah, Dathan and Abiram incited a rebellion against Moses. God told them and their followers to bring their incense burners to the Tabernacle. The ground opened up and swallowed the men. The fire raged from the burners and consumed the men offering incense. The people muttered about the incident and God brought a plague, killing 14,700 until Moses and Aaron interceded.

NUMBERS 17

Because of complaints from the tribe over who was holy and who was not, God asked that one staff from each leader of each tribe be put in front of the ark. Aaron's budded and produced almonds, confirming that they were the official tribe of God's choosing.

NUMBERS 18

God outlined the duties of the priests and Levites who were in charge of the tabernacle. God spoke about redeeming the firstborn and the giving of tithes. Also, the Levites received no land inheritance, but were paid by the food and gifts given to God.

NUMBERS 19

God gave instructions for the sacrifice of a red heifer, whose ashes were mixed into the water of cleansing. He also detailed rules of purification after a death for people, clothes and tents.

NUMBERS 20

Miriam died. There was no water in the wilderness of Zin so the people complained. God told Moses to command the rock to produce water. Moses, angrily, struck the rock twice with his staff while yelling at the people. God barred him from entering the Promised Land because of his leadership gaff. The people arrived at Mount Hor. Aaron's garments were given to his son Eleazar, transferring the high priest role to him, then Aaron died.

NUMBERS 21

The Israelites defeated the Canaanites, then they murmured about dying in the wilderness and hating manna. God sent poisonous snakes that bit people and killed them. After the people cried out, God had Moses make a bronze snake and put it on a pole. When people looked at the bronze snake, they would be healed. King Sihon of the Ammorites refused to allow the Israelites to cross through his land so he attacked them. The Israelites won and took all their towns, settling in them. King Og of Bashan also attacked and was killed.

NUMBERS 22

The Israelites traveled to Moab and the King of Moab, Balak, felt threatened. He called on Balaam, a prophet, to curse the Israelites. Balaam heard from God who told him not to curse the Israelites. Balak pressed Balaam again so Balaam went to meet Balak. God put an angel in his path that only the donkey saw, steering away. After Balaam beat the donkey three times, the donkey spoke saying he was trying to protect his master, like a loyal servant. Then an angel spoke, telling Balaam he had sinned. God gave Balaam permission to speak to Balak, who showed Balaam the Israelites from a mountain.

NUMBERS 23

Balak told Balaam three times to curse the Israelites from three different mountains, but God told Balaam to bless the Israelites instead. Balak was furious.

NUMBERS 24

Balaam prophesied for Israel one more time. Balak refused to pay Balaam, but Balaam didn't want money. Balaam gave a prophecy for Moab. This prophecy mentioned a king whose star would come out of Judah.

NUMBERS 25

The Israelites were seduced by the Moabite women into worshipping Baal. God's anger blazed. An Israelite man brought a Midianite woman to his house right in front of Moses. Phineas took a spear and killed both of them, ceasing God's anger that had become a plague. God loved Phineas' zeal.

NUMBERS 26

While camped in Moab, on the Jordan, across from Jericho, God asked Moses to take a second census of the tribes. Then, according to the population, Moses divided the land according to tribal size – more land to bigger tribes, less land to smaller tribes (except for the Levites). Not one person in the census had been alive when they left Egypt, except Joshua and Caleb.

NUMBERS 27

The daughters of Zelophehad questioned the right of sons only receiving an inheritance of land after their father died. God allowed daughters to receive an equal inheritance in cases such as this. Moses knew he would die soon and God confirmed that Joshua would lead the Israelites. Before the whole community, Moses transferred power to Joshua with Eleazar the priest present.

NUMBERS 28

God gave Moses instructions regarding daily, Sabbath, monthly, Passover and Harvest offerings.

NUMBERS 29

God gave Moses specific instructions regarding the Festival of Trumpets, Day of Atonement and the Festival of Tabernacles offerings.

NUMBERS 30

God told Moses if a man made a vow, he can't break it. For a woman, her vows have to be approved by her father or husband.

NUMBERS 31

God told Moses, as his last act of leadership, to command the Israelites to fight against the Midianites as vengeance on leading them into idolatry. They defeated them, plundering the Midianites and dividing up the spoils – from livestock to gold – equally among everyone.

NUMBERS 32

Since they had vast amounts of livestock, the tribes of Reuben, Gad and the half tribe of Manasseh saw the land of east of the Jordan and wanted to settle there. Moses was furious until the tribes suggested that their men cross over and battle with the other tribes to overtake the land. Once the land was subdued, they would return. Everyone agreed.

NUMBERS 33

This chapter gives the itinerary for the Israelites' stops during their 40 years in the wilderness. It remembers the Lord's command to wipe out all the people who worship the pagan shrines.

NUMBERS 34

God outlined the boundaries for the nation and nominated the leaders who would determine their tribe's possession.

NUMBERS 35

God laid out the plan for the cities of refuge, Levite cities that a murderer can escape to and not be avenged. While there, justice can be served to see if the crime was premeditated, accidental or if he was guilty at all. The Levites received no land but these 48 cities.

NUMBERS 36

A command was given to families with daughters like Zelophehad with no male ancestors, who could marry outside their tribe and transfer land to them. The Lord agreed that they must marry within their tribe. The book ended with the Israelites camped on the plains of Moab besides the Jordan River, across from Jericho.

DEUTERONOMY

Number of Chapters: 34
Most likely author: Moses
Approximate time span: 1405 BC (One month)

DEUTERONOMY 1
Moses addressed the Israelites one last time, east of the Jordan. He remembered God's promise to Abraham to occupy the land and Moses leading them to it. He recalled the incident with the twelve scouts, the people's lack of trust to defeat the inhabitants of Canaan and the subsequent banishment of one generation from inhabiting the land. Also, Moses reminded them of that generation's unsuccessful attack against the Amorites.

DEUTERONOMY 2
Moses remembered the great enemies they faced (Emites, Anakites, Amorites and the army of King Sihon).

DEUTERONOMY 3
Moses remembered their victory over Og of Bashan and the division of land to the east of the Jordan. Moses could not enter the Promised Land but was allowed to speak from Pisgah Peak.

DEUTERONOMY 4
Moses encouraged the people to obey God's laws, for no other god had ever taken a nation and made it his own. So why worship those gods?

DEUTERONOMY 5
Moses reiterated the 10 Commandments and pleaded with the people to obey all God's commands so they could live long and prosperous lives.

DEUTERONOMY 6
Moses urged the people to obey everything God told them and to love God with all their heart, soul and strength.

They must not worship other nation's gods. They must pass down God's legacy to the next generation and remind them of His great power.

DEUTERONOMY 7

Moses told the Israelites that God would clear out all their enemies, going before them. He loved this nation, not because they were a large nation, but just because he loved them. If the nation obeyed, God would prosper them. Also, burn those idols!

DEUTERONOMY 8

Moses recalled how God took care of them in the wilderness providing them with manna to teach them that man does not live on bread alone. God promised to take care of them in the Promised Land. The land flowed with fruit and precious metals. If they forgot about God once their houses were built, their flocks were large and the gold multiplied, they would become proud. Don't forget God!

DEUTERONOMY 9

Moses walked through the moment on Mount Sinai when he received the Ten Commandments in stone, then found the Israelites worshipping a golden calf. He pleaded with God not to destroy them. Moses remembered other places where they made God furious and Moses stepped in to save them. God did not choose them because they were more numerous. He chose them because he made a promise to their ancestors.

DEUTERONOMY 10

Moses remembered taking the Ten Commandments and placed them in a wooden ark. He recalled Aaron dying, the Levite tribe being set apart and staying on the mountain another forty days to plead for them. Moses again pleaded for them to fear God, to live according to his will and love him. He is the God of gods and the Lord of lords.

DEUTERONOMY 11

Moses emphasized the need to love God with all your heart and soul and obey all the commands. He reminded them of God's power to drown the Egyptians in the Red Sea and swallow up those who complained.

DEUTERONOMY 12

Moses wanted to make sure they did not worship the gods of other nations, in fact, the people must smash all their altars. He differentiated between offering worship to God and worship of other gods, for example not eating the blood of sacrifices.

DEUTERONOMY 13

Moses gave warnings against false prophets and those that lead others to worship other gods. They must be put to death.

DEUTERONOMY 14

A list of the qualities of clean and unclean animals, fish, birds, insects. Also, rules for the giving of tithes – one tenth of all grain, new wine, olive oil and firstborn males of flocks and herds.

DEUTERONOMY 15

Every seven years debts were canceled with fellow Hebrews. Hebrew slaves were released after six years of service with the option of staying or leaving. Also, rules of sacrificing the firstborn male from flocks and herds – an animal without defect, lame or blind.

DEUTERONOMY 16

Moses went over the instructions for Passover, the Festival of Unleavened Bread, the Festival of the Harvest/Weeks and the Festival of the Tabernacles/Shelters. He also told them to appoint judges to rule fairly.

DEUTERONOMY 17

     Instructions were given for stoning someone accused of worshipping another god. Also, Moses gave guidelines for putting a king in power: they must not accumulate too much stuff, they must be an Israelite and they must copy the law down by hand in front of the priests.

DEUTERONOMY 18

     Instructions given for the priests to eat from the offerings since they do not receive an inheritance from the land. Moses urged them not to engage in the practices of sorcery or witchcraft. He told them to listen to the true prophets sent by God but not to the false prophets whose warnings do not come true.

DEUTERONOMY 19

     Moses outlined the rules for the cities of refuge and what constituted involuntarily manslaughter from voluntary. Also, anyone accused of a crime must have two to three witnesses.

DEUTERONOMY 20

     Moses gave them instructions for fighting war, including reasons for soldiers to be excused from war. Also, when attacking a faraway city, they must kill the men of distant cities and have the option of taking the women, children and plunder for themselves, but, for nearby cities, they must destroy everyone. Trees must not be cut down during battle.

DEUTERONOMY 21

     Moses gave various instructions including how to cleanse a town of unsolved murder by offering a sacrifice of a heifer and the leaders of the town washing their hands over it. Instructions for marrying a captive woman, a firstborn's inheritance, the stoning of a rebellious son and what to do with a body hung on a tree (it cannot stay overnight).

DEUTERONOMY 22

     Various instructions for helping a neighbor and returning his lost animals and possessions. Rules about mixing various items like animals when plowing, fabrics and crops. Also, commands about sexual purity, rape and adultery.

DEUTERONOMY 23
Lots of specific regulations including building a latrine, not becoming a temple prostitute, not charging interest to fellow Israelites and fulfilling your vows.

DEUTERONOMY 24
More specific regulations including not drafting a newly married man to war, kidnapping, skin diseases, getting back an item that was borrowed, justice shown to foreigners and parents not being put to death for the sins of their children.

DEUTERONOMY 25
More instructions including no floggings must exceed forty lashes, a widow marrying her brother in law to keep the inheritance in the family, using accurate scales and a charge to kill the Amalekites.

DEUTERONOMY 26
Moses gave the Israelites instructions on how to present the harvest offering and what to say in the presence of the Lord. Every third year they were to give a special offering for the Levites, foreigners, orphans and widows. Another call to obedience was made to make Israel a great nation.

DEUTERONOMY 27
Moses told them to set up an altar when they crossed the Jordan and to also proclaim curses on people who violated God's commands, from stealing to sexual immorality, from assassinations to despising your mother and father.

DEUTERONOMY 28
Moses told them about the incredible blessings that would occur in the nation if they were obedient. God would bless them with material abundance. Moses also gave dire warning for disobedience, from poverty to occupation by an

enemy. Nothing would seem to work out and the Israelites could lose everything.

DEUTERONOMY 29

Moses called the Israelites to commit to this covenant of obedience. He reminded them of God's faithfulness, but if they disobeyed, God would destroy them and generations to come would hear of their devastation.

DEUTERONOMY 30

Moses told them that every time they returned to God he would show them mercy. Moses gave them a choice between prosperity and disaster, life or death, blessings or curses. Choose God.

DEUTERONOMY 31

Moses, at 120 years old, realized he could not go on so he handed the leadership over to Joshua. He told Joshua to be strong and courageous. Moses said to read the law aloud to the public every seven years and to teach the Israelites a song he was about to write. Moses wrote everything down in the law.

DEUTERONOMY 32

Moses wrote a theme song that spoke of God's great power, mercy and love. He spoke of Israel's disobedience. God's desire was to show other nations how powerful he was by building this nation and using them to take vengeance on those enemies. Moses passed these commands to Joshua emphasizing their importance. God told Moses to climb Mount Nebo and see the land he had promised, but he would die right there on the mountain.

DEUTERONOMY 33

Moses blessed the tribes individually (Simeon left out), then told Israel how blessed they were to have God.

DEUTERONOMY 34

Moses climbed Mount Nebo and God showed him the Promised Land. Moses died at 120 years old, still with good eye sight. God buried Moses in a place nobody knows. Joshua, full of the spirit, took over. There was never another prophet like Moses who knew God face-to-face.

JOSHUA

Number of Chapters: 24
Most likely author: Joshua
Approximate time span: 1405-1390 BC (15 years)

JOSHUA 1

God commissioned Joshua to lead the Israelites, telling him to be "strong and courageous." God commands Joshua to mediate on the law day and night and to obey it always. The families of the three tribes settling in the east side of the Jordan were to remain while the soldiers crossed.

JOSHUA 2

Two Israelite spies scouted out Jericho and stayed at the house of Rahab the prostitute. When the city found out the spies were at her house, she lied and said they were gone. She had actually hidden them on the roof. Rahab asked for a promise from the spies that her family not be killed in the war. By marking her home with a scarlet rope, the army would know not to harm her.

JOSHUA 3

God gave the Israelites instructions for crossing the Jordan. The ark went first, carried by the priests. When they stepped into the flowing river, the water backed up upstream until everyone safely crossed to dry land.

JOSHUA 4

God told twelve leaders from the twelve tribes to get twelve stones from the middle of the Jordan and place them as a monument to God's power as a reminder to their children of that day.

JOSHUA 5

Since none of the Israelite men were circumcised, Joshua led a campaign to make sure they all were. After resting from the surgery, they celebrated Passover. Joshua saw a man with a sword, a commander in the Lord's army. Joshua bowed before him and asked him if he was for or against them. The angel responded, "Neither."

JOSHUA 6

The Israelites marched once around Jericho for six days, carrying the ark and ram's horns in silence. On the seventh day, they marched around the city seven times, then blew the horns and shouted. The walls fell down. They killed everyone inside including the livestock. They only took the gold, silver, bronze and iron which would then be given to the Lord. Rahab and her family were saved.

JOSHUA 7

Achan stole some of devoted items that God said should be set aside for him. The spies scouted out Ai, a small city, and said there would be no problem defeating them. But Ai overwhelmed the Israelites with a small army. God told Joshua someone stole something that should be for God. After singling out the tribe of Judah and going tent to tent, Achan was discovered. They stoned him, appeasing God's anger.

JOSHUA 8

The Israelites ambushed Ai and successfully defeated them. God said they could take the cattle and the goods this time. Only the king survived but was later hung. Joshua copied the law onto a stone altar and read it aloud.

JOSHUA 9

The nations in the area began to panic and organize against the Israelites, but the Gibeonites pretended to be a nation from far away by wearing old clothes and carrying moldy bread. They deceived the Israelites into making a treaty with them, when the truth was they lived right there in the Promised Land. The Israelites did not consult the Lord first. So Joshua allowed them to live, giving them the servant jobs of woodcutting and water carrying.

JOSHUA 10

The kings of Jerusalem, Hebron, Jarmuth, Lachish and Eglon attacked Gibeon, since they made a treaty with the Israelites. So Joshua's army came to the rescue. Along the way, they defeated the Amorites with God also throwing a terrible hailstorm at them. Joshua prayed for the sun to stand still and it did. They moved on and defeated the five armies and the kings all hid in a cave. Joshua pulled them out and killed them himself. They took out the cities of Makkedah, Libnah, Lachish, Gezer, Eglon, Hebron, Debir, all the nations of the western region and north hill country. They returned to their camp in Gilgal.

JOSHUA 11

The Israelites defeated their enemies to the north, destroying every living thing. They then finally had rest from war.

JOSHUA 12

The list of thirty-one kings Israel conquered.

JOSHUA 13

Joshua was getting old, but more enemies need to be defeated. In the meantime, the land east of the Jordan divided up among the tribes of Reuben, Gad and Manasseh, with specific boundaries given in detail. The Levites received no land inheritance.

JOSHUA 14

Caleb asked for his division of the land where the feared Anakites lived, reminding everyone that as a spy forty-five years ago he trusted God completely.

JOSHUA 15

The boundaries of the land for the tribe of Judah detailed precisely. Caleb was assigned Hebron. He battled the Anakites. He gave his daughter to anyone who defeated the city of Kiriath-sepher. Othniel conquered it and married her. All the cities he received were listed, but only the Jebusites in the city of Jerusalem were not driven out.

JOSHUA 16

The tribe of Joseph through his son Ephraim got their allotment, which included Jericho and Bethel.

JOSHUA 17

The tribe of Joseph through his son Manasseh got their allotment east of the Jordan. They didn't feel they received enough land so they were encouraged to clear out the forest land of the hills.

JOSHUA 18

Three men from each tribe were sent out to survey the land. When they returned, the rest of the tribes received their allotment through the casting of lots, starting with the tribe of Benjamin, who received the town of Jebus (Jerusalem).

JOSHUA 19

The tribes of Simeon, Zebulun, Issachar, Asher, Naphtali and Dan received their specific allotment. Joshua got a special piece of land.

JOSHUA 20

The purpose of the cities of refuge was described as places where someone can go if they caused an accidental death. The accused can run to the city, plead their case before the leaders then be tried before the victim's family can get revenge.

JOSHUA 21

Each tribe gave the Levites designated cities. Each clan in the Levites (Gershon, Kohathite, Merari) received their own allotment. A total number of 48 cities were given to the Levites.

JOSHUA 22

Reubenites, Gadites and the half tribe of Manasseh were dismissed from their promise to help the other tribes occupy the land west of the Jordan. But when they arrived home, the three tribes built an altar that made the other tribes think they were separating from them. A delegation arrived before war broke out and the three tribes said they built the altar as a memorial, not a substitute or an act of separation. They wanted their descendants to know that they worship the same God as their brothers on the other side of the Jordan. Satisfied, the tribes backed down.

JOSHUA 23

Joshua, now old, gave final instructions, imploring the people to follow God's commandments or be destroyed. He reminded them that God faithfully kept every promise.

JOSHUA 24

Joshua's final words reminded the Israelites what God had done from Abraham through Moses. He made them promise to be faithful to God and God alone. The people swore they would. Joshua died and was buried. Joseph's bones were also buried. Eleazar the priest also died.

JUDGES

Number of Chapters: 21
Author Unknown: Possibly Samuel
Approximate time span: 1375-1050 BC (nearly 350 years)

JUDGES 1

A summary of events after Joshua died. Judah attacked the Canaanites first, capturing Jerusalem, then moving to other towns. Othniel, Caleb's nephew, conquered Kiriath-sepher and received Caleb's daughter in return. All the tribes failed to drive out all the former inhabitants, so their influence continued during occupation.

JUDGES 2

An angel came to the people at Bokim and pointed out their disobedience by making covenants with the enemies and not destroying their altars. Joshua died and the people began worshipping other gods. God got angry but raised up judges who saved the people, until they fell back into their old patterns.

JUDGES 3

Certain nations, including the Canaanites, Hittites, Amorites, Jebusites and others were left to live in Israel, tempting the Israelites. Othniel defeated the king of Aram giving Israel peace for forty years. When the Moabites attacked Israel and took over Jericho, the Israelites were subject to King Moab for eight years. Ehud, a left handed man, told Eglon he had a private message and drove a dagger into his fat belly. The servants didn't disturb the king, thinking he was relieving himself, until they entered the room and discovered him dead. Ehud defeated the Moabites and they had peace for eighty years. Shamgar then killed six hundred Philistines with an ox goad.

JUDGES 4

King Jabin of the Canaanites, with Sisera as his army's commander, took over Israel. Deborah, the judge, told Barak that he would have victory over the Canaanites. But when Barak insisted that Deborah came with them, the plan changed and

Deborah said a woman would defeat the army. So after Barak's campaign crippled the Canaanites, Sisera escaped to the tent of a woman named Jael. She gave him some milk and a warm blanket. As Sisera slept, Jael drove a tent peg into his head. Jabin's army was subdued.

JUDGES 5

Deborah and Barak sang a song of victory, giving more details about the defeat of Sisera and King Jabin. The nation had peace for forty years.

JUDGES 6

The Midianites used to ravage the land during harvest, stealing all the livestock and crops. The Israelites would hide in the mountains for defense. God called Gideon to destroy the Midianites. An angel delivered the message and proved it was God by setting his offering ablaze. Gideon knocked down the altar of Baal and the Asherah pole. The town wasn't happy. Gideon's dad told them to let Baal defend himself. Gideon then asked for one more sign from the Lord – he set out a fleece and asked it to be wet and the ground dry. After it happened the next morning, he asked for the fleece to be dry and the ground wet. It too was so.

JUDGES 7

God thought Gideon had too many warriors so Gideon told all those who were scared to go home. 22,000 did. Then he separated those who lapped up water with their hands from those who knelt down to drink. 300 brought the water to their mouths. Those 300 took torches, ram's horns and clay jars, surrounded the Midianites and smashed the jars, revealing the torches and blowing the horns. The Midianites fought against each other and were defeated. Gideon hunted down and killed two Midianite leaders, Oreb and Zeeb.

JUDGES 8

Gideon's army chased two more Midianite leaders, Zebah and Zalmunna, to Succoth and Gideon asked the town to feed his army. They refused and Gideon swore he would return to torment them with thorns and briers. He went to the people of Peniel and got the same answer. He swore he would tear down the tower. Finally Gideon hunted down Zebah and Zalmunna, two Midianite kings. He returned to Succoth and punished them with briers and thorns. Gideon tore down Peniel and killed all the men. Gideon refused to be Israel's leader (saying God would do that) but asked for earrings from the treasuries. He used the earrings to make a gold ephod. During the rest of Gideon's lifetime, forty years, Israel was at peace. He had seventy sons, one named Abimelek from a concubine. Gideon died and the people returned to worshipping gods.

JUDGES 9

Abimelek, Gideon's son, asked the people of Shechem who they would rather have rule over them – one man or seventy brothers? The town said one man so Abimelek murdered all his brothers. Only one brother, Jotham, escaped. Jotham told a parable about trees asking for a leader, then Jotham escaped and hid. Shechem began to question Abimelek so he attacked the city. When they took refuge in a tower, he burned it down. He moved on to the city of Thebez and, while preparing to burn down the tower, a woman threw a millstone down and cracked his skull. His armor bearer killed him so it wouldn't be said a woman killed Abimelek. God punished Abimelek and Shechem for killing Gideon's sons.

JUDGES 10

After Abimelek, Tola rescued Israel for twenty-three years. He was from the tribe of Issachar. Then Jair from Gilead judged for twenty-two years, with his thirty sons who rode on thirty donkeys. Then the people of Israel worshipped the gods of their enemies. God's anger burned. When the people cried out, God refused to help them and told them to cry out to their own gods.

JUDGES 11

Gilead had a child with a prostitute. The boy was named Jephthah and Gilead's half-brothers kicked him out, not wanting him to share in the inheritance. Then, the Ammonites threatened the region, the elders asked Jephthah to lead the army against the Ammonites. Jephthah made them swear he would be their leader. They agreed. After Jephthah sent a threat to the Ammonites that was ignored, he went to war, making a vow that when he returned home he would sacrifice the first thing that came through the door. After destroying twenty cities, Jephthah returned home and his daughter was first through the door. She agreed that the vow had to be carried through, but wanted two months to weep in the mountains with her friends.

JUDGES 12

The Ephraimites were upset that the Gileadites attacked the Ammonites without their help. When they threatened Jephthah, he went to war and struck them down. They set up stations to test the accents of travelers and if they pronounced the word "Shibboleth" "Sibboleth" they were struck down. 43,000 Ephraimites were killed. Ibzan the judge had thirty sons and married off thirty daughters to other clans. He led for seven years. Elon led Israel for ten years. Abdon had forty sons and thirty daughters who rode seventy donkeys. He led Israel for eight years.

JUDGES 13

The Israelites did evil once again. Philistines took power for forty years. A Danite named Manoah and his wife were sterile and childless. The angel of the Lord appeared to her and told her that she would have a son, but he must not drink wine or any fermented drink, must stay away from anything unclean and no razor can come to his head. When his wife told Manoah what happened, he wanted confirmation and asked to meet with the man. The angel arrived and repeated the command. Then when the couple gave a sacrifice, the angel disappeared in the flames to the sky. They realized this was God! Samson was born and the spirit stirred in him.

JUDGES 14

Samson told his parents he wanted a wife from among the Philistines. As they all went to get her, a lion attacked and Samson tore it apart with his bare hands. Later, as he walked by the carcass, he saw a swarm of bees inside and scooped out the honey. He told a riddle to the Philistines about the honey soaked lion, offering a prize of thirty sets of clothes and garments. Samson refused to give them the answer. After his wife complained, Samson explained the riddle to her. When she told the people the answer, Samson got furious and killed thirty men and gave their clothes to the ones who solved the riddle. Samson's wife was given to another man.

JUDGES 15

Samson went to get his wife and discovered she had been given to another. Irate, Samson tied three hundred foxes together and put a torch in between them. They scurried around and lit up all the fields, vineyards and olive groves. Samson retreated into Judah. The Philistines came to capture him and Judah agreed to get him themselves. Three thousand men from Judah asked Samson if they could turn him over. He agreed if they tied his hands. When the Philistines came to get him, the Spirit of the Lord came upon him and he killed a thousand men with a donkey jawbone. He was thirsty and God open up a spring.

JUDGES 16

Samson met a prostitute in Gaza. When the locals came to arrest him he tore off their city gates and deposited them near Hebron. He fell in love with a woman name Delilah and the Philistines bribed her to find out Samson's secret of his strength. She nagged him and Samson told her three lies – seven fresh bowstrings not dried, new ropes never used, seven braids of his hair woven in a loom. Finally he told her that no razor had come to his head. When they shaved his head, his strength left him. They gouged out his eyes and put him in prison to grind grain. Samson's hair began to grow. As they put him in their god Dagon's temple for entertainment, Samson pleaded with God for one more opportunity to serve him. He pushed down the pillars and killed 3,000. Samson had judged for six years.

JUDGES 17

A man from Ephraim, Micah, made an idol from shekels and put it in his house with an ephod and other idols. Israel had no leader and everyone did what they wanted. Micah met a Levite and hired him to be his personal priest.

JUDGES 18

The Danites, looking for a land to call their own, attacked Ephraim and enter Micah's city. They went to Micah's house and took his idol and priest. Micah could not overpower them. The Danites rebuilt Laish and called it Dan. They set up the idol to worship.

JUDGES 19

A Levite and his concubine left Bethlehem and travelled to Gibeah in Benjamin. They stopped in the city square but no one took them in. Finally a man from Ephraim allowed to stay at his place. That night, evil men of the city wanted to have sex with the stranger. The host offered his virgin daughters. The crowd refused. The Levite offered his concubine. They raped her and left her for dead. The Levite cut the woman in twelve pieces and sent them to all areas of Israel.

JUDGES 20

The tribes reacted in horror to the body parts sent to them, so the tribes surrounded Gibeah and the Benjamites. They asked for the evil men, but Benjamin refused to release them. The tribes inquired of the Lord who encouraged them to move ahead. After two setbacks, Benjamin was destroyed, putting the town to the sword.

JUDGES 21

The tribes lamented the destruction of Benjamin and the gap in the tribes, but they made a solemn oath that no one would give their daughter to a Benjamite in marriage. The tribes of Israel gathered at Mizpah and discovered one group from Jabesh Gilead failed to show up. The tribes sent 12,000 fighting men to kill every male and woman who was not a virgin in Jabesh Gilead. They took 400 virgins and gave them to the surviving

Benjamites. There was not enough women. So they encouraged the Benjamites to kidnap the girls of Shiloh and take them home to rebuild the tribe. In those days there was no king and everyone did what they saw fit.

RUTH

Number of Chapters: *4*
Author Unknown: *?*
Approximate time span: 1300-1280 BC (around 12 years)

RUTH 1

A famine caused Elimelek and his wife Naomi to move to Moab with her sons. The sons married two Moabite women, Orpah and Ruth. When her husband and sons died, Naomi decided to return to Bethlehem and told her daughter in laws they should stay in Moab. Only Ruth agreed to go with her. Orpah returned to Moab. When Naomi arrived home, the town was amazed. She asked to be called Mara because of her bitterness.

RUTH 2

Ruth gleaned grain in the fields and met Boaz who caught his eye. He asked the others who she was and gave her special treatment and protection. Naomi rejoiced over the grain Ruth picked and called Boaz a kinsmen-redeemer, a close relative.

RUTH 3

Naomi encouraged Ruth to present herself to Boaz by laying at his feet on the threshing floor. Ruth did so and pleased Boaz who called her kind. He offered to help her.

RUTH 4

Boaz settled legal matters with the true kinsman-redeemer, next in line to acquire Elimelek's and his sons' land. However, the transaction included Ruth, who the kinsman-redeemer refused. Boaz acquired the property and Ruth. They married and had a son, Obed. Obed's son was Jesse, whose son was David.

1 SAMUEL

Number of Chapters: *31*
Author Unknown: *Possibly Samuel, Nathan, Gad*
Approximate time span: 1105-1011 BC (94 years)

1 SAMUEL 1

A man named Elkanah had two wives, Hannah and Peninnah. Hannah could not have children and Peninnah teased her. Hannah went to pray at the temple to pray for a child while Eli watched her. Because of her passionate prayer, Eli misinterpreted her behavior for drunkenness. When she told him her request, he affirmed it and Hannah promised to dedicate the child to the Lord. After Hannah conceived and gave birth, she made good on her promise and gave her son Samuel to Eli.

1 SAMUEL 2

Hannah sang a song of praise to God. Eli's sons were wicked, eating the choice parts of the offering and sleeping with women who served at the Tent of Meeting. Eli prayed for Hannah to have more children and she had five more while Samuel grew and served the Lord. A man of God prophesied that both of Eli's sons would die the same day since they disgraced God.

1 SAMUEL 3

Samuel heard someone calling him three times, thinking it was Eli. Finally Eli told him it was probably God and to answer. The fourth time Samuel did and God told him that Eli's time as priest would end soon.

1 SAMUEL 4

Israel attacked the Philistines, but the Philistines fought back, killing about 4,000 of them. The Israelites decided to bring the ark to camp, but that did not deter the Philistines, who slaughtered 30,000, captured the ark. Eli's sons, Hophi and Phinehas, died. When Eli heard the news, he fell off his chair and broke his neck (apparently he was old, blind and fat).

Phinehas' wife gave birth to a son, who she named Ichabod, which means "the glory of the Lord has departed Israel."

1 SAMUEL 5

The Philistines placed the ark in the temple of their god, Dagon, but when they woke up in the morning, the idol was face down before the ark, with its head and hands broken off. Tumors began to spread among the people. The Philistines moved the ark to Gath and the same outbreak occurred. So they move the ark to Ekron and more died. Tumors broke out on those that did not die.

1 SAMUEL 6

After seven months, the Philistines returned the ark on a cart and pointed it towards Beth Shemesh. Inside the ark they put five gold rats and five gold tumors, representing the rulers and cities inflicted with the plague. When the ark arrived, the people rejoiced, but seventy men looked inside the ark and died.

1 SAMUEL 7

The men of Kiriath Jearim took the ark to Abinadab's house. During the 20 years the ark was there, Samuel pleaded for people throw away their idols. The Philistines threatened, but God scared them with thunder and panic. The Israelites pursued the Philistines and killed them. Samuel set up a stone and called it Ebenezer, meaning the Lord has helped us. Samuel remained as judge over Israel all the days of his life.

1 SAMUEL 8

Samuel's sons were corrupt and Samuel was getting old, so the people asked for a king. God warned them saying a king would take a lot from them, but they still demanded. God said, "Give them a king."

1 SAMUEL 9

Saul, a Benjamite, went looking for his father's lost donkeys. Unsuccessful, they decided to ask the local seer, Samuel. God had told Samuel that on that day he would send the next king of Israel. Samuel met Saul and prepared to anoint him.

1 SAMUEL 10

Samuel anointed Saul as king, then told him where to find the donkeys. God changed Saul's heart. Saul joined a procession of prophets and began prophesying, shocking those who knew him. Samuel announced to the people that Saul was their new king. They proclaimed, "Long live the king!"

1 SAMUEL 11

King Nahash the Ammonite led his army to Jabesh Gilead and threatened to kill them. When they asked for a treaty, he offered to gouge out their right eyes. Saul rescued the city of Jabesh and the nation crowned him as king.

1 SAMUEL 12

Samuel addressed the people, confirming with them that he was an honest man who never stole from them. They agreed. He warned them about following idols and chastised them about asking for a king. Samuel prayed for rain and it came, causing the people to realize their sin.

1 SAMUEL 13

Before a scary stand-off with the Philistines in which the Israelites were outnumbered, the army waited for Samuel's arrival. Impatient, Saul made the burnt offering himself just as Samuel arrived. Samuel announced that another king would rule instead, a man after God's heart. Saul's army did not have weapons as they prepared to fight the Philistines.

1 SAMUEL 14

Jonathan performed a solo sneak attack on the Philistines, causing chaos in their camp. When Saul's army also attacked, the Philistines were killing each other and in confusion. Saul told his army not to eat food before their enemies have fallen. Not knowing about the curse, Jonathan ate honey. When told, Jonathan thought the command was foolish. When Saul asked God for permission to attack the Philistines, he got no answer and decided to cast lots to figure out the problem. It landed on Jonathan, who confessed to eating the honey. Saul wanted to kill him, but the soldiers protested. Saul had military success. His family lineage is outlined.

1 SAMUEL 15

Samuel told Saul to defeat the Amalekites and to destroy everything and everyone in the nation. Saul defeated the Amalekites, but did not kill the best livestock and King Agag, who he brought back to the camp. Samuel arrived and heard the bleating of sheep. Samuel told Saul that God rejected him as king and was sorry he ever made him king. Samuel killed King Agag.

1 SAMUEL 16

Tired of Saul, God told Samuel to go to Bethlehem to see the man God had chosen to be king. God directed him to Jesse and his sons, telling Samuel to not judge by outward appearances. God judges a person's thoughts and intentions. After seeing all the sons, Samuel didn't feel God's approval until Jesse called for his youngest son David who was tending sheep. Samuel anointed him. The Spirit of God left Saul and he was tormented by spirits. Samuel's servants suggested music to calm him. David, who played harp, was hired and Saul was pleased and made him an armor-bearer too.

1 SAMUEL 17

The Israelite and Philistine army faced off at the Valley of Elah. Goliath, a giant, challenged anyone from the Israelite army to fight him. The winner won the entire battle. No one took up the offer. David, delivering food and messages to his brothers at the front lines, heard of the insults coming from Goliath and offered to fight him. Saul tried to dress him in armor but David said he had killed lions and bears as a shepherd. Goliath mocked David, until David charged him with a sling and planted a stone in his forehead. David cut off Goliath's head and the Israelites routed the Philistines.

1 SAMUEL 18

David and Jonathan bonded. The people credited David with ten times more deaths than Saul, making Saul jealous. Saul raved like a madman, throwing his spear at David to kill him. Saul gave his daughter Merab to David, as his other daughter Michal fell in love with him. David refused marriage to a king's daughter, wondering how his humble family could afford the bride price. Saul asked for one hundred Philistine foreskins. David brought two hundred. Saul gave David Michal.

1 SAMUEL 19

Jonathan warned David about his father. Saul promised not to kill him, but when David arrived to play the harp, an evil spirit caused Sault to hurl a spear at him. Saul even sent troops to David's house. Michal warned David and helped him escape, then set up a fake idol with goat hair to pretend David was asleep in bed. The troops arrived and discovered he was gone. When word got out that David was in Naoith, Saul sent troops there, but all three battalions began prophesying with prophets. When Saul himself went to Naoith, he too prophesied, laying naked on the ground all night.

1 SAMUEL 20

Jonathan and David set up a signal with arrows to indicate whether Saul was angry at David or not. At dinner, Saul flew into a rage at Jonathan saying, "David must die" and threw a spear at his son. Jonathan delivered the signal and David went on the run.

1 SAMUEL 21

David asked Ahimelek the priest for bread for his men. Ahimelek gave him all that he had – the consecrated bread. Doeg the Edomite witnessed this. Ahimelek gave David Goliath's sword. David traveled to Gath and met King Achish. David acted insane around the king to fool him so he could stay.

1 SAMUEL 22

Saul was furious at his men since they had done nothing to stop David. Doeg told Saul about Ahimelek giving David bread. Saul had Ahimelek brought to him and accused him of treason. After none of Saul's officials agreed to kill Ahimelek, Saul asked Doeg who killed the priest then eighty-five other priests and a whole town of priests. Abiathar, Ahimelek's son, escaped and told David about the massacre.

1 SAMUEL 23

David inquired of God if he should save the city of Keilah from the Philistines. God gave him permission. Saul pursued him but God never gave David over to him. Jonathan met with David to encourage him. David slipped into En Gedi.

1 SAMUEL 24

In a cave in En Gedi, Saul went in to relieve himself. David, hiding in the shadows, crept up and cut off a corner of Saul's robe. As Saul left, David, conscience-stricken, stepped out and apologized to Saul for his act. Saul could not believe David was being so kind to him, when he was being so vindictive towards David. Saul admitted that David was more righteous than he was and would ultimately be king.

1 SAMUEL 25

Samuel died. David approached Nabal, a rich livestock owner, for food for his troops. Nabal told him to get lost. Nabal's wife, Abigail, quickly prepared food and met David's troops marching to kill Nabal. David was touched by her kindness. After hearing what Abigail did, Nabal died and David married Abigail, in addition to another woman, Ahinoam. Saul had given Michal away to a man named Paltiel.

1 SAMUEL 26

David snuck into Saul's camp with Abishai. Abishai wanted to kill the king but David stopped him. They stole Saul's spear and water jug, then called out to Abner, Saul's bodyguard, telling him he was inept in protecting God's anointed. Saul was once again convicted by David's loyalty.

1 SAMUEL 27

David hid out with the Philistines to keep distance between he and Saul. King Achish allowed David, his six hundred soldiers and their families to live in Ziklag. David would live there then head out to conquer Geshurites, Girzites and Amalekites. He killed everyone he attacked so no one could inform on them. Each time he returned to this Philistine controlled area.

1 SAMUEL 28

Achish, king of Gath, asked David to fight against Israel, as his lifetime bodyguard. Saul, unable to hear from God through a prophet, dreams or Urim, visited a medium at Endor. She called up a spirit who was Samuel. Samuel chastised Saul saying this was exactly why Israel was taken from him. He promised that tomorrow Saul and his sons would be given over to the Philistines. Saul mourned.

1 SAMUEL 29

The Philistine commanders grew uneasy about David joining their ranks and asked the king to dismiss him. Achish defended David but relented and asked David not to join in battle.

1 SAMUEL 30

David and his men arrived in Ziklag and found that the Amalekites had burned the city and captured all the women and children, including David's wives. Some of his army were too weak to fight and stayed back while the others defeated the Amalekites and retrieved their families and everything stolen from them. David defended those who stayed behind and allowed them to share in the plunder.

1 SAMUEL 31

Saul fought the Philistines. Jonathan and Saul's two other sons killed and Saul was wounded by archers. He asked the armor bearer to kill him, but the armor bearer refused. Saul fell on his own sword. The Philistines beheaded Saul and hung his body on the wall at Beth Shan. They put his armor in the temple of the Ashtoreths. The people of Jabesh Gilead removed Saul's body and gave him a proper burial.

2 SAMUEL

Number of Chapters: 24
Author Unknown: Possibly Nathan/Gad
Approximate time span: 1010-970 BC (40 years)

2 SAMUEL 1

An Amalekite said he found Saul on his spear and Saul asked the man to kill him. The Amalekite said he did and brought David Saul's crown. When David heard the news, he tore his robes and had the messenger killed who said/lied that he killed Saul, God's anointed. David sang a lament for Saul and Jonathan.

2 SAMUEL 2

David anointed king over Judah. Meanwhile, Saul's son Ish-bosheth was declared king of Israel by Abner, Saul's commander. David's and Saul's army fight a little twelve-on-twelve battle. Abner kills Asahel, Joab's brother, who refused to stop chasing him, even after Joab warned him. Joab and Abishai pursued Abner, who called for a truce.

2 SAMUEL 3

Abner, offended by Ish-Bosheth's comment that he slept with Saul's concubine, defected to David's side. David asked for Michal back, while her husband cried. Joab, after he heard Abner came to David's side, called Abner a spy. He and his brother Abishai killed Abner for killing their brother Asahel.

2 SAMUEL 4

When a nurse heard of the death of Saul and Jonathan, she hurriedly picked up the son of Jonathan to run, but dropped him, causing him to become lame in both feet. Ish-Bosheth was killed while lying in bed by Recab and Baanah, who brought his head to David. David had Recab and Baanah killed and hung their bodies outside.

2 SAMUEL 5

David anointed King of Israel. David marched into Jerusalem and took it from the Jebusites. He captured the fortress of Zion and called it the City of David. The King of Tyre sent cedar and workers to build a palace for David. God told David to defeat the Philistines at the Valley of Rephaim.

2 SAMUEL 6

David led a huge procession with the ark from the house of Abinadab, putting it on a new cart pulled by oxen. But when the oxen stumbled, Uzzah reached out to grab the ark. He touched it and God was angry at his irreverent act. Uzzah died. David was angry at God. They parked the ark at the house of Obed-Edom for three months. His house prospered during that time. Then, wearing only a linen ephod, David led another procession (this time they carried the ark), sacrificing along the way and dancing with all his might. His wife Michal saw him dance disrespectfully, half naked. David said he would be humiliated before his own eyes so God could be honored. Michal had no more children from that day on.

2 SAMUEL 7

David realized he sat in a cedar palace and the ark sat in a tent. God came to Nathan and encouraged David to build a temple, promising that someone from his line would sit on the throne forever (a prophecy that led to Jesus from his family line). David was humbled that God would choose him for this honor.

2 SAMUEL 8

David had great victories against the Philistines, Moabites and the Arameans. He dedicated great quantities of gold, silver and bronze to the Lord. God gave him all these victories.

2 SAMUEL 9

David asked Ziba if there was anyone he could show kindness to in the line of Jonathan. Ziba mentioned Mephibosheth, crippled in both feet. David brought him in and promised to restore his position and allow him to eat his table. Mephibosheth, humbled, called himself nothing but a dead dog.

2 SAMUEL 10

David reached out to the Ammonites when their king died, but they humiliated the envoys by shaving off half their beards. David was furious. The Ammonites hired Aramean soldiers to defend themselves, but David beat them all in battle.

2 SAMUEL 11

David should be at war fighting the Ammonites who besieged Rabbah, but he stayed behind. One night he looked outside and saw Bathsheba bathing on the roof. He sent for her and slept with her. When she announced that she was pregnant, David tried to get her husband Uriah to come home from battle and sleep with his wife. Dedicated to his soldiers, he refused. So David had the army pull back, leaving him behind and defenseless. Uriah was killed. The news was broken to David and Bathsheba mourned. After the time of mourning, he married her. God wasn't too happy.

2 SAMUEL 12

The prophet Nathan told David a story about a rich man who took a poor man's sheep to feed a traveler when the rich man had flocks and flocks. David was outraged at the rich man from the story until Nathan said, "You are that man." David understood the gravity of his sin. Nathan announced that the child he conceived with Bathsheba would die. David fasted and mourned until the child died. Bathsheba became pregnant again and had Solomon. David went to Rabbah and helped the troops defeat the Ammonites.

2 SAMUEL 13

David's son Amnon fell in love with his half-sister, Tamar. An adviser told Amnon to act sick and have Tamar bring him food in bed. He did so and raped her. After he raped her, he hated her and had her sent away. She mourned the loss of her virginity. Absalom knew what happened and had Amnon killed.

Word got back to David that all his sons were dead, but it was only Amnon. Absalom ran away and hid.

2 SAMUEL 14

Joab sent a wise woman in disguise to David to discover his heart about Absalom. David realized he must make amends with Absalom. Absalom returned to the city but did not see the king for two years. Absalom was handsome, flawless from head to toe. He had beautiful hair that had to be cut because it was so heavy. Absalom wanted to see the king so he called for Joab who didn't return his calls. Absalom had his servants set fire to Joab's fields. Joab finally showed up and Absalom asked him to set up a meeting with David. They met and David kissed him.

2 SAMUEL 15

Absalom sat by the city gates, advising and consoling people so their hearts turned to him. He asked to go to Hebron where he set himself as the heir to the throne. Instead of fighting his own son, David fled as Absalom entered the city. David left the ark, ten concubines and the priests in the city.

2 SAMUEL 16

David gave Ziba Mephibosheth's possessions, when Ziba told him Mephibosheth wanted the kingdom to return to him. Shimei cursed and threw rocks at David, but David allowed him to, believing God instructed him to. Absalom was advised by Ahithophel to sleep with David's concubines, in plain sight of all of Israel.

2 SAMUEL 17

Absalom's adviser Ahithophel told Absalom to attack David with 12,000 men. Hushai gave different advice, saying gather all Israel, from Dan to Beersheba, creating a bigger army. Absalom agreed with Hushai, but it was the Lord's plan so Absalom could fail. When Ahithophel saw his advice was not followed, he hung himself. David was informed of Absalom's plans by two messengers and prepared for battle.

2 SAMUEL 18

David divided his troops under three commanders: Joab, Abishai and Ittai. As the battle heated up, Absalom, riding his mule, got stuck in a tree by his hair and was hanging there. No one wanted to kill the king's son. So Joab took three javelins and killed him. Two messengers delivered the news to David. David mourned in his room.

2 SAMUEL 19

Joab rebuked David for mourning Absalom, saying David would rather his rebellious son live and one of them die. David put Amasa, Absalom's commander, in charge over Joab. After the people wondered who was in charge, David returned to Jerusalem and restored the kingdom. Shimei came out and apologized to the king for defaming him. David allowed him to live. Mephibosheth also met David and told him Ziba his servant betrayed him. Barzillai the Gileadite, an old man who showed great kindness to David and his troops, was asked to join David as he entered Jerusalem. Barzillai politely declined.

2 SAMUEL 20

The men of Israel led by Shea rebelled against David, except for the men of Judah. David gave Amasa a task to mobilize the men of Judah. Amasa took longer than the assigned three days. Joab found Amasa and killed him, telling Amasa's men to follow him instead. David's men pursued Sheba to a city and sieged it. A wise woman negotiated with Joab and they threw Sheba's head over the wall to stop the attack.

2 SAMUEL 21

Because of a famine in Israel, David asked God why it was happening and God said because Saul attacked the Gibeonites, who the Israelites had a treaty with since the days of Joshua. In return, the Gibeonites asked for seven male descendants of Saul for payment. David gave them seven descendants. David was getting too old to battle, but his men fought some impressive battles, especially against giants and freakish six digit men.

2 SAMUEL 22

David sang a song about being delivered from his enemies because of the awesome power of God.

2 SAMUEL 23

The last words of David, plus a quick history of the deeds of his mighty men.

2 SAMUEL 24

God punished David for the census of his army. God gave him three options for punishment. David couldn't choose so God chose for him. David cried out during the plague for it to stop. David built an altar on the threshing floor of Araunah after he saw an angel of the Lord standing there. Araunah offered it to David for free but David said how can it be a sacrifice if it cost him nothing?

1 KINGS

Number of Chapters: *22*
Author Unknown: *Possibly Jeremiah*
Approximate time span: 970-850 BC (130 years)

1 KINGS 1

Since David was getting old, his associates brought in Abishag, a beautiful young girl, to keep him warm (though he never had sexual relations with her). Adonijah, David's son by Haggith, positioned himself to be king, causing Zadok the priest and Nathan the prophet to be concerned. David swore to Bathsheba that he would make Solomon king. Zadok anointed Solomon. Adonijah heard the news and panicked, asking Solomon for forgiveness and received it.

1 KINGS 2

Before David died he gave Solomon advice to walk in the ways of God and reminded Solomon of David's enemies. When David passed away, Solomon took care of all of David's enemies. Adonijah asked Bathsheba for Abishag. Solomon refused and had Adonijah killed by Benaiah. He allowed the priest Abiathar to live since he carried the ark. Solomon then had traitors like Joab killed and then Shimei, who disobeyed Solomon's request for him to stay outside Jerusalem.

1 KINGS 3

Solomon had a dream in Gibeon that God came to him and asked him what Solomon wanted God to give him. Solomon recognized how difficult it was to lead these people so he asked for wisdom. God agreed, acknowledging all the things Solomon did not ask for (long life, riches, death for enemies), but gave those things to him anyway. Solomon's wisdom was displayed when two prostitutes argued over a child and Solomon revealed the true mother by offering to cut the child in two.

1 KINGS 4

A list of Solomon's officials and governors. The time of Solomon's reign was very peaceful. Solomon's wisdom of plant life, animals, birds, reptiles and fish became world renown and people came from all over to listen to him.

1 KINGS 5

Solomon negotiated with King Hiram of Tyre to collect cedars and cut stone for the temple. Solomon hired 30,000 laborers, 70,000 carriers, 80,000 stonecutters and 3,300 foremen to do the work.

1 KINGS 6

480 years after the Israelites left Egypt and four years into Solomon's reign, Solomon began building the temple. Made of cedar, gold and olive wood, the temple was finished after seven years. God promised Solomon that if he followed his laws and kept his commands, he would honor the promise he made to Solomon's father David and keep a descendant on the throne.

1 KINGS 7

Solomon built his palace, taking a total of thirteen years. The work required a lot of detail, done by a guy from Tyre named Huram. When all the work was done, Solomon brought his father's silver and gold into the temple treasuries.

1 KINGS 8

The ark was brought into the temple with great fanfare and sacrifice. Solomon dedicated the temple with prayer and thousands of sacrifices. The glory of the Lord showed up and the party lasted fourteen days.

1 KINGS 9

God warned Solomon about turning away or God would turn the temple into rubble. Solomon gave ten towns to the King of Tyre, but the king was not pleased with them. Solomon conscripted labor from many of their enemies, but the Israelites did not act as slaves. Solomon built ships to get gold from Ophir.

1 KINGS 10

Queen of Sheba stopped by to admire Solomon's wisdom. Solomon grew in riches, receiving 666 talents a year in gold. Solomon accumulated shields, chariots, horses and built a huge throne. He had so much gold, silver was considered worthless. People came from all over to hear his wisdom, bringing more and more gifts.

1 KINGS 11

Solomon tied the knot 700 times, with 300 concubines thrown in too. His wives led him astray with high places and false idols such as Ashtoreth, Molek and Chemosh. Because of Solomon's disobedience by intermarrying and his worshipping of foreign gods, God raised up adversaries such as Hadad and Rezon. Jeroboam, a foreman on the city wall, was told by the prophet Ahijah that God would tear the kingdom away and give him ten nations. God promised to bless that new nation if Jeroboam followed closely to God's ways. Solomon died after forty years of reign. His son Rehoboam succeeded him.

1 KINGS 12

Rehoboam became king and rejected the advice of wise advisers who asked him to lighten the load on the people. Instead, he made things harder. The people rejected him and turned to Jeroboam. Ten nations followed Jeroboam and two (Judah and Benjamin) followed Rehoboam. God refused Rehoboam permission to attack his fellow Israelites to the north. Jeroboam, worried that people would go to Jerusalem to make sacrifices, set up two golden calves in an altar in Bethel and Dan, telling the people to worship their gods there.

1 KINGS 13

A man of God cursed the altar in Bethel. Jeroboam reached out his hand to the man, but Jeroboam's hand shriveled up. The altar split apart. The man of God interceded for Jeroboam and his hand was restored. Jeroboam wanted to eat with the man of God but the man was told by God not to eat with anyone. A prophet deceived the man of God by inviting him to eat. The prophet declared a curse on the old prophet. A lion killed the man of God for disobeying his directive to not eat with anyone. The lion and the man's donkey stood over his body in the road.

1 KINGS 14

Jeroboam's son Abijah got sick so Jeroboam asked his wife to disguise herself and go inquire of the prophet Ahijah what would happen to him. Ahijah's prophesized against Jeroboam about his son dying and his entire kingdom falling apart, eventually being eaten by dogs and birds. When Jeroboam's wife arrived home, her son Abijah died. Jeroboam died after twenty-two years in power. Rehoboam's kingdom was also sinful, worshipping other gods. God allowed Shishak king of Egypt to attack Jerusalem and steal the treasuries of the temple. Rehoboam died and his son Abijah succeeded him.

1 KINGS 15

Abijah King of Judah was not fully devoted to God. He died. His son Asa King of Judah did what was right in God's eyes and expelled the temple prostitutes, even his queen mother Maacah because she made an Asherah pole. But, he kept the high places. Asa and Baasha fought, so Asa gave all the temple treasuries to Ben-Hadad of Aram to help him. Asa and Aram overpowered Baasha. Jeroboam's son Nadab succeeded him as king. Baasha killed Nadab and all of Jeroboam's family in accordance to the prophecy of Ahijah. Baasha King of Israel did evil in the eyes of the Lord.

1 KINGS 16

God told the prophet Jehu that Baasha's ancestors would be wiped out. After Baasha died, Elah King of Israel (the son of Baasha), was killed by Zimri, one of his officials, and became king for seven days. Zimri was overthrown by Omri King of Israel, the commander of his army. He ruled twelve years and his son Ahab King of Israel became king. He was the husband of Jezebel. Omri built Samaria and Ahab built a temple to Baal there. During Ahab's tenure, Hiel of Bethel rebuilt Jericho and his son died, according to the prophecy of Joshua that anyone who tried to rebuild Jericho would lose their firstborn son.

1 KINGS 17

A prophet Elijah announced a drought on the land. In the meantime, ravens fed him meat and bread by a brook. God directed him to the house of a widow who was promised a multiplying supply of oil and flour to keep them all alive. Her son became gravely ill and died, but Elijah stretched out over him and raised her son from death.

1 KINGS 18

Following God's orders, Elijah went to meet Ahab and along the way met Obadiah, a devout believer and palace administrator who hid 100 of God's prophets in caves away from Jezebel who was threatening to kill them all. Elijah challenged Ahab to a duel, 450 prophets of Baal and 400 prophets of Asherah versus Elijah. Elijah told them to set up a sacrifice on Mount Carmel and pray to their god to light the fire for the sacrifice. The 450 prophets of Baal danced and cut themselves for hours. The whole time Elijah taunted them. Then he set up an altar with twelve stones and had it soaked with water. After he prayed to God, fire fell from the sky and lit everything on fire. The people of Israel who witnessed the event proclaimed the Lord as the only God! The prophets of Baal were slaughtered in the valley of Kishon. A small rain cloud appeared in the distance and Elijah on foot outran Ahab in a chariot.

1 KINGS 19

After hearing that Jezebel wanted him dead for killing all the prophets, Elijah fled to Beersheba. An angel woke him and made him something to eat. Elijah walked forty days to Mount Horeb. God wondered what he was doing there. God ministered to him, speaking to him, not in the wind or the earthquake or the fire, but in a whisper. God told Elijah to anoint Hazael king of Aram, Jehu king of Israel and Elisha. Elijah found Elisha plowing and put his mantle over Elisha's shoulders. Elisha killed his oxen and burned his plow equipment and followed Elijah.

1 KINGS 20

Ben-Hadad from Aram attacked Samaria. A man of God came to Ahab and said Israel would win and know who the true

God was. But, Ahab must not to allow Ben-Hadad to live. When the Israelites defeated the Arameans, two times, Ahab disobeyed and allowed Ben-Hadad (who he called his brother) to live and another prophet pronounced judgment on him.

1 KINGS 21

Ahab asked Naboth, a farmer whose vineyard bordered Ahab's palace, to trade or sell his vineyard so Ahab could plant a vegetable garden. Naboth refused. Jezebel told Ahab that was no way for king to act. So Jezebel had Naboth killed for his vineyard after being falsely accused for blasphemy by two scoundrels. He was taken out and stoned. Ahab took possession of the vineyard. Elijah prophesied that dogs would lick up his blood and eat Jezebel's body. Ahab humbled himself and God delayed the punishment.

1 KINGS 22

Jehoshaphat King of Judah aligned with Ahab to go to war with Aram over the city Ramoth Gilead. Four hundred prophets said go fight. One prophet, who never said anything good to Ahab, Micaiah, predicted the war would go well but Israel would be scattered. Micaiah saw God talk to all the spirits about sending a deceiving spirit to all the prophets. Micaiah was slapped by Zedekiah then imprisoned. Israel and Judah attacked Ramoth Gilead. Ahab fought in disguise, but a random arrow killed him. Dogs licked up his blood that had spilled into a prostitute's pool, just as Elijah predicted. Jehoshaphat King of Judah followed the good ways of his father Asa but did not remove the high places. His son Jehoram succeeded him. When Ahab died, his son Ahaziah King of Israel followed the ways of his evil parents.

2 KINGS

Number of Chapters: 25
Author Unknown: Possibly Jeremiah
Approximate time span: 850-560 BC (290 years)

2 KINGS 1

King Ahaziah of Israel fell through the lattice and was injured. He wanted to inquire of the god Baal-Zebub whether he would recover. Elijah intercepted the messengers and prophesied that he would die in bed since he did not inquire of God. Two times the king sent a company of men to arrest Elijah and those soldiers burned up with fire from heaven. The third company pleaded for mercy and Elijah went with them to the king to pass on the message face-to-face. Ahaziah died. He had no son so Joram succeeded him.

2 KINGS 2

Elisha and a company of prophets all knew that Elijah was about to go to heaven. Elisha followed Elijah to Bethel, Jericho and the Jordan. Elijah parted the Jordan River with his cloak. Elisha asked for a double portion of what Elijah had. A chariot of fire took Elijah away. Fifty prophets showed up and offered to go look for Elijah, thinking maybe he was dropped off at some mountain. Elisha said don't bother but permitted them when they insisted. They didn't find Elijah and Elisha said "I told you so." Elisha healed the bad city water by adding salt. Elisha was jeered by some youths who called him "Baldy" so Elisha cursed them. Two bears mauled the teens.

2 KINGS 3

Joram King of Israel became king. Moab rebelled against Israel, not paying their tribute of lambs and wool. Angry, Joram asked Jehoshaphat to join him (and the nation of Edom) to attack Moab. When the armies couldn't find water for days, Jehoshaphat asked for a prophet's permission first. Elisha was suggested and when he arrived, he showed favor to the kings because of Jehoshaphat. Elisha told them to dig ditches in the valley and in the morning they would be full of water. They obeyed, but when the Moabites woke up and saw the ditches, the valley water looked like pools of blood. Thinking the enemies slaughtered themselves they celebrated, but the Israelites attacked and devastated the land.

2 KINGS 4

A prophet's widow needed income or her boys would be sold into slavery, so Elisha told her to pour oil into all the jars she could collect. The oil kept multiplying until she had enough to pay off her debts. Elisha paid back a wealthy Shunammite women's hospitality (she had a room made for Elisha that was his anytime he visited) by prophesying that she would have a son. She did, but when the boy was one year old, he had a massive headache and died. The woman called for Elisha and he stretched out over him and the boy lived. A company of prophets made a stew, but unknowingly it had a poison herb. After the prophets took a couple bites, Elisha healed the pot of deadly stew by adding flour. Elisha multiplied bread, feeding hundreds of people.

2 KINGS 5

Naaman, a commander of the army of Aram, had leprosy. He went to the king of Israel with a letter of permission to find Elisha. The king tore his robes, wondering why Aram was trying to pick a fight. Elisha heard about this and told Naaman to wash in the Jordan, seven times. Naaman did and was healed. Elisha refused any compensation but his servant Gehazi, thinking Elisha was too easy on Naaman, went and accepted some money which he kept for himself. Elisha confronted Gehazi and said the leprosy would be on him forever.

2 KINGS 6

When the prophets were cutting down trees, an axe head fell off into the Jordan. Elisha caused the axe head to float by throwing a stick into the water. King of Aram went to war with Israel. He sent troops to get Elisha. The Lord caused the army to go blind, while the Lord surrounded Elisha with an army of horses and chariots of fire. Elisha led the blind army into Israel but instead of having them killed, he told the king of Israel to throw them a feast when the blindness was lifted. Later, the King of Aram laid siege on Samaria. The famine inside was so bad they were eating the children and selling donkey heads for an inflated price.

2 KINGS 7

Elisha promised that the siege would be over tomorrow and prices would return to normal. Four men with leprosy inside Samaria decided it was better to die at the enemy's camp then at Samaria. So they went to the camp and found it empty. The army had heard the sounds of chariots and horses and thought the Egyptians were coming. They ran for their lives. The men with leprosy told the Samarians the good news and prices returned to normal.

2 KINGS 8

Elisha told the Shunammite woman there would be a great famine and to go away for seven years. She did and when she returned, the king gave her back her land. Ben-Hadad of Aram was ill and sent Hazael to Elisha to find out whether he would recover. Elisha prophesized that Hazael would become king of Aram and do great destruction to Israel. Hazael murdered Ben-Hadad. Jehoram King of Judah fought the Edomites in a chariot battle. Ahaziah King of Judah, whose mother was Athaliah, fought alongside Joram King of Israel against Aram at Ramoth Gilead. Ahaziah followed in the ways of Ahab because he was related to his family. Ahaziah visited Joram when he got injured.

2 KINGS 9

Elisha had Jehu anointed King of Israel and told him to wipe out the lineage of Ahab. Jehu killed Joram, Ahab's son, and Ahaziah, King of Judah, an ally of Jehu. Jehu found Jezebel in a tower with her servants, putting on her make-up. Her servants threw her off the tower and dogs completely devoured her body until nothing was left but her skull, her feet and her hands.

2 KINGS 10

King Jehu of Israel called the officials at Jezreel to kill all seventy sons of Ahab living in the land. They brought the heads of those sons to Jehu. Then a traveling group of Ahaziah's family came into town and they were killed too. Jehu pretended to be interested in worshipping Baal and called all the servants of Baal. Jehu had the guards cut them all down in the shrine. Their bodies were burned on a sacred stone which people later used as a latrine.

2 KINGS 11

Athaliah, Ahaziah's mom, saw that her son Ahaziah was dead and began to wipe out the entire family line, but a relative named Jehosheba had Joash and his nurse hidden for six years in the temple. Jehoiada, the priest, order the commanders to protect the inauguration of Joash as king. Queen Athaliah was brought out and killed and King Joash of Judah was seven years old when his reign began.

2 KINGS 12

Joash repaired the temple with money that had been dedicated but never used. The workman worked in complete honesty. King Aram attacked Jerusalem but Joash gave him the sacred articles to ward him off. Joash was assassinated by two officials after reigning forty years.

2 KINGS 13

Jehoahaz King of Israel was kept under the power of the king of Aram, but God provided a deliverer for them to escape. The fight with Aram debilitated their army and they never turned away from their sins. Jehoash King of Israel went down to see Elisha when he heard he was dying. Elisha had him shoot an arrow out the window to declare his victory over the Arameans. Then he told him to hit the arrow on the ground. Jehoash only hit the ground three times, which meant he would only defeat the Arameans three times. Elisha then died. A man buried next to Elisha came to life when his body touched Elisha's bones.

2 KINGS 14

Amaziah King of Judah did what was right in the eyes of the Lord but did not tear down the high places. He called out King Jehoash of Israel into battle, lost the fight and was captured. Sections of Jerusalem's wall were knocked down and the treasures from the temple taken. Amaziah's officials kill him and the people made his son, Azariah, king. Jeroboam II king of Israel reigned forty-two years.

2 KINGS 15

Azariah King of Judah was sixteen when his reign began and he was afflicted with leprosy. Zechariah King of Israel was killed by Shallum, who was then assassinated after reigning as king for one month by Menahem. Menahem paid Pul King of Assyria a thousand talents to back off, receiving tributes from the wealthy to keep the enemy away. Menachem son's Pekahiah became King of Israel but was assassinated by Pekah who was assassinated by Hoshea. Jotham son of Azariah became king of Judah and did what was right but did not remove the high places.

2 KINGS 16

Ahaz King of Judah followed the corrupt ways of the kings of Israel, even sacrificing his own son in the fire. When Aram and Israel attacked, Ahaz turned to Assyria for help by paying Assyria with treasures from the temple. When visiting Tiglath-Pileser king of Assyria, Ahaz liked an altar he saw there, sketched it and asked his priest Uriah to build one. When Ahaz returned to Jerusalem, he tore up God's temple in the process. Ahaz died and his son Hezekiah replaced him.

2 KINGS 17

Hoshea was the last king of Israel and he was seized by Shalmaneser king of Assyria. Assyria invaded Israel and laid siege to Samaria for three years. The people were deported to Assyria and people from other nations were told to settle in the cities of Samaria. When those people refused to worship God, God sent lions to attack the land of Israel. The Assyrians believed God was angry so they had a priest sent back to make sure there was more worship of God going on. However, the people worshipped other gods still. This went completely against what God intended when he brought his people out of Egypt.

2 KINGS 18

Hezekiah King of Judah smashed all the high places, Asherah poles and Moses' bronze snake, which people were still worshipping. After taking over Israel/Samaria, Assyria moved closer to Judah, attacking the fortified cities. Hezekiah paid him off with the temple treasures, but Assyria wanted more. The commander of Assyria's army tried to intimidate Hezekiah's army with tough words.

2 KINGS 19

The Prophet Isaiah told Hezekiah not to listen to the King of Assyria. Sennacherib King of Assyria threatened Judah once again in a letter. Hezekiah took the letter and prayed in the temple to God. Isaiah said God heard his prayer and Sennacherib would fall for his blasphemy. An angel of the Lord attacked the Assyrians and 185,000 were found dead the next morning in the Assyrian camp. Sennacherib returned to Nineveh. Sennacherib's sons kill him while he was worshipping his god, Nisroch.

2 KINGS 20

Hezekiah got sick and Isaiah warned him that he would die. Hezekiah prayed and received fifteen more years of life, confirmed by the shadow going backwards ten steps. Hezekiah showed off his storehouses to envoys from Babylon. Isaiah said God was unhappy by that and promised that Babylon would carry away all those treasures to their kingdom.

2 KINGS 21

Manasseh King of Judah was twelve when he became king and he reigned fifty-five years. He worshipped Baals and the starry hosts, putting an Asherah pole in the temple. Manasseh even sacrificed his son in fire. His other son Amon, who next became King of Judah, was assassinated by his officials after only two years and his son Josiah became king.

2 KINGS 22

Josiah King of Judah was only eight when he became king. He repaired the temple. Hilkiah the high priest found the Book of the Law in the temple and read it to the king. The king tore his robes. A prophetess named Huldah told Josiah that God would not bring disaster during his kingdom.

2 KINGS 23

Josiah renewed his covenant with God. The book of the law was read to the people. Josiah removed idols, wiped out the altars, got rid of male shrine prostitutes, removed the high places, stopped sacrifices of children, slaughtered false priests, and kicked out the mediums, spiritists and household gods. He restored Passover. Josiah died facing Pharaoh Necho King of Egypt at Megiddo. His son Jehoahaz King of Judah became king for three months until Necho put him in chains. Necho made Josiah's other son Eliakim king and changed his name to Jehoiakim.

2 KINGS 24

Nebuchadnezzar king of Babylon invaded Judah and allowed Jehoiakim to be his vassal for three years, until he rebelled. Egypt backed off while Babylon ruled. Jehoiachin King of Judah surrendered to Nebuchadnezzar. Nebuchadnezzar carried off items from the temple and the officers, fighting men, skilled workers and artisans to Babylon, leaving only the poor people to care for the vineyards and fields. He made Mattaniah, Jehoiachin's uncle, king and changed his name to Zedekiah King of Judah. Zedekiah rebelled though.

2 KINGS 25

Because of Zedekiah's rebellion, Nebuchadnezzar laid siege to Jerusalem. The city experienced a great famine. The army and Zedekiah, with his family, tried to escape but they are captured and his sons are killed before him. Jerusalem was ransacked by the Babylonians and everything – the temple, the palace, the important buildings – were all burned to the ground. Gedaliah was made governor, but he was assassinated by his own people when he told everyone to accept the Babylonians.

Many fled to Egypt. Jehoiachin was released from prison and Awel-Marduk, now King of Babylon, treated him kindly and allowed him to sit with him at dinner.

1 CHRONICLES

Number of Chapters: 29
Author Unknown: Possibly Ezra
Approximate time span: From creation to 1010-960 BC

1 CHRONICLES 1
A genealogy from Adam to Abraham, detailing the sons of Noah (through Japheth, Ham and Shem), and the descendants of Abraham (through Hagar, Keturah, Sarah), then Esau and the Edomite kings.

1 CHRONICLES 2
The sons of Israel, focusing on Judah, his five sons and those children born through those sons, down to Caleb.

1 CHRONICLES 3
The sons of David (and his wives) and the kings of Judah, followed by David's line after the exile.

1 CHRONICLES 4
Other descendants in the line of Judah, including Jabez. The tribe of Simeon outlined also.

1 CHRONICLES 5
The family line of Reuben, Gad and the half tribe of Manasseh. Reuben lost the rights of the firstborn because he defiled his father's bed, so those rights were given to Joseph instead. Pul King of Assyria took these three tribes captive and marched them into exile.

1 CHRONICLES 6
The family line of Levi through his sons of Kohath (including Aaron, Moses, Miriam), Gershon and Merari down to Samuel. A list of temple musicians and cities of refuge.

1 CHRONICLES 7
The family line of Issachar, Benjamin, Naphtali, Manasseh, Ephraim, Asher.

1 CHRONICLES 8

The family line of Benjamin down to Saul and Jonathan.

1 CHRONICLES 9

The people who returned to Jerusalem after the Babylonian captivity, highlighting those who worked the temple (priests, gatekeepers, bread makers, musicians). A short genealogy of Saul.

1 CHRONICLES 10

The Philistines overwhelmed the Israelites, killing Jonathan and injuring Saul. Saul fell on his sword and his kingdom was turned over to David. He died because he was unfaithful to God.

1 CHRONICLES 11

David became king at Hebron. He marched into Jerusalem, then called Jebus (inhabited by the Jebusites), defeated it and took up residence in the fortress, then called the City of David. The exploits and names of David's mighty warriors were outlined, including Eleazar, Abishai and Benaiah.

1 CHRONICLES 12

Other warriors joined David, from Saul's family line of Benjamin and others from the tribe of Gad and Manasseh. The experience, loyalty and participation of David's army made it unstoppable.

1 CHRONICLES 13

David led the ark from Abinadab's house. When the oxen stumbled with the cart holding the ark, Uzzah reached out to steady it. The Lord struck him down and David was angry. The ark was parked at Obed-Edom's house and the household was blessed.

1 CHRONICLES 14

David's family grew while in Jerusalem, with more wives and more sons. Philistines attacked David's army two times and David defeated them both times, because he inquired of the Lord who gave him permission to attack.

1 CHRONICLES 15

This time David led the ark into Jerusalem the right way. He asked the Levites to carry the ark on their shoulders while musicians played joyfully. David danced in the process and his wife Michal despised him when she saw him.

1 CHRONICLES 16

The ark was placed in a tent in Jerusalem while sacrifices were given. David sang a song of praise. David left the priests and his associates in charge of the ark.

1 CHRONICLES 17

David could not comprehend why he lived in a house of cedar while the ark sat in a tent. Nathan reported to David that God promised to build a house for Himself in Jerusalem. It would not happen with David, but through his son. David prayed to God with thanksgiving and humility, unable to believe that God would use him for such a task.

1 CHRONICLES 18

David was victorious against many enemies, including the Philistines, the Moabites, the Arameans and Hadadezer king of Zobah. Tou, King of Hamath, heard about his victories and sent him gold, silver and bronze. David dedicated it all to the Lord.

1 CHRONICLES 19

David tried to show kindness to the Ammonites by sending envoys when their king died. The Ammonites thought they were spies, so they shaved them, cut their garments at the buttocks and sent them back humiliated. Fearing retaliation, the Ammonites hired the Arameans to help, but David's army defeated them both. The Arameans refused to ever help the Ammonites again.

1 CHRONICLES 20

David, who was supposed to go to war in the spring time, received a crown from Joab after the defeat of Rabbah. The brother of Goliath was defeated by Elhanan. David's nephew, Jonathan, killed another giant with six digits on each hand and foot.

1 CHRONICLES 21

David took a census of his troops despite the objection of Joab, his commander. Gad gave David three choices of punishment for such pride, but David preferred to be in God's hands. God allowed a plague which struck 70,000 people. The angel of death relented after David pleaded for mercy. David built an altar on the threshing floor where he saw an angel.

1 CHRONICLES 22

On the spot where he saw the angel, David prepared to build the temple, gathering the materials. Because he shed so much blood, David could not build the temple, so he passed the duties on to Solomon. David began to accumulate the materials needed.

1 CHRONICLES 23

David passed the reign over to Solomon. He gathered the priests and Levites, the descendants of Levi, the Gershonites, the Kohathites and the Merarites. The duties and purpose of the Levites were outlined.

1 CHRONICLES 24

The divisions of the priests were detailed with the order of the priests who would serve chosen by lot.

1 CHRONICLES 25

A detailed list of the musicians who led the praise music while they prophesied and thanked God.

1 CHRONICLES 26

A detailed list of the gatekeepers watching each gate into the city of Jerusalem, along with the treasurers and other officials.

1 CHRONICLES 27

A list of the divisions of the army, the leaders of the tribes and the various cabinet leaders who served under David. There were twelve divisions of 24,000 soldiers each who served one month a year.

1 CHRONICLES 28

David communicated his plans (God's plans) for the temple to the officials. He handed the plans to his son Solomon, urging him to be obedient to the Lord all the days of his life.

1 CHRONICLES 29

David relinquished his gifts for the temple (gold, silver, bronze, iron, wood, fine stones and marble). His leaders also gave to the building project. David praised God for the gifts. Solomon was accepted as king by the people and David died after forty years of rule.

2 CHRONICLES

Number of Chapters: *36*
Author Unknown: *Possibly Ezra*
Approximate time span: 970-538 BC (over 430 years)

2 CHRONICLES 1
Solomon went to Gibeon where the Tent of Meeting and the altar were located and asked God for wisdom and knowledge. God gave him that plus riches, wealth and honor. Solomon accumulated chariots and horses and he made gold and silver as common as stones in Jerusalem.

2 CHRONICLES 2
Solomon asked the King of Tyre to help him construct the temple. Tyre sent skilled craftsmen and building materials while Solomon enlisted foreigners to do the work.

2 CHRONICLES 3
Solomon began building the temple on Mount Moriah, on the threshing floor that David purchased, starting with the foundation, the main hall, the Most Holy Place, the curtain and pillars.

2 CHRONICLES 4
A detailed list of the temple furnishings, the altar, basins, lampstands, tables, pots, shovels and bowls.

2 CHRONICLES 5
The ark was brought into the temple by the Levites with great fanfare. While the musicians played, the priests prepared to serve, but the glory of the Lord so filled the temple, they were unable to do anything.

2 CHRONICLES 6
At the opening of the temple, Solomon prayed to God that he would hear the cries of his people and forgive them.

2 CHRONICLES 7

A huge grand opening of the temple, with thousands of sacrifices. The party lasted fourteen days. God urged Solomon to have the people called by His name to humble themselves and pray, seeking his face. He directly told Solomon not to turn to other gods or God would reject the temple.

2 CHRONICLES 8

Solomon's many other building projects and duties kept the city and temple running. He made sure the festivals were honored. He conscripted slave labor from the enemies and not the Israelites.

2 CHRONICLES 9

The Queen of Sheba stopped by with gifts to see how wise Solomon really was. She left praising him for his incredible wisdom. An outline of Solomon's possessions and the many items made of gold (shields, throne, goblets) showed why he was greater in riches than any other king on the earth. Solomon had thousands of horses and chariots. Solomon died and his son Rehoboam succeeded him.

2 CHRONICLES 10

After Jeroboam spoke up for a group of people asking for relief from the years of hard labor and high taxes Solomon put on them, King Rehoboam consulted his father's elders, but chose instead to follow his own friends, turning up the workload and pressuring the people. Rebellion occurred as a group of people rejected Rehoboam.

2 CHRONICLES 11

Rehoboam prepared to battle against Israel, but Shemaiah, a man of God, told him not to. Rehoboam fortified many of the cities around Judah and Benjamin. The Levites sided with Rehoboam, since Jeroboam refused to use them as priests in their temples. A small family line of Rehoboam is detailed, including Abijah, his son, who he made crown prince.

2 CHRONICLES 12

Judah abandoned the law of God, so God allowed Shishak king of Egypt to attack Jerusalem. Rehoboam's leaders were humbled. God gave Shishak permission to attack, but not to overrun, so only the temple treasuries were taken, including the gold shields made by Solomon. Rehoboam eventually died and Abijah, his son, became king.

2 CHRONICLES 13

Abijah called out to Jeroboam's army, establishing Judah's right to be in charge since they were following God's requirements. Jeroboam tried to flank them. Judah cried out to God and God helped them defeat the army that outnumbered them twice as much. Jeroboam died.

2 CHRONICLES 14

Asa, his son, succeeded Abijah as king. Asa removed the high places and smashed the idols. Asa fortified the towns and went out to war against the Cushites who had marched against them. Asa cried out to the Lord and the Cushites were crushed.

2 CHRONICLES 15

The prophet Azariah told Asa to keep following the Lord. Asa removed more idols and repaired the temple. All of Judah and Benjamin gathered to worship and sacrifice to God. Asa even deposed his own grandmother for making an Asherah pole.

2 CHRONICLES 16

After Israel went up against Judah, King Asa asked Ben-Hadad King of Aram to break his treaty with Baasha King of Israel to fight against them. He gave him silver and gold out of God's temple treasuries. Ben-Hadad agreed. God was displeased that Asa asked Aram for help and didn't turn to God. Asa got angry at the seer who delivered the news. Asa was afflicted with a foot disease. In total, Asa ruled forty-one years.

2 CHRONICLES 17

King Jehoshaphat succeeded his father Asa and sought God's help regularly. His power was so great his enemies sought his favor. Jehoshaphat sent officials to all the towns of Judah to teach the law of the Lord.

2 CHRONICLES 18

Jehoshaphat, married to Ahab's (the king of Israel) daughter, was asked by Ahab to go to war against the Arameans at Ramoth Gilead. Jehoshaphat sought the counsel of God, yet these 400 prophets seemed like Ahab's yes-men. Only Micaiah, the true prophet, told them that they would be scattered by Aram and that a deceiving spirit was put in the mouths of the other prophets. Arab punished Micaiah and went to war anyway. God protected Jehoshaphat during the war, but Ahab the King of Israel, who fought in disguise, was hit by a random arrow and died.

2 CHRONICLES 19

Jehoshaphat appointed judges to help resolve conflicts in the towns of Judah. He also sent priests and teachers of the law to teach them about God.

2 CHRONICLES 20

An army of Moabites and Ammonites waged war against Judah. Jehoshaphat asked the people to fast. Then he prayed mightily and boldly. He asked the people to sing and praise as he went to war. They won easily and the other nations were now afraid. Jehoshaphat had great peace during his final years. He cleaned up the nation but left the high places.

2 CHRONICLES 21

Jehoshaphat's son, Jehoram, succeeded him as king. Jehoram killed all his brothers. Elijah condemned him in a letter, promising that God would strike his family and give Jehoram a bowel disease. The Philistines and Arabs attacked Judah and carried off all the king's goods, wives and sons, except for the youngest, Ahaziah. Jehoram got a bowel disease and died. The city did not mourn.

2 CHRONICLES 22

Jehoram's youngest son, Ahaziah, escaped capture and became king. He retained Ahab's advisers and married his daughter. His mother, Athaliah, encouraged him to act wickedly. Ahaziah went to visit Joram, king of Israel, who was wounded in war. Jehu, executed judgment on the house of Ahab and killed Ahaziah. In retaliation, Athaliah began to destroy the whole royal family, killing everyone but Ahaziah's son Joash. Joash was stolen by a nurse named Jehosheba, Joash's sister and the wife of Jehoiada the priest, and hidden for six years in the temple while Athaliah ruled.

2 CHRONICLES 23

Jehoiada, a priest, organized the leaders to put one of David's descendants on the throne. Armed with swords in the temple, the priests anointed Joash as king and put Athaliah to death. Jehoiada had the Baal temples torn down and idol altars smashed. Priests and gatekeepers were put into position all around the city.

2 CHRONICLES 24

Joash became king at the age of seven. Sometime later, he asked that the temple be repaired from funds collected at the gate. The chest overflowed because the people gave gladly. The priest Jehoiada died an old man and, after his death, Judah abandoned the temple. Zechariah son of Jehoiada was filled with the spirit and confronted the people but he was put to death by Joash. As a result of their sin, God allowed Aram to invade Judah and Jerusalem and kill all the leaders. Joash, wounded in the battle, laid in bed and was killed by his officials.

2 CHRONICLES 25

Amaziah, Joash's son, succeeded him as king. He built up the army and hired men from Israel. A man of God warned him not to align with Israel. Amaziah dismissed the soldiers from Israel. After slaughtering the Edomites, Amaziah brought back their gods and worshipped them. A prophet warned him but Amaziah rejected his warning. Amaziah challenged Jehoash king of Israel to war. Israel defeated Judah and Amaziah was captured. A portion of Jerusalem's wall was torn down and the temple treasures taken. The invaders returned to Samaria. Later Amaziah fled from conspirators and was killed in Lachish.

2 CHRONICLES 26

Amaziah's son Uzziah was made king. He sought God and was given success in battles and building projects. However, his pride led to his downfall and he improperly burned incense in the temple. When confronted by the priests, leprosy broke out on Uzziah's forehead, a disease that afflicted him until this death.

2 CHRONICLES 27

Uzziah's son Jotham became king and did right before the Lord. He was given success in war (the Ammonites) because he walk steadfastly before the Lord.

2 CHRONICLES 28

Jotham's son Ahaz became king but he made idols for the Baals, burned sacrifices and sacrificed his children in the fire. God gave him over to the Arameans and the Israelites, killing 125,000 soldiers and capturing 200,000 wives, sons and daughters. A prophet named Oded intercepted the army from Israel and warned them about taking the wives, sons and daughters slaves from fellow Israelites. The soldiers returned the people and plunder, fearing God's wrath. The Edomites and Philistines attacked too, so Jotham turned to the Assyrians for help, who ended up becoming more trouble. Instead of being humble before God, Ahaz turned away, building more high places and shutting the temple down.

2 CHRONICLES 29

Ahaz's son Hezekiah became king and he opened the doors of the temple, purifying it and offering sacrifices during the first month of his administration. Many sacrifices were brought, more than the priests could handle.

2 CHRONICLES 30

Hezekiah sent out a proclamation for everyone to celebrate Passover. There was great joy in Jerusalem, unlike anything since the days of David and Solomon. The people extended Passover for seven more days.

2 CHRONICLES 31

The people went through the land, smashing all the idols. Hezekiah encouraged the people to give to the priests and they gave more than enough, gathering it in huge piles. The priests were given their appropriate duties and everyone undertook their proper service in the temple.

2 CHRONICLES 32

Threatened by Sennacherib king of Assyria, Hezekiah fortified the city. Sennacherib wondered why Hezekiah's God was any different than the gods of other nations he destroyed. Hezekiah prayed and Sennacherib's army was devastated by an angel. Hezekiah got ill, prayed and God healed him, but Hezekiah's heart was proud. God tested his heart by allowing Babylonian envoys to meet with Hezekiah. He showed off his riches to them. Hezekiah died and his son Manasseh succeeded him.

2 CHRONICLES 33

Hezekiah's son Manasseh became king. He did evil, putting the high places, altars of Baal and Asherah poles back into Jerusalem and the temple. He sacrificed children, practiced witchcraft and sought spiritists. Manasseh ignored God's warnings. The king of Assyria captured Manasseh, putting a hook in his nose and dragging him to Assyria. Finally Manasseh humbled himself and prayed. God relented and returned Manasseh to Jerusalem. Manasseh fortified Jerusalem and got rid of all the foreign gods. Manasseh's son Amon became king. He too did evil and his officials assassinated him.

2 CHRONICLES 34

Manasseh's son Josiah became king at eight years old. He cleaned out Judah of the idols, altars and high places. He began to repair the temple. Hilkiah the priest found the Book of the Law in the temple. Shaphan the secretary brought it to Josiah and read it. Josiah was convicted and desired that Judah follow everything the book said they should be doing. Josiah read the book to the people.

2 CHRONICLES 35

Josiah celebrated Passover in a big way. He had the ark put back in the temple. Everybody, from priests to Levities and musicians, performed their duties. It was the greatest Passover since the days of Samuel. Necho king of Egypt went out to fight at the Euphrates and Josiah went out to meet him. Necho had no quarrel with Josiah and asked him to turn away. Josiah refused and disguised himself during battle. An archer shot Josiah and he died. Jeremiah wrote laments for the death of Josiah and the nation mourned.

2 CHRONICLES 36

Josiah's son Jehoahaz became king. The king of Egypt dethroned him and made Eliakim, Jehoahaz's brother, king, changing his name to Jehoiakim. Jehoahaz was then carried off to Egypt. Jehoiakim did evil. Nebuchadnezzar king of Babylon attacked him and put Jehoiakim in shackles, carrying him and the articles of the temple off to Babylon. Jehoiakim's son Jehoiachin became king. He too did evil. Nebuchadnezzar made his uncle, Zedekiah, king of Judah and Jerusalem. Zedekiah did evil and refused to humble himself, despite the words of Jeremiah. Zedekiah rebelled against Babylon. The people lost faith and mocked God's messengers. God allowed Nebuchadnezzar to wipe out Judah, killing the people and taking the temple articles away. The temple was burned down and the walls torn to the ground. Many people were carried into exile in Babylon for seventy years, giving a Sabbath rest to the land according to Jeremiah. Then Cyrus king of Persia rose to power, fulfilled the word of God and instructed that the temple be rebuilt.

EZRA

Number of Chapters: *10*
Most likely author: *Ezra*
Approximate time span: 538-516, 458 BC (covering a time span
of 80 years, but specifically 23 years)

EZRA 1
Cyrus King of Persian decreed that the temple be rebuilt in Jerusalem, just as Jeremiah predicted. Family heads of Judah and Benjamin, priests and Levites prepared to return with the articles of the temple Nebuchadnezzar stole. People gave freewill offerings towards the effort to rebuild the temple.

EZRA 2
A list of the exiles according to their descendant and also by their job title (musician, gatekeeper, singers). 42,360 in total. Offerings were also collected.

EZRA 3
When they arrived in Jerusalem, the priests Joshua and Zerubbabel built the altar and celebrated festivals and offerings. As the money came in, they began to build the temple. When the foundation was laid, a great celebration went up. Many who had seen the former temple wept aloud.

EZRA 4
Opposition leaders asked to help build the temple, but were refused. The opposition created fear, gave bribes and slowed down construction. During the reigns of Xerxes and Artaxerxes they lodged accusations and wrote letters accusing the Israelites of rebellion in the past, refusing to pay tributes and taxes. Artaxerxes agreed with them and made sure that the work stopped.

EZRA 5
After prophecies by Haggai and Zechariah, Zerubbabel started construction on the house of God again. Tattenai, the governor of Trans-Euphrates, sent a letter to King Darius telling

him the Jews had restarted construction. He asked the king to search the royal records to see if Cyrus had authorized this work to be done.

EZRA 6

Darius searched the archives and found Cyrus' authorization to rebuild the temple. He wrote back and told Tattenai to not hinder the work and to give them whatever they needed, including the funds and any food. The temple was completed and dedicated with sacrifices. The priests went to work and the Passover was held.

EZRA 7

During the reign of Artaxerxes, Ezra, a Levite, received permission to come to Jerusalem. He arrived from Babylon with other Israelites, including priests, Levites and others. King Artaxerxes gave him a letter – a permission slip to make executive decisions – along with gold, silver, wine, wheat and olive oil. The priests, Levites and temple workers were granted a tax-free status.

EZRA 8

A list of the heads of the families who came from Babylon to Jerusalem with Ezra. Ezra assembled the exiles to fast and pray before they left. They didn't ask the king for soldiers since Ezra said God was with them. Ezra gathered the priests and weighed out the financial offerings to God. They arrived in Jerusalem and sacrificed offerings to God.

EZRA 9

The leaders confided to Ezra about the Jews (and the priests) marrying foreign wives. Ezra tore his robe and prayed, ashamed for his people.

EZRA 10

A crowd of Israelites gathered around Ezra and wept also. They repented for their sins of marrying foreign women. Everyone in Judah and Jerusalem were told to assemble within three days. Everyone who married a foreign woman needed to end those relationships. A list of priests who married foreign women ends the book.

NEHEMIAH

Number of Chapters: 13
The Author: Nehemiah
Approximate time span: 445-425 BC (20 years)

NEHEMIAH 1

Nehemiah, a cupbearer for the King of Persia at the citadel of Susa, asked his brother and others who returned from Jerusalem how the exiles were doing. He was told that the walls were down and the gates were burnt with fire. Nehemiah mourned and prayed for his nation's sins.

NEHEMIAH 2

King Artaxerxes noticed Nehemiah's sadness and asked why. Nehemiah told him that his people's city, Jerusalem, was in great peril and that he wanted to go to Jerusalem to help rebuild it. The King gave Nehemiah letters for passage and permission to go. Sanballat and Tobiah did not like to hear this news that Jerusalem would be rebuilt. Nehemiah arrived in Jerusalem and examined the gates. He gathered the officials and they agreed to get to work. Sanballat, Tobiah and Geshem mocked this idea. Nehemiah told them to stay out.

NEHEMIAH 3

A list of the people who worked on the specific gates. The gates were named Sheep, Fish, Jeshanah/Old, Valley, Dung, Fountain, Water, Horse and East. Everybody from many different backgrounds got into the act.

NEHEMIAH 4

Sanballat and Tobiah raised opposition against the Jews when they heard the walls were being rebuilt. Nehemiah, writing in first person, explained how morale dropped with fear. He stationed guards to protect the builders. They worked with weapons in one hand and carried materials in the other.

NEHEMIAH 5

Many Jews slipped into debt because fellow Jews lent them money at high interest. Nehemiah asked the borrowers to give back the interest and they did. As governor, Nehemiah refused to take the costly food allotted to the governor and lived and worked like the others.

NEHEMIAH 6

Opposition leaders tried to meet with Nehemiah to harm him, but he refused to stop working on the wall. They accused the Jews of revolt, which Nehemiah rejected. Shemaiah tried to get Nehemiah to hide in the temple, but Nehemiah knew this was a set-up to disgrace his name. The wall was finally completed in fifty-two days. The surrounding nations, upon hearing this, grew afraid.

NEHEMIAH 7

The workers were put into place. Nehemiah found the genealogical record of all the people who exiled there (Ezra 2). This extensive genealogical list totaled 42,360.

NEHEMIAH 8

Ezra read the Book of the Law to the people. The people wept, but the leaders told them to be joyful. They read and understood about the festival of the Tabernacles, a holy celebration when they slept in shelters like their ancestors. They gathered branches and celebrated it for seven days.

NEHEMIAH 9

The Israelites fasted and wore sackcloth, confessing their sins. The priests led a prayer, outlining God's faithfulness through Abraham, Moses, to the occupation of Israel and the rejection of God's prophets.

NEHEMIAH 10

The people made a binding agreement, which a number of leaders sealed. They promised to carefully follow the commands, not to give their daughters in marriage to outsiders, not to work on the Sabbath, to tithe and to follow the feasts and offerings.

NEHEMIAH 11

Lots were cast to bring one out of every ten people to live inside Jerusalem. A list of those who moved into Jerusalem along with a list of towns where people lived in Judah.

NEHEMIAH 12

A list of the priests and Levites who returned with Zerubbabel. Musicians and two choirs walked in opposite directions along the top of the wall for its dedication. Portions and tithes were set aside for the priests, musicians and gatekeepers.

NEHEMIAH 13

After Nehemiah returned to Babylon to work for King Artaxerxes, he heard that Tobiah, an Ammonite, was given a room in a courtyard storehouse and lived inside the city (the Book of the Law said no Ammonite or Moabite should do so). Nehemiah returned and threw Tobiah out. He also found that the Levites were not being provided for and the people worked on the Sabbath. Nehemiah had the city gates shut on the Sabbath. He discovered men who had taken wives from Ashdod, Ammon and Moab. Nehemiah beat them and pulled their hair. He purified the priests and Levites and assigned them duties. Nehemiah asked God to remember his faithfulness.

ESTHER

Number of Chapters: *10*
Author Unknown: *Possibly Mordecai/Ezra/Nehemiah*
Approximate time span: 483-473 BC (10 years)

ESTHER 1

Persian king Xerxes gave a banquet for his nobles and officials. He asked for his wife Vashti, who was also holding a banquet for the women, to come out so he could show her off. She refused. Afraid other women would hear of her disrespect and refuse their own husbands, the officials suggested a royal decree that barred Vashti from entering the presence of Xerxes.

ESTHER 2

A search began for the new queen. Mordecai nominated his orphan cousin Esther (also known as Hadassah) who instantly gained approval and received twelve months of beauty treatments. Mordecai told her not to mention her nationality. The king was attracted to her more than any other woman. He set the royal crown on her head. Later, Mordecai overheard a conspiracy by two of the king's officers who wanted to assassinate the king. He reported it to Queen Esther, who told Xerxes. Mordecai's action were reported in the book of annals.

ESTHER 3

King Xerxes gave Haman the highest position available. Everyone bowed to pay him honor except Mordecai. When Haman heard that Mordecai was a Jew, he plotted to kill all the Jews. Haman warned Xerxes about these separate and different people who disobeyed the king's laws. He suggested a decree to have them destroyed. The king gave Haman his signet ring to seal the decree and make it happen. Couriers sent word out that on a single day – the thirteenth day of the twelfth month of Adar – that all Jews could be murdered and plundered of all goods. The town was bewildered.

ESTHER 4

Mordecai tore his clothes, put on sackcloth and wailed bitterly in the city. He communicated to Esther about the edict and asked that she talk to the king. Esther said no one could approach the king without being summoned. Mordecai warned her that she could die too and maybe she attained this position of queen for such a time as this. She asked for prayer, willing to approach the king, whether she died or not.

ESTHER 5

Esther showed up at the palace and Xerxes extended his scepter, offering half his kingdom if she requested it. She requested Xerxes' attendance at a banquet with Haman. Xerxes enjoyed the banquet and asked Esther for any other request. She offered another banquet where she would reveal her true request. Haman left the banquet and saw Mordecai, who disrespected him. Enraged, he asked his wife and friends what he should do. They told him to build a gallows to hang (or a pole to impale) Mordecai on.

ESTHER 6

That night, King Xerxes could not sleep so he asked that the royal records be read to him. He heard from the records about Mordecai thwarting the assassination and realized nothing had been done for him. Xerxes asked Haman how a king should honor someone who delighted him. Haman, thinking the king wanted to honor him, suggested the royal robe be put on him, mounted on a horse and paraded in the streets. The king loved the idea and told Haman to show that honor to Mordecai, leading him through the streets, proclaiming "This man delights the king." Haman grieved at home as the attendants arrived to take him to the banquet.

ESTHER 7

At her second banquet, Esther revealed her nationality, the dire fate of her people and the man behind it all, Haman. Haman pleaded with Esther for mercy, but his begging looked like molesting to the king. Xerxes had Haman impaled/hung on the pole/gallows Haman had made for Mordecai.

ESTHER 8

King Xerxes gave Esther Haman's estate and Mordecai received Haman's job. Xerxes, who couldn't stop his previous edict for all the Jews to be killed on a certain day, allowed Mordecai to create a new edict, allowing the Jews to assemble and protect themselves when attacked. The other nationalities then feared the Jews.

ESTHER 9

When the fateful day arrived, the Jews overpowered their enemies (but didn't touch the plunder). Mordecai's reputation spread far and quickly. Haman's ten sons were executed. After killing thousands of attackers, the Jews celebrated on a day of feasting and giving presents to one another. Mordecai established this day called Purim after the lots (or pur) Haman cast to pick the day of their demise, which turned into the Jew's day of victory.

ESTHER 10

King Xerxes' acts and the greatness of Mordecai were all recorded in the book of the annals of the kings of Media and Persia.

JOB

Number of Chapters: *42*
Author Unknown: *?*
Approximately written: *Around 2000 BC*

JOB 1

In the land of Uz, a blameless and upright man named Job lived. He was very wealthy and very blessed. The angels presented themselves before God and God questioned Satan about Job, asking if Satan had ever considered his servant Job. Satan complained that he could not touch Job because God put a hedge of protection around him. God allowed Satan to persecute Job, but his physical body was off limits. In one day Job's sons and daughters were killed when the roof collapsed, the Sabeans killed his servants and stole donkeys and oxen, fire fell from the sky and burned up sheep and servants, and the Chaldeans stole his camels. In the end, Job replied "Naked I came from the womb and naked I will depart. The Lord gives and the Lord takes away."

JOB 2

God again challenged Satan about Job who maintained his integrity despite all the suffering Satan caused. Satan complained saying things would be different if Satan had access to Job's health. God allowed Satan to touch Job's body but not take his life. Job broke out in painful sores all over his body. Job's wife wanted him to curse God. Job's three friends – Eliphaz the Temanite, Bildad the Shuhite and Zophar the Naamathite – sat with Job in silence, grieving with their friend.

JOB 3

Job cursed the day of his birth, wishing it never happened.

JOB 4

Eliphaz remembered how helpful Job was to others, now he needed help. He observed that those who plow evil, receive evil in return. Eliphaz claimed to have been visited by a spirit who said no man is more righteous than God.

JOB 5

Eliphaz continued talking about a fool whose house was cursed and his children in court. Trouble, he believed, always came from God so he encouraged Job to appeal to God, the creator and guide of all things, and accept his discipline. If Job did, Eliphaz said Job would not need to fear anything and die a fulfilled man.

JOB 6

Job replied describing his deep anguish, desiring death. He can't believe his friends are not being any help and begged them to show him where he was wrong.

JOB 7

Job continued by saying life is hard and right now this was what he had been allotted. Soon, Job believed, his life would end and his friends would see him no more. He cried out, wondering why he was God's target.

JOB 8

Bildad spoke saying Job's children deserved what they got for their sin and God would restore Job's fortune if he was pure and upright. If people forget God, they would wither, Bildad explained. He can't fathom God hurting the good and helping the bad.

JOB 9

Job replied wondering how man can prove their innocence before such a powerful God. Job did not believe he could argue with God or get an answer from him without being crushed, even though he claimed his innocence. If only someone could mediate between him and God!

JOB 10

Job expressed his displeasure for life. He wanted God to show the charges against him. Job wished he was never born or that he died at childbirth.

JOB 11

Zophar spoke against Job's claim of innocence before God. He encouraged Job to devote his heart to God and put away the sin, then Job could stand once again.

JOB 12

Job felt he had become a laughingstock to his friends. He confirmed his friend's statement that God was very powerful and had everything in his grasp.

JOB 13

Job continued by saying he desired to speak to God and argue his case. He called his friends liars and wished they would shut up. Job had confidence in God feeling he would have hope in Him even if He slayed him. Job listed a few questions he would ask God if he could.

JOB 14

Job continued with more questions for God. He wished for God to hide him in a grave. He knew that God did not keep track of his sin.

JOB 15

Eliphaz answered, calling Job's words useless and prompted by sin. He felt the old and wise agreed with Job's friends. He described the wicked, tormented their whole lives with distress and anguish. They shake their fists at God. They would wither away.

JOB 16

Job replied, chastising them for being miserable comforters. He promised he would encourage them if they were in his shoes instead of lecturing them. Job felt God turned on him, but he's still Job's friend. Soon, Job sensed he would die.

JOB 17

Job's spirit was broken. He felt surrounded by his enemies and at the end of his rope.

JOB 18

Bildad wanted Job to end these speeches, feeling offended by Job's rebukes. Bildad said that wicked men face calamity and disaster, their names erased from the world.

JOB 19

Job wondered how long his friends would torment him. He felt God had wronged him, stripped him of his honor and became the target of God's anger, escaping only by the skin of his teeth. Job communicated his feelings of alienation from the world. He pleaded for mercy from his friends. Job knew that on resurrection day he would see God in the flesh.

JOB 20

Zophar jumped in, disturbed, needing to answer. He replied saying the wicked live short lives and they would perish forever, unfulfilled.

JOB 21

Job knew the wicked live prosperous lives, with secure homes and successful businesses, yet they reject God. That's life. Some die healthy, others in misery, but both meet the same fate. Job found his friends' word nothing but nonsense.

JOB 22

Eliphaz jumped in, questioning whether man can be a benefit to God. God would not punish Job if he were righteous. Eliphaz accused Job of stripping people naked, not showing compassion to the needy. This was why everything happened to Job! Does he not know God sees him? Eliphaz told Job to accept God's instruction and be restored. God would hear him!

JOB 23

Job wanted to present his case before God, even though he would be terrified to do so. Job still felt God would find nothing wrong with him.

JOB 24

Job felt there was a lot of evil and sad circumstances in the world, yet many go unpunished.

JOB 25

Bildad responded, saying man was not righteous, but a mere maggot or worm.

JOB 26

Job told his friends they have no wisdom. God has great wisdom and power and there's no way to understand him.

JOB 27

Job stood by his integrity. God would punish the wicked and strip them of everything.

JOB 28

Just like God creates priceless riches deep in the rocks, his wisdom is just as hidden. God's wisdom far out values any precious metal. Wisdom only comes from one place, God. The fear of the Lord, Job stated, is wisdom.

JOB 29

Job remembered how much God blessed him, how people respected him and how much good he did for the poor and fatherless.

JOB 30

But now, Job continued, he was mocked and attacked. His life slipped away and God would not answer him.

JOB 31

Job felt that if he had been sinful, then he deserved to lose everything. Job's word ended here.

JOB 32

The three friends stopped talking to Job because he was righteous in his own eyes. Elihu, listening to the entire encounter, grew angry because Job justified himself and not God and because the three friends condemned Job but could not prove him wrong. Being younger, he waited his turn to speak. Now, like a bottle uncorked, Elihu was ready to speak his mind.

JOB 33

Elihu did not think Job should call himself pure and free from guilt before God. He didn't think God had to answer Job either. God can speak any way he wants. God spares people from the pit of death.

JOB 34

Elihu stated that God gives man what they deserve. God cannot do wrong. He shows no partiality. He knows our every step. God can do what he wants. Elihu still contested that Job spoke without full knowledge of his situation and God.

JOB 35

Elihu presented the idea that our sinfulness and righteousness affect only us, not God. God does not have to answer us. He felt Job spoke with empty talk.

JOB 36

Elihu said that God does not despise mankind. He helps the afflicted. He corrects the unrighteous. God is powerful and no one can understand his ways.

JOB 37

Elihu concluded by proclaiming God's power in nature. He is beyond our reach and does no wrong. Elihu pleaded with Job to consider God's wonders.

JOB 38

God replied to Job, asking him what he knew about every aspect of the earth – from the physical specifications, to weather and animals. It's a quiz and every answer is "God" or when challenged if Job had any hand in creating the world, Job must answer "no."

JOB 39

God continued his power and knowledge challenge to Job, with more questions about animal life, specifically the mountain goat, wild donkey, wild ox, ostrich, horse, hawk and eagle.

JOB 40

God asked if Job could correct God. Job repented, unworthy to answer God. Silence, he believed, was best. God then asked if Job was like God, with God detailing more powerful qualities. God then questioned Job about his power over the Behemoth, a large, untamable animal.

JOB 41

God spoke more about his power to contain an animal like the Leviathan and make it his pet. God could do that. Job couldn't.

JOB 42

Job gave God all the credit and glory. God told Eliphaz, Bildad and Zophar to make sacrifices and God would hear Job's prayer for mercy over them. Job's fortunes were restored more plentifully than before, his family grew and were beautiful. Job lived to be 140 years old.

PSALMS

Number of Chapters: *150*
List of authors: *David, Asaph, sons of Korah, Solomon,*
                           Moses, Heman, Ethan, anonymous
Approximate time span: From the time of Moses to the
                           Babylonian captivity

ABOUT THIS BOOK: It's impossible to cover all the information in every chapter of Psalms. A brief summary of each chapter is given, emphasizing the unique and predominant thoughts.

BOOK I

PSALM 1
A man is blessed if he stays away from sinners and mockers, but he'll be fruitful if he mediates on God's law.

PSALM 2
Nations stand against God. God laughs at them.

PSALM 3
The writer had many foes but God sustained him.

PSALM 4
The writer desired that God hear his cry and protect him in his sleep.

PSALM 5
The writer called out to God in the morning. His bloodthirsty enemies were evil and have throats like open graves.

PSALM 6
The writer begged for mercy, his bones in agony, worn out from groaning. The Lord had heard his groaning and his enemies would be overwhelmed.

PSALM 7

The writer felt that if he had done something wrong, he deserved his enemies' wrath. He asked for God's anger to rise up against his enemies. God is a righteous judge who displays his wrath every day.

PSALM 8

When the writer gazed at the heavens, he wondered why God even considers mankind.

PSALM 9

The writer praised God and told of his wonder. He knew that God would not forsake those who seek him. He was also assured to know that evil nations and wicked people get what they deserve.

PSALM 10

The prideful think everything would be great as they hurt innocent victims. God sees the wicked even though they think he doesn't. The writer pleaded that the evil get punished.

PSALM 11

God is in his temple and he has his eyes on everyone – the righteous and the wicked.

PSALM 12

The writer cried for help since no one was faithful. Because of the oppression of the weak, God promised to rise and protect them.

PSALM 13

The writer wondered why God was, but promised to trust in his unfailing love.

PSALM 14

A fool says there is no God. God looks down from heaven for those who understand or seek God, but there's no one who does good.

PSALM 15

Who can dwell with God? Only someone whose walk is blameless and they do no wrong.

PSALM 16

The writer asked to be kept safe. By confirming his relationship and love to the Lord, he felt he would never be abandoned, especially in the grave.

PSALM 17

The writer called out to God in the midst of his enemies. He pleaded that God keep him as the apple of his eye and bring down the enemies.

PSALM 18

While the cords of death entangle the writer, he called God his rock, fortress, deliverer, shield, horn of salvation and stronghold. God had dealt with him according to his righteousness and delivered the writer from the attacks of people.

PSALM 19

The heavens proclaim the glory of God, pouring out the evidence of God's power. His law is perfect, trustworthy and right. The writer asked that the words of his mouth and the meditations of his heart be pleasing to God.

PSALM 20

The writer hoped that God answered him in his distress. While some trust in chariots and some in horses, the writer trusted in the name of God.

PSALM 21

A song of praise from a king, who trusted in the Lord to defeat his enemies.

PSALM 22

The writer wondered why God had forsaken him. He cried out but God did not help. His enemies surrounded him. Jesus quoted the opening line of this verse from the cross, which mentions his bones not being broken and his garments being divided up.

PSALM 23

The writer was comforted knowing that the Lord was his shepherd. He felt he didn't really need anything because he was being watched over so lovingly.

PSALM 24

The earth is the Lord's and everything in it, so who can stand up to God. The writer asked who was this king of glory – the Lord almighty was his name.

PSALM 25

The writer trusted God. He pleaded with God to show him all his ways. He asked that his sins from his youth be forgotten. He wanted God to see his afflictions and take away his sins.

PSALM 26

The writer asked to be tested, tried and examined. The writer felt he stayed away from sinners, praised God when he could and loved the Lord's house.

PSALM 27

The writer confidently expressed that the Lord was his light and salvation so there was no one to fear. One thing he asked and that was to dwell in the house of the Lord forever.

PSALM 28

The writer pleaded for mercy and asked not to be dragged away by evil. He praised God as his shepherd.

PSALM 29

The writer described the voice of the Lord, powerful, earth-shattering, causing thunder and lightning. It shakes the earth.

PSALM 30

The writer felt God had saved him from the pit of death. God turned his wailing into dancing.

PSALM 31

The writer, in distress, called to God for strength. He asked God to shine his face on him. He trusted God and praised him for his goodness.

PSALM 32

The writer confessed his sins and knew he was forgiven. A blessed feeling! He called God his hiding place. He asked that everyone who was godly to pray to Him.

PSALM 33

God made the heavens, so only his plans will stand firm. Blessed is the nation who God has his eyes on.

PSALM 34

The writer sought the Lord and He answered. He asked people to taste and see that the Lord is good. The Lord hears the righteous and is close to the brokenhearted.

PSALM 35

The writer asked God to fight against those who fight against him. He asked for his enemies to be shamed and defeated.

PSALM 36

God's love reaches to the heavens. His righteousness to the skies. In God is the fountain of life.

PSALM 37

If you delight in the Lord, he will give you the desires of your heart. Be still before him and wait patiently. The meek will inherit the earth. Wait for the Lord. Don't be the like the wicked.

PSALM 38

The writer asked that God not rebuke him in anger or discipline him in wrath. He was very heavy with guilt. He asked God not to be far from him.

PSALM 39

The writer asked to be shown the number of his days. From God's perspective, a man's life is just a breath. The writer wanted to make sure God heard him.

PSALM 40

The writer rejoiced that God heard his cry, lifted him from the pit and put his feet on solid rock. He knew that God did not desire sacrifice and offerings, but righteousness.

PSALM 41

Blessed is the one who takes the weak into consideration. God will bless him. The writer felt betrayed, even by a close friend who he shared bread with.

BOOK II

PSALM 42

Just as a deer pants for water, the writer's soul panted for God, thirsty for the living God. Why would a soul be downcast? Put all your hope in God.

PSALM 43

The writer needed God's light and truth to guide him. His hope was in God. No time for his soul to be downcast.

PSALM 44

The writer felt God had rejected his armies and given up on his people. While all this happened, God was not forgotten. He asked for God wake up and not hide from them any longer.

PSALM 45

The writer praised God, the king, on his throne, whose kingdom will last forever.

PSALM 46

God is a refuge and strength, always present in times of trouble. Come and see what he has done. Be still and know He is God.

PSALM 47

The writer encouraged the nations to praise God for he is the king of the earth.

PSALM 48

The writer expressed that God was worthy of praise and that praise reached to the end of the earth.

PSALM 49

Why, the writer asked, should a person fear the days to come against wicked people who cannot redeem their own lives? Man cannot endure. They are all destined for the grave. But God can save us from the grave!

PSALM 50

God controls the heavens and the earth. He doesn't need sacrifices. He owns all the cattle on a thousand hills. But a warning to the wicked, don't forget God, or else.

PSALM 51

The psalmist pleaded for mercy, knowing God has great compassion. He wanted his sins washed away, so he can be whiter than snow. He asked for God to create in him a clean heart and not to push him away from God's presence. The writer wanted that joy of salvation back once again.

PSALM 52

The writer asked for all prideful, mighty man to be destroyed by God. Those that trust in wealth are uprooted.

PSALM 53

The writer said that God looks down from heaven and cannot see anyone who seeks or understands him. Everyone is corrupt.

PSALM 54

The psalmist was overwhelmed by attacks from strangers and asked God to save him.

PSALM 55

The writer was anguished, wanting to run away. He saw violence all around him and he wanted his enemies dead. He cried out to God all day and night.

PSALM 56

The psalmist wondered why he was afraid. He trusted in God so what can man do to him?

PSALM 57

Even in the midst of his enemies, the psalmist praised God for his great love and faithfulness that reached to the skies.

PSALM 58

The writer described the wicked, asking God to break their teeth. The righteous will be rewarded.

PSALM 59

The psalmist asked for deliverance from his enemies. He believed God would go before him. He wanted the sinful to be caught up in their own pride and wrath.

PSALM 60

The writer felt that God had rejected them and shown them desperate times. God had triumphed over all the enemies, describing Edom as a simple washbasin. Only victory comes through him.

PSALM 61

God was the writer's refuge. He longed to dwell in the shelter of God's wings. He desired to sing praise to God's name day after day.

PSALM 62

God was the writer's rock, salvation and fortress. He trusted in him at all times.

PSALM 63

The writer's soul thirsted and clung to God.

PSALM 64

The wicked fire away at innocent men. They encourage others with evil plans. But God will take them out.

PSALM 65

The psalmist knew that God blessed those he chose. He answers with deeds of righteousness.

PSALM 66

Shout for joy all the earth! Praise God, people! God listens to his people!

PSALM 67

May God be gracious to us and bless us and make his face shine on us!

PSALM 68

The psalmist expressed that God protected the fatherless and widows. When God marches, the earth shakes. God saves his people against the enemies. Summon your power, God!

PSALM 69

The writer felt like he was drowning. He was worn out, outnumbered. He had endured scorn and shame. He cried out for God's help. The writer stated that they had put gall in his food and given vinegar for his thirst. He wanted God to pour out his wrath on his enemies.

PSALM 70

May those who seek God rejoice and be glad. Let God be exalted!

PSALM 71

The psalmist's enemies were after him, but he knew God had watched over him since birth. The accusers thought God had abandoned him. Not true. The psalmist felt confident God would restore his life again.

PSALM 72

The writer asked God to bless the king, so that during his days the righteous would flourish. He prayed that the king's name endured forever. (This concluded the prayers of David, son of Jesse)

BOOK III

PSALM 73

The writer envied the wicked who prosper. They seemed carefree. But, the writer felt they were the ones in trouble. He confessed to being arrogant. He had God and that's all he needed.

PSALM 74

The enemy had smashed and burned the sanctuary, mocking God. The writer knew that God was in control and pleaded for Him to rise up.

PSALM 75

When the world shook, the psalmist knew that God held it all together. God judges and exalts.

PSALM 76

God alone is to be feared. Who can stand against him? We should fulfill our vows to him.

PSALM 77

The psalmist cried out to God for help. He remembered God and groaned. God won't reject him forever, so he meditated on his great deeds and miracles, such as parting the Red Sea with Moses and Aaron.

PSALM 78

The writer said God will speak with a parable. He will not hide things from people. God makes his plans clear, so people can pass on God's deeds to future generations and do not become arrogant. God has always done his miracles in plain sight, such as all the miracles he did for the Israelites going to the Promised Land. God also showed his patience against such rebellious people, especially when they were disloyal as they settled in the Promised Land. Finally he chose David to shepherd the people.

PSALM 79

How long will God be angry at these nations who have defiled Jerusalem and killed its people? The psalmist cried out for God to forgive their own sins. We are the sheep of God's pasture.

PSALM 80

How long God will you make Israel the mockery of their enemies? The psalmist asked for the restoration of God's people and his nation so they could be saved.

PSALM 81

The psalmist heard a voice saying that God removed the burden from the people's shoulders, saving them from Egypt. He told the people not to worship other gods but they would not listen.

PSALM 82

God judges the gods who know nothing and understand nothing.

PSALM 83

The psalmist asked God to hear his cry regarding his enemies, who all plotted together. He wanted God to turn the enemies into tumbleweed and chaff.

PSALM 84

The writer yearned for God's dwelling place, his heart and flesh crying out. Better is one day in God's courts than a thousand days anywhere else.

PSALM 85

God once showed favor to his people, so the psalmist asked for that restoration again. He asked that God's wrath subside so he could show his unfailing love.

PSALM 86

The writer asked God to hear him. He knew God was forgiving and good. The writer sought His teaching and wanted an undivided heart. He needed mercy.

PSALM 87

God founded Zion, the city on the hill, established by the Most High.

PSALM 88

The psalmist was overwhelmed with troubles, feeling an end to his life. He called out to God every day, but felt rejected. God had taken his closest friends from him. He only friend was darkness.

PSALM 89

The writer promised to sing of God's love forever. Nobody in the skies or in heaven could compare to Him. Blessed are people who rejoice in Him. God once established a servant named David. God's hand strengthened him. David called God his Father so God established his throne forever. Any of David's sons who disobeyed his laws would be punished. The anointed one was rejected and suffered by the hands of his foes.

BOOK IV

PSALM 90

God has been in power forever. He can turn people to dust. A thousand years to God is like a day. Our years, though, number only seventy or eighty. We need to number our days. Lord we need your compassion.

PSALM 91

God will protect you like a bird protects its young. No need to fear the night, disease or thousands of enemies. If you truly believe the Lord is your refuge, no harm will come. If you love God, he will rescue you.

PSALM 92

How great it is to praise the Lord. People without sense don't understand. All enemies will perish and the righteous will flourish.

PSALM 93

The Lord reigns. His throne secure. His statutes stand firm.

PSALM 94

Avenge the wicked, God. Senseless people don't stand a chance. God disciplines those he loves. He stands up for us against the wicked. The Lord is my fortress and my rock.

PSALM 95

Shout for joy to the Lord. Kneel before him in worship. Do not harden your heart against him like those in the wilderness did.

PSALM 96

Sing to the Lord a new song. Praise him all the nations. Let heaven and earth rejoice.

PSALM 97

The Lord reigns. He displays his power in this world. On earth he is exalted above everything else.

PSALM 98

Sing to the Lord a new song. He has made his salvation known to all the nations. All the earth should burst forth in song.

PSALM 99

The Lord reigns and the nations should tremble. God loves justice. Some great men from the past (Moses, Aaron, Samuel) called on God and he answered them.

PSALM 100

The earth should shout for joy and worship with gladness. God made us and we are his. Someday we will enter his gates praising him.

PSALM 101

The psalmist wanted to lead a blameless life. He hated what faithless people do, slandering and being all proud. Deceitful people are not allowed in.

PSALM 102

The psalmist knew his days were short and he was miserable. His enemies sought after him and he cried in his food. But God was on his throne and he will rebuild Zion. God is always the same.

PSALM 103

Praise God who forgives our sins, as far as the east is from the west, who heals our diseases and has compassion on those who fear him.

PSALM 104

God is the creator of this world. He takes care of everything from the sky, moon and sun to the birds, grass and trees.

PSALM 105

Give praise and give glory to the Lord. Remember all that he has done, his miracles, his covenants and his work throughout history as seen from the time of Abraham to Moses.

PSALM 106

Despite Israel's history of rebelling against God, as told in detail from their time with Moses to their occupation of the Promised Land, God showed mercy to the Israelites. Save us again, O Lord!

BOOK V

PSALM 107

While people endured their most troubling times—hunger, thirst, darkness, drought, storms, oppression, sorrow—God saved them from distress.

PSALM 108

God's love is great, higher than the heavens. He will save us.

PSALM 109

My enemies oppose me, God, so appoint someone evil to oppose them. Pour out your curses on them. As for me, poor and needy, help me and I will praise you.

PSALM 110

In a passage that he quoted from Psalm 110, Jesus gave proof to the idea of the Trinity in the Old Testament where it says, "The Lord said to my Lord, sit at my right hand." The Lord will not change his mind.

PSALM 111

The Lord's works are great and glorious. They are established forever. The fear of the Lord is the beginning of wisdom.

PSALM 112

Those who fear the Lord and love his commandments will be blessed through their children and their wealth. Quite a different story for the wicked.

PSALM 113

Praise the Lord over all the nations. No one is like him. He lifts up the poor and seats them with royalty. He gives children to a childless mother.

PSALM 114

The earth trembles at God's presence.

PSALM 115

You get the glory Lord. Other nations wonder where you are, but they worship idols. God will bless those who fear him. If you make an idol, you will become like it.

PSALM 116

The cords of death entangle me but I cry out to the Lord to save me. God allows me to walk among the living. The death of a saint is precious in God's sight.

PSALM 117

The shortest chapter in the Bible says all the nations should praise God.

PSALM 118

Why be afraid if God is with you? Trust God not men. Even if nations surround you, God is your defense. The stone the builders rejected has become the cornerstone. Blessed are all who come in the name of the Lord.

PSALM 119

The longest chapter in the Bible says those who are blameless walk according to the law, his precepts and his decrees. They must hide his word in their heart and meditate on his words. God's word is eternal. It is a lamp for our feet. A light for our path.

PSALM 120

The writer called on the Lord. He called himself a person of peace but lived among those who were not.

PSALM 121

The writer lifted his eyes to the mountain, looking for help. The Lord watches over us and keeps us from harm.

PSALM 122

Pray for the peace of Jerusalem.

PSALM 123

I look to you, God. Have mercy on us.

PSALM 124

If the Lord had not been on our side, we would be overwhelmed by the flood of our enemies' attacks.

PSALM 125

Lord, do good to the do-gooders. Banish the evildoers.

PSALM 126

When God restored Zion, he turned tears into joy. He has done great things for us.

PSALM 127

God must build your house or it will be in vain. Your children are a reward. Blessed is the man who has a quiver full of children.

PSALM 128

If you walk in obedience with the Lord, your labor, wife and children will be blessed.

PSALM 129

People oppress Israel, but God has cut it free from its enemies. Anyone who hates Zion will wither away.

PSALM 130

I cry out to you, thankful that you don't keep a record of sins. I wait for the Lord.

PSALM 131

I am not proud, but like a calm, weaned child. Israel put your hope in the Lord.

PSALM 132

David swore an oath to build a place for the Lord. The Lord swore to David that his descendants would always be on the throne.

PSALM 133

When God's people are united, it's like an anointing of blessing.

PSALM 134

Praise all those who serve in God's house.

PSALM 135

Praise all those servants who minister in the house of the Lord. God is great and he does what he pleases. He strikes down his enemies and is greater than the idols. His name endures forever. Praise him.

PSALM 136

Give thanks to the Lord, for he is good. His love endures forever. He created this earth and brought Israel out of Egypt with great signs and wonders.

PSALM 137

The captors in Babylon asked for songs about Zion, but how could they sing while in a foreign land. Remember Lord what the Edomites did to Jerusalem. That nation was doomed.

PSALM 138

The psalmist will praise God with all his heart. God always answered him and saved him from my enemies.

PSALM 139

The writer wanted God to search him and know him intimately. God always knew what he was doing and what he was going to say. He couldn't go anywhere without God there. He created him and put him together. He was fearfully and wonderfully made. He saw the writer in his mother's womb. God's thoughts are precious and plentiful. The writer wanted his heart searched and known, asking for anything offensive inside him to be pointed out.

PSALM 140

The psalmist wanted God to rescue him and keep him safe from the wicked. Don't give the wicked what they desire.

PSALM 141

The writer wanted his mouth guarded and his heart protected from evil. He wanted a righteous man to strike him so that the evil could learn a lesson.

PSALM 142

The psalmist cried out to God. He wanted to be heard because he was desperate, stuck in his own prison.

PSALM 143

The writer wanted his prayer heard. He thirsted for God. He needed a quick answer. He wanted to be rescued and his life preserved.

PSALM 144

Praise God for caring for humans. The writer needed God to reach down and rescue him. He would sing a new song about how he blessed us.

PSALM 145

The psalmist said the Lord was worthy of praise. He was good to all. All his works tell of his glory. He knew God as trustworthy, who fulfilled all the desires of those who fear him.

PSALM 146

The writer warned against trusting in princes or human beings. All our hope needed to be put in God, the maker of heaven and earth, who loves the oppressed, sets prisoners free and watches over the fatherless.

PSALM 147

The Lord built up Jerusalem. He is in control of the stars (and names them), the clouds and the animals. He delights in those that love him. God is the strength of Jerusalem.

PSALM 148

The writer told everything in the world to praise God.

PSALM 149

Let Israel rejoice in their maker. May praise be in their mouth while a sword is in their hand to inflict vengeance on the nations.

PSALM 150

Praise God with every instrument you can find. Let everything that breathes praise the Lord.

PROVERBS

Number of Chapters: *31*
List of Authors: *Solomon, Hezekiah, Agur, Lemuel*
Approximately written: *950-700 BC*

PROVERBS 1
- Once you fear the Lord, knowledge truly begins.
- Fools despise knowledge.
- Listen to your parents.
- Don't let sinful men entice you to do wrong.
- Wisdom cries out for you to listen, but once it's too late, wisdom won't listen.

PROVERBS 2
- Apply wisdom to your life. It's better than silver.
- The Lord gives wisdom.
- Wisdom will save you from wicked men and adulterous women.

PROVERBS 3
- Love and faithfulness need to be near our hearts.
- Trust God and not your understanding.
- Don't be self-wise.
- Honor God with your wealth.
- Accept God's discipline.
- Wisdom is priceless.
- Wisdom gives long life.
- If you can help a neighbor now, do it. Don't put it off.
- The Lord curses the house of the wicked.

PROVERBS 4
- Listen to your father. He learned from his father.
- The wisest thing to do is to get wisdom.
- With wisdom you will get to where you want to go.
- Guard your heart.

PROVERBS 5

- Stay away from an adulterous woman. She leads only to death.
- Stay away from her house or you will regret it to your death.
- Be faithful and only drink water from your own cistern. Don't share your wife with others.
- Be intoxicated only by the wife of your youth.

PROVERBS 6

- Don't make any pledge of money with a neighbor or stranger, because it's like being an animal in a trap.
- If you're lazy, watch the ants for they work and have no boss.
- If you're lazy, poverty sneaks up on you like a thief.
- God really hates troublemakers, arrogant people, liars, murderers, schemers, evil doers, and gossipers.
- Stay away from your neighbor's wife. You're only playing with fire.

PROVERBS 7

- Don't be drawn into the home of an adulterous woman no matter what she says or how good the opportunity is. You are only digging your own grave.
- She has a list of many victims.

PROVERBS 8

- Wisdom calls out for you to listen.
- Prudence, knowledge, discretion, counsel and sound judgment all come with wisdom.
- Wisdom was around before creation and with wisdom God created everything.
- Find wisdom and find life.

PROVERBS 9

- Wisdom has built her house and invites you in.
- Mockers and the wicked don't like to be told what to do. The wise love to be rebuked and grow wiser still.

- The fear of the Lord begins the quest for knowledge.
- By wisdom you will live longer.
- Folly stirs up trouble.

PROVERBS 10
- Many comparisons between the wise and the foolish.
- Many comparisons between the righteous and the wicked.
- Hatred only stirs up more hatred. Love is best.
- Watch what you say and be wise. A fool cannot control his tongue.

PROVERBS 11
- The righteous prosper. Even the city rejoices.
- The wicked are brought down by evil desires.
- Don't gossip.
- Kindness and generosity are always best.
- A beautiful woman with no discretion is like a gold ring in a pig's snout.

PROVERBS 12
- The righteous stand firm. They even care for their animals.
- The unrighteous are uprooted.
- The wise listen to advice. They overlook insults. They keep their knowledge to themselves.
- The fool shows annoyance. He blurts out folly.
- Anxiety weighs a heart down, but a kind word cheers it up.

PROVERBS 13
- Better to pretend to be poor and having great wealth, then to pretend to be rich and have nothing.
- Listen to instruction. It is life. Hang out with the wise.
- If you love your child, discipline him.

PROVERBS 14
- A fool lashes out with pride. Stay away from him.

- The poor are shunned. Be kind to the needy. Oppress them and you show contempt for God.
- The fear of the Lord is life.

PROVERBS 15

- A gentle answer turns away wrath. A soothing tongue is life.
- Harsh words stir up anger and quarrels.
- Plans fail for lack of counsel. Get many advisers.

PROVERBS 16

- Humans may have plans, but ultimately it's what God wants that matters.
- God doesn't like pride. It causes the fall of many.
- Kings like honesty and hate wrongdoing.
- Gray hair is a crown of splendor.

PROVERBS 17

- Don't cause strife or stir up trouble.
- God tests the heart.
- A cheerful heart is good medicine.
- A friend loves but a brother is always there for you.
- A foolish child brings grief to his parents.

PROVERBS 18

- The fool's mouth brings strife, invites a beating, becomes their undoing and is a snare to their very lives.
- The name of the Lord is like a strong tower. Run to it and be safe.
- Don't answer before listening. Acquire knowledge.

PROVERBS 19

- You need desire and knowledge together.
- Wealthy people attract a lot of friends, but the poor are shunned.
- A quarrelsome wife is like a leaky roof.
- Laziness brings hunger and poverty.

- Discipline your child or you will be a party to their death.
- Flog and penalize mockers.

PROVERBS 20

- Wine and beer lead to fights.
- The Lord hates dishonest scales.
- Food gained by fraudulent measures tastes sweet at first, but turns to dirt in your mouth later.
- A person's steps are directed by the Lord.
- Gray hair gives splendor to the old.

PROVERBS 21

- You make think your way is best, but God weighs your heart.
- If you are diligent, you will succeed. If you are lazy, you will die.
- If you love pleasure and fine foods, you will go poor.
- Don't ignore the poor.
- It's better to live on the roof of your house or in the desert than with a quarrelsome wife.

PROVERBS 22

- It's better to have a good name than riches.
- Start your child off in the way he should go and when he is older he will not depart from it.
- Don't oppress the poor.
- Don't make friends with a hot-tempered man.
- Don't make promises you can't keep.
- Don't move ancient boundary stones.

PROVERBS 23

- Don't give in to gluttony or crave delicacies.
- Don't wear yourself out getting rich. Wealth is fleeting.
- Grow in wisdom.
- Don't withhold discipline from a child. You could save them from death.
- Don't envy sinners.

- Don't drink too much or crave wine. You will do stupid things when drunk.
- Listen to your mom and dad.

PROVERBS 24
- A house is built by wisdom. Knowledge fills the rooms.
- Wisdom is as sweet as honey.
- Don't gloat when your enemy falls.
- The field of a sluggard is covered in thorns and weeds. Poverty comes quickly and quietly like a thief.

PROVERBS 25
- Don't try to exalt yourself around a king. Let him call you forward.
- The rebuke of a wise judge is very valuable.
- Don't eat too much honey. Don't abuse too much of a good thing.
- If your enemy is hungry or thirsty, help him.
- Self-control is like the walls around your city.

PROVERBS 26
- Don't answer a fool or listen to him. Don't associate or even try to understand.
- Dogs go back and eat their vomit. Fools do the same thing over and over again.
- Lazy people get nowhere in life.
- Quarrelsome and gossipy people cause so many problems.
- Beware your enemies and their clever speech.

PROVERBS 27
- Don't boast about tomorrow. You don't know what's going to happen.
- Don't praise yourself. Let others do that.
- A friend can wound you and it's okay. Their heartfelt advice is pleasant.
- Your life is reflected in your heart.
- As iron sharpens iron, we keep each other sharp.

- Know the condition of your flocks. Nothing is secure forever.

PROVERBS 28
- A ruthless ruler is destructive. Many innocent get hurt.
- Better to be poor and blameless than rich and perverse.
- If you do right, you will be blessed. Do wrong and you are cursed.
- Don't show partiality. Be kind to the poor.

PROVERBS 29
- Evildoers get caught up in their own sin. They don't care about the poor.
- A child needs to be disciplined or he will bring disgrace to his parents.
- People need revelation and a vision or they will do what they want.
- An angry person commits many sins.

PROVERBS 30
- Every word of God is flawless. Don't ever add to it.
- Keep poverty or riches away from me. Give me only my daily bread.
- Four things are never satisfied: the grave, the barren womb, a thirsty land and fire.
- Four things are amazing: an eagle, a snake, a ship and a man with a young woman.
- Four things are small but wise: ants, hyraxes, locusts and a lizard.

PROVERBS 31
- Kings should not crave wine or beer. Leave that for those in anguish.
- A wife of noble character is a great find. Her husband loves her and has full confidence in her.
- A wife of noble character works very hard day and night, supplying for her family's daily needs.

- A wife of noble character is an investor and a maker of fine items.
- Everyone in her family sings her praises.

ECCLESIASTES

Number of Chapters: *12*
Most likely author: *Solomon*
Approximately written: *935 BC*

ECCLESIASTES 1

The son of David, the teacher and king of Jerusalem called everything utterly meaningless. He claimed there was nothing new under the sun. Attaining wisdom, the teacher said, was nothing more than chasing after wind and with more knowledge came nothing but more grief.

ECCLESIASTES 2

The teacher tried to find meaning in pleasure and partying. Meaningless. He tried to find meaning in great building projects and lots of laborers. Meaningless. Everything he wanted he took and he denied himself nothing. Meaningless. The wise and fool have the same fate, so what's the use. The best answer the teacher felt was to eat and drink and enjoy one's toil.

ECCLESIASTES 3

There's a time for everything. God has placed eternity (time) on the hearts of men. Man wants to enjoy life during his time on earth. God shows man that time is limited. Death awaits us all, even the animals. We will all, eventually, turn to dust.

ECCLESIASTES 4

The teacher saw all the oppression, toil, envy and loneliness in this world. What's the use? Two are always better than one. We all need someone to pick us up.

ECCLESIASTES 5

When you go to God, don't be so quick to speak. When you make a vow, honor it. Gaining money does not do any good either. Hard work and enjoying the fruits of your labor is the way to go, not gaining more and more, because when you die, you can't take it with you. We all arrive naked into this world and we will all leave the same way.

ECCLESIASTES 6
God gives people wealth but they can't enjoy it. What's the use? All people do is try to satisfy their hunger.

ECCLESIASTES 7
The writer gave some proverbial sayings of wisdom (much like Proverbs) about the meaninglessness of life. Topics include wisdom over foolishness and righteousness over wickedness.

ECCLESIASTES 8
The writer encouraged the readers to obey the king, though nobody really has the power to control war or death. The writer had seen the wicked and the righteous getting what the other deserved. Who can understand it? People need to enjoy their labor instead of getting no sleep.

ECCLESIASTES 9
The righteous and the wicked all share a common destiny – death overtakes them all. There is also evil in everything in this world. And when you die, you know nothing and you don't have another chance. So enjoy life. Work hard. You never know when your hour will come. It's better to be quiet and wise than a loud fool.

ECCLESIASTES 10
Proverbs about life, wisdom, laziness and folly.

ECCLESIASTES 11
Proverbs about wise business, farming and taking advantage of your youth while you still can.

ECCLESIASTES 12
The teacher encouraged people to remember their Creator before they got too old and things begin to fall apart over time. In the end, the Teacher announced the conclusion of this

entire matter – fear God and obey his commandments. God will judge us all in the end.

SONG OF SONGS

Number of Chapters: *8*
Most likely author: *Solomon*
Approximately written: *970-960 BC*

ABOUT THIS BOOK: Song of Songs (also known as Song of Solomon) is a chorus of marital bliss, as two lovers sing about love and sex. A woman and a man (who is a king and probably Solomon himself) exchange detailed descriptions of what they love about each other bodies, while a chorus of friends supports their feelings and vows to each other.

SONG OF SONGS 1

The woman didn't want people staring at her because her skin was so dark. The man compared her to a mare from Pharaoh's horses. He complimented her cheeks, neck and eyes. She said he smelled like myrrh and henna blossoms. A chorus of friends support their union.

SONG OF SONGS 2

The woman called herself a Rose of Sharon. She wanted to be taken to his banquet hall, strengthened by food and taken into his arms. She did not want love awakened before the time was right. The man wanted to see her face and hear her voice. The woman claimed him as her own and gave herself to be his.

SONG OF SONGS 3

The woman went looking for her man. The watchman had not seen him. Then, immediately, she found him and took him to her mother's house, to the bed where she was conceived. Solomon's carriage arrived in all its splendor.

SONG OF SONGS 4

The man detailed different parts of her body – her eyes, hair, teeth, lips, mouth, temples, neck and breasts – in poetic detail. He called her beautiful and perfect. He said she stole his heart. She's better than fine wine. Under her tongue were milk and honey. The man called his woman a garden. She told him to come into her garden.

SONG OF SONGS 5

The friends encourage the lovers to take their fill of each other. The woman was ready for her man to come to her, but he had disappeared. She looked for him but could not find him. The woman described her man in great detail, including his eyes, cheeks, lips, arms, body, legs and mouth.

SONG OF SONGS 6

The woman found the man in the garden. He described her again as lovely and beautiful, detailing her hair, teeth and temples. Out of numerous queens, concubines and virgins, he called her unique. The friends wanted to gaze on her, the Shulammite woman.

SONG OF SONGS 7

The man continued his detailed description of the woman, including her feet, legs, navel, waist, breasts, neck, eyes, nose, head, hair and overall stature. She said she would give him her love in the vineyards.

SONG OF SONGS 8

The lovers embraced. Their love was unquenchable.

ISAIAH

Number of Chapters: *66*
The Author: *Isaiah*
Approximate time span: 740-680 BC (during the destruction of
                          Jerusalem and the exile to Babylon)

ISAIAH 1

Isaiah saw a vision regarding Judah and Jerusalem, during the reigns of Uzziah, Jotham, Ahaz, Hezekiah. The nation had become detestable to God, the people's sacrifices and festivals were meaningless to Him. God saw them as a burden, their hands full of blood. Even though these nations sinned, God would restore them, cleansing their sins to be white as snow. The city would once again be restored, after God purged the dross.

ISAIAH 2

Isaiah saw the Lord's temple, in the last days, being established and raised up high, people streaming to it. People would travel there to be taught. A place where peace reigned. However, as of now, Isaiah expressed how God had abandoned them. They thought they were rich, but God would humble the proud. The detestable idols would be tossed and God exalted.

ISAIAH 3

God was about to bring judgment down on Jerusalem and Judah. The women of Zion were haughty and enticing. Soon, it would all be humbled and destroyed.

ISAIAH 4

Isaiah looked forward to the Branch of the Lord who will cleanse the people. The Lord will wash away the filth and protect the people at Mount Zion.

ISAIAH 5

A song about the vineyard that was once fertile, now it produced bad grapes. Because of that, the hedge and the wall of protection would be removed. That vineyard was the nation of

Israel. All attempts at making it productive would fail. Isaiah expressed woes on the wicked, the perverters of justice, those who party. God called on those from distant nations and gave them permission to attack easily and swiftly.

ISAIAH 6

Isaiah had a vision of God on his throne, with seraphim praising God. While seeing this, Isaiah fell apart and mourned his unclean lips. One of the seraphim took a hot coal and touched Isaiah's mouth, cleaning Isaiah from guilt. When God asked who would take on a mission for God, Isaiah accepted, asking that he be sent. God told him to tell the people that they hear but don't understand and that their hearts were calloused.

ISAIAH 7

Aram and Israel threatened Judah, but God had Israel deliver a message to king Ahaz of Judah telling him not to worry. God spoke to Ahaz and said that he would give him a sign – the virgin would conceive and give birth to a son and would call him Immanuel. Before that child knew right from wrong, their enemies would be no more.

ISAIAH 8

Isaiah made love with the prophetess and she conceived and gave birth to a son named Maher-Shalal-Hash-Baz. However, before the boy could speak, God said Samaria would be carried off by Assyria. Isaiah and his children were the signs for Judah's future. God told Isaiah not to follow the people. God would be the stone that caused people to stumble. Those from Jerusalem would call him a trap and a snare. Isaiah warned people not to consult mediums and spiritists.

ISAIAH 9

Isaiah promised no more gloom for those in distress for in the future he would honor Galilee. A great light would be seen by those in the darkness. A child would be born, a son, and the government will be on his shoulders. They will call him Wonderful Counselor, Mighty God, Everlasting Father, Prince of Peace. His rule will be peaceful and it will never end. God, though, was angry at Israel. Prideful, they tried to rebuild, but God was against their efforts.

ISAIAH 10

Woe to nations who hurt their people, taking advantage of the poor and widows. There would be judgment on Assyria and its king for his willful pride and the haughty look in his eyes. There is encouragement for a remnant of Israel who would return one day. Do not fear the Assyrians. God's wrath would end against his people and be directed to their enemies.

ISAIAH 11

The Branch from Jesse would come and bear fruit. The Spirit of the Lord would rest on him. He will judge with righteousness and strike the earth with the rod of his mouth. When he comes, he will bring peace, such as when a lion lies down with a lamb. The nations will rally to the Root of Jesse. He will gather the remnant and raise a banner for them.

ISAIAH 12

Praise God for he is my salvation. I will not be afraid. Praise God for his glorious deeds.

ISAIAH 13

A prophecy against Babylon who, though they were once a threat, would be destroyed by the Medes, as predicted by Isaiah.

ISAIAH 14

God would have compassion on Israel and devastate her enemies, especially Babylon and the Philistines. Isaiah seemed to compare Babylon to Satan in this chapter, once a beautiful morning star, now reduced to the ground.

ISAIAH 15

A prophecy against Moab, where great grief would occur in its cities.

ISAIAH 16

The prophecy against Moab continued, predicting that in three years Moab would be devastated.

ISAIAH 17

A prophecy against Damascus, predicting the day when this great city would be a heap of ruins.

ISAIAH 18

A prophecy against the tall, smooth skinned people along the rivers of Cush.

ISAIAH 19

A prophecy against Egypt, saying they would be oppressed by a cruel leader and the waters would dry up causing distress. Egypt would become dizzy and weak. In the end, Egypt and Assyria would worship God.

ISAIAH 20

God told Isaiah to walk around stripped and barefoot as a sign that the king of Assyria would lead the officials of Egypt and Cush away stripped and barefoot.

ISAIAH 21

A prophecy against Babylon, Edom and Arabia.

ISAIAH 22

A prophecy against Jerusalem. God was about to roll them up and toss them out. A person named Eliakim would come and be a father to all those living in Jerusalem.

ISAIAH 23

A prophecy against Tyre and its destruction. It was once a wealthy town of prosperity and revelry, now it would be forgotten for seventy years, the span of one king's life.

ISAIAH 24

An apocalyptic view of the earth's devastation. God will destroy it all one day, punishing the earth for its sins.

ISAIAH 25

God is to be revered by the strong and the ruthless nations. In those last days, God will provide and protect those on his mountain with a great feast, swallowing up death and wiping away every tear.

ISAIAH 26

A praise song that would be sung in Judah, where salvation dwells and the righteous enter. Let the wicked see God's zeal. One day the dead will live and rise, but for now, God's wrath is coming to the sinful.

ISAIAH 27

God promised judgment on those cities that have struck his people.

ISAIAH 28

God would bring judgment on Ephraim and Judah, especially those spiritual leaders drunk with power. God would speak to his people nonetheless. God placed a precious cornerstone, a foundation, a righteous plumb line so people can build their lives in righteousness. God would plant and produce carefully and according to his instructions.

ISAIAH 29

Woe to the city, Ariel, where David settled. God promised to bring it to ruin through enemy nations. The people came with words from their mouths, but their hearts were far away. Clay can't turn to the potter and say, "You didn't make me." In a short time, God would restore the city of Zion and the people would turn around.

ISAIAH 30

How dare God's people think that Egypt can protect them! That's a useless country. The people wanted the prophets and priests to give them pleasant illusions. Repentance and rest are where salvation is found. God would be gracious. He promised to hear and to guide them to the left or to the right. He would send rain. His wrath would pour out on Assyria.

ISAIAH 31

Do not put your reliance on Egypt – their horses or chariots. They were mere mortals. Assyria would fall, but not by a human, mortal sword.

ISAIAH 32

Justice would come to the land. People would see and understand clearly. The fool would no longer be called noble. The complacent women needed to be afraid and cry out until God's spirit was poured down and peace came to the land.

ISAIAH 33

Woe to those who destroy and betray. God is our sure foundation. Once things seemed hopeless, then God would arise. A new king would come and replace those former arrogant leaders. The Lord is our judge, lawgiver and king.

ISAIAH 34

The Lord was going to pour out his wrath on all the nations, especially Edom.

ISAIAH 35

A time of perfect peace was coming. The people will see the glory and splendor of God. Everyone would be healed and the land would be restored.

ISAIAH 36

Sennacherib King of Assyria attacked Judah and the fortified cities. A field commander negotiated with representatives from King Hezekiah and said it was no use fighting Assyria, just surrender. He said don't rely on Egypt or any of your gods. They did not do any good for any other nation they've conquered.

ISAIAH 37

Isaiah was told of the Assyrian threat and told Hezekiah not to worry. God would send Sennacherib a certain report that would cause him to return to his own country. Sennacherib heard that the King of Egypt was marching out to fight him.

Hezekiah prayed for God to protect them. Isaiah confirmed that God heard his prayer. An angel of the Lord visited the Assyrian camp and put 185,000 to death. Sennacherib was killed by his own sons while worshipping his god.

ISAIAH 38

Isaiah told Hezekiah that he would die, but when Hezekiah prayed, God gave him fifteen more years of life. The sign—the shadow moved back across the ten steps it just went down. Hezekiah sang a song of praise for God saving him from death. Isaiah commanded that a poultice of figs be applied to the Hezekiah's boil.

ISAIAH 39

Babylon sent envoys to wish Hezekiah good health. Hezekiah showed off his treasures to them. Isaiah protested, telling Hezekiah that because of his action the kingdom would be stripped someday of all those treasures and taken to Babylon.

ISAIAH 40

God provides comfort and strength to his people. There's a voice calling in the desert to prepare the way for the Lord. We, like grass and flowers, wither but the word of the Lord endures forever. Good news is coming. The Lord has power. Who can compare to him? Look to the heavens. He has every star in place. He doesn't grow weary. If you have hope in the Lord, you will soar on the wings of eagles.

ISAIAH 41

God told Israel not to be afraid of any enemy. Their enemies would be disgraced. God promised to make rivers flow in barren places and pools of water in desert spots. Idols can't help you.

ISAIAH 42

God vowed to send a servant (Jesus) to establish new things. He would be peaceful and establish justice. God would be a light for the Gentiles, open the eyes of the blind and free captives from prison. God explained why he should be praised.

Israel was blind and deaf. They saw many things and did not pay attention, so God poured out his anger on them.

ISAIAH 43

God promised to be with Israel through fire or high water. He loves them. God wanted to bring his people back from the four corners of the earth. He wanted to forget the past and move on to new things, but Israel would not worship him.

ISAIAH 44

God promised to take care of Israel and restore it. However, they needed to stop allowing worthless idols to be made. These idols were made by human effort with products all around them, and yet these idols received so much glory. People thought these idols could save their lives. But God, the maker of all things, who fought the false prophets and fools, would allow Jerusalem to be inhabited once again.

ISAIAH 45

God promised to use King Cyrus and Persia to subdue the existing nation. God would help defeat Cyrus' enemies. Only God could do this. There is no one like him. He created everything above and below. Don't quarrel with God. What good will it do? Why trust in idols? Turn to God and be saved.

ISAIAH 46

God promised to love and sustain the remnant of Israel. Can an idol do that? Don't forget what God has done. What he plans will come about.

ISAIAH 47

The great queen city of the Babylonians would soon be exposed. This great city of pleasure would soon see suffering in full measures. Good luck with your sorceries and spells. They can't save people.

ISAIAH 48

God told the Israelites he would save them but they stubbornly resisted. He did these things so the idols would not get credit. The Israelites should have listened to God and things would have been much more peaceful.

ISAIAH 49

A servant was coming to bring Jacob back to him. He would be a light to the Gentiles, so God's salvation could reach the ends of the earth. God would restore the land and bring back the people and the joy.

ISAIAH 50

The people got into this situation because of their sin, not because God couldn't rescue them. God offered himself and the people beat, mocked and spat on him.

ISAIAH 51

God promised to bless Zion and bring joy and singing to her once again. The people must wake up and listen to God's instruction. God would strengthen and comfort them. Do not forget him! Jerusalem drank a cup of God's wrath before, but God would hand that cup over to their enemies.

ISAIAH 52

The people were told to rejoice as they returned to Zion. God promised to go before them and watch their backs. God's servant would act wisely, despite how much he appalled them with his disfigured appearance.

ISAIAH 53

This Suffering Servant grew up normally, with nothing really attractive about him. He was familiar with suffering and pain and took up our pain and suffering through punishment by God. He was pierced for our transgressions, but by his wounds we were healed. We have wandered away from God, like sheep do. But this person did not protest the punishment he received. He died and was assigned a grave with the wicked and the rich. He didn't do anything wrong. It was God's will this had to happen. He poured out his life for many and interceded for us sinners.

ISAIAH 54

God promised things would get better. He rejected his people for a little while, but he had compassion. Things can fall apart yet God's unfailing love for us can never be shaken. He will rebuild. No enemy can stop him.

ISAIAH 55

God invited all who were thirsty to come to him for he would make an everlasting covenant with everyone. Seek God while there's still time. His thoughts and ways are not our thoughts and ways. Every word that comes from his mouth does not return null and void.

ISAIAH 56

God told the people to hold on and keep the commands, which includes all the eunuchs and foreigners too. He will give them joy in his house of prayer, which is for all nations. Israel's leaders were described as mute watchdogs who lie around and dream.

ISAIAH 57

The righteous find peace in death, however the wicked will be judged by their lives, mocking God, sacrificing their children and worshipping false idols which will not save them from God's wrath. God will heal the holy and bring them to comfort. There is no peace for the wicked.

ISAIAH 58

God challenged the people's idea of fasting, which in those days always ended with strife and fighting. True fasting humbles and leads people to help others in need. If the people do that, they would be blessed.

ISAIAH 59

The people's sins separated them from God. Everyone's hands were stained with blood and their feet rushed into sin. They don't know peace or justice. God was not pleased but he promised to keep his covenant. His words must always be on their lips.

ISAIAH 60

God promised to rebuild the city, despite their disobedience. He would bring prosperity once again, coming via the nations around the world. Once again, this city would be respected by the world, bowing down to it. God promised to be the light of the restored city.

ISAIAH 61

Isaiah proclaimed that the spirit of God was on him, to proclaim good news to the poor, bind up the brokenhearted, to proclaim freedom for the captives and release the prisoners from darkness. God would rebuild lives and remove the shame.

ISAIAH 62

God promised that Jerusalem would no longer be deserted. He would carry the city like a groom carries a bride. He would post watchmen on the walls, watching day and night. No longer would foreigners eat their harvest. Open up the gates and highways!

ISAIAH 63

Isaiah saw one robed in splendor, but splattered with blood from trampling the nations in anger. This Lord had done many good things for Israel, showing them compassion, love and mercy, even though they rebelled and grieved the Holy Spirit.

ISAIAH 64

The writer pleaded with God to come down from heaven and cause the nations to tremble. God's people had become unclean, their righteous acts like filthy rags. They've turned from God and hidden their faces. Don't be angry forever, Lord. The cities have become wastelands. The temple burned with fire. Don't keep silent, Lord!

ISAIAH 65

God revealed himself to nations who did not ask for God to reveal himself to them. All day God holds out his hands to obstinate people who openly defy him. However, there would be a day of vengeance for all who did evil in God's sight. In that day, God promised to take care of his servants, providing blessings for them. He will create a new heaven and new earth. The old will all pass away. In this new world, there will be life, houses, vineyards and peace.

ISAIAH 66

Heaven is God's throne and earth is a mere footstool. God loves those who are humble, but hates those who selfishly offer sacrifices. Praise God and receive his comfort. All the nations will eventually bow down. Those who declare God as their own and follow him will not face death.

JEREMIAH

Number of Chapters: *52*
The Author: *Jeremiah*
Approximate time span: 627-580 BC (during the final days of
                                  Jerusalem and the exile to Babylon)

ABOUT THIS BOOK: The prophecies of Jeremiah were not compiled in chronological order. Careful attention needs to be paid as to when each prophesy was spoken.

JEREMIAH 1
     God called Jeremiah, a priest, to be a prophet during Israel's exile. Jeremiah thought he was too young, but God replied that he knew what he was doing. After Jeremiah witnessed a couple things in a vision, God told him to get ready and not to be afraid for God would protect them.

JEREMIAH 2
     God told Jeremiah to speak to those in Jerusalem. The people were once devoted to God, but they followed worthless idols. God brought them to a fertile land and they follow other gods then turn to other nations for help.

JEREMIAH 3
     God compared Israel to unashamed men who wait on the side of the road for the next prostitute. He couldn't believe Judah fell into the same adulteries. God asked for faithless Israel to return to him, calling himself their husband and Father.

JEREMIAH 4
     God asked Israel to return to him. He warned Judah of an enemy coming down from the north. God lamented the destruction that would happen, his heart breaking. The coming disaster would cause the land to be completely destroyed.

JEREMIAH 5
     If they could find one honest person in Jerusalem, God said he wouldn't destroy them. The city was full of unrepentant

fools. God needed to punish them with a distant nation that would devour everything. The people needed to start fearing God.

JEREMIAH 6

God told Jerusalem to flee for safety because a battle was coming. But, God wondered, who would listen to him? From the least to the greatest, prophet or priest? They were all wicked. So a mighty army was coming their way.

JEREMIAH 7

God told Jeremiah to stand at the gate and plead for the people to reform their ways and not sin. His temple had become a den of robbers. God invited the people to go to Shiloh, where the tabernacle once stood, and see what he did to those detestable people. God promised to turn their high places, where they sacrificed their own children, into a valley of slaughter filled with their own bones.

JEREMIAH 8

God said that the bones of priests, prophets, kings and officials would become like dung on the ground. Everybody had turned away to do their own thing. Nobody listened. Nobody was ashamed of their sin. God promised to take it all away. Jeremiah was crushed by this news, crying out for healing.

JEREMIAH 9

The people lied, sinned and betrayed their friends. They worshipped idols. God said he would scatter them and cause much weeping. Much death was coming their way.

JEREMIAH 10

God called their idols worthless, completely fabricated by man and had no creative powers themselves. God made the earth. Listen to him! But, because they didn't, there was a destruction coming soon. Jeremiah prayed for God's discipline and wrath.

JEREMIAH 11

God told Jeremiah to proclaim to those in the towns of Judah and the streets of Jerusalem that they have broken the covenant with God because they were stubborn and followed other gods. God then revealed an assassination plot against Jeremiah by the people of Anathoth. God promised to wipe them out.

JEREMIAH 12

Jeremiah couldn't believe the wicked prospered and the faithless lived the easy life. God replied that he was willing to give up his people and sacrifice his inheritance. He would have to uproot them but later have compassion on them.

JEREMIAH 13

God told Jeremiah to take a linen belt and hide it in the rocks. Later, when Jeremiah dug the belt up, it was ruined and God compared it to Judah and Jerusalem – completely useless. God threatened them with captivity, saying they would be in pain, scattered and shamed.

JEREMIAH 14

A drought hit the area and the people suffered. Jeremiah pleaded for God to help. God told Jeremiah not to pray for the well-being of the people. He would destroy them with sword, famine and plague. But Jeremiah said the prophets were saying this would not happen. God called them liars. Jeremiah tried to intercede for the people, but God said don't bother.

JEREMIAH 15

God said he would make Jerusalem abhorrent. He was tired of holding back on them. Destruction and death was coming. However, they still had a chance if they repented. Only then would he save them.

JEREMIAH 16

God told Jeremiah not to marry or have children. He told Jeremiah not to mourn or celebrate at parties because great calamity was coming. If they asked why this happened to them,

Jeremiah was to say because they forsook God and worshipped idols.

JEREMIAH 17

Judah's sin was great and God was ready to give away their inheritance. A nation is blessed if their confidence is in God. God examines the heart and rewards people according to their deeds. Jeremiah pleaded for healing because he had been faithful. God told Jeremiah to watch the city gates and make sure people weren't carrying loads and doing work on the Sabbath.

JEREMIAH 18

God directed Jeremiah to go to a potter's house and watch him shape and reshape clay into a pot. God said that he would do the same thing to Israel – tear it down and shape it up. God was bringing a terrible disaster to them. He warned Jeremiah that his life would be threatened by this message. Jeremiah asked for his enemies to be punished.

JEREMIAH 19

God told Jeremiah to buy a clay jar from the potter then take the elders and priests to the Valley of Ben Hinnom where he proclaimed God's judgment on the land for worshipping other gods. Jeremiah was then to smash the jar into pieces, like God would smash this nation.

JEREMIAH 20

A priest named Pashur had Jeremiah put in stocks because of his negative prophecies. When released, Jeremiah told Pashur that God would turn Israel over to Babylon and Pashur and all his friends would die in exile. Jeremiah then complained to God about all the ridicule he received because of his prophecies. Everybody whispered and attacked him. Jeremiah wished he hadn't been born.

JEREMIAH 21

King Zedekiah asked Jeremiah to intervene with God regarding Nebuchadnezzar. Jeremiah said those who stay in

Jerusalem would die because of the Babylonian siege, either by sword, famine or plague. Those who surrender would live. God told the royal house of Judah to administer justice because God would judge according to their deeds.

JEREMIAH 22

God sent Jeremiah to the king's palace to proclaim judgment. He told the officials to do what was right and continue their reign or die. The palace, God promised, would be destroyed. People would pass by and wonder why God would do such a thing. The answer: they forsook their covenant with God and worshipped other idols. To King Shallum, God said this palace was built with greed. To King Jehoiakim, God said his death would not be mourned. To King Jehoiachin, God said he would turn him over to the Babylonians.

JEREMIAH 23

God hated the shepherds who led his people astray. God promised to gather them and bring them back to pasture. A day would be coming when a righteous member of David's family tree would reign wisely and his name would be the Lord our Righteous Savior. God hated the lying prophets who went around telling people what God said. He never spoke to them! He urged the people not to listen to them. God would punish them greatly.

JEREMIAH 24

After Jehoiachin and others were carried away by Nebuchadnezzar, God showed Jeremiah two baskets of figs – one good and the other inedible. The good figs represented the exiles to Babylon who God promised to watch over and bring back to Jerusalem. The bad represented King Zedekiah, his officials and the survivors from Jerusalem.

JEREMIAH 25

During the first year of Nebuchadnezzar's reign, Jeremiah had been prophesizing for twenty-three years but no one listened, so God promised to use Babylon to completely destroy the land. Then, after seventy years, God would punish

Babylon and make them desolate forever. Many nations would drink the cup of God's wrath. God was going to punish his own city—why not theirs? A terrible storm was coming.

JEREMIAH 26

God told Jeremiah to preach in the temple that he would curse Jerusalem and the temple. The priests, prophets and people wanted Jeremiah killed. Some defended Jeremiah, saying other prophets (Micah and Uriah) had said the same thing and his death could bring a greater curse.

JEREMIAH 27

During the reign of Zedekiah, God told Jeremiah to make a yolk and wear it, then say that all nations must surrender to Nebuchadnezzar. He told them not to listen to their prophets, diviners, mediums or sorcerers. The articles from the Lord's house would not be returning soon from Babylon.

JEREMIAH 28

The false prophet Hananiah said God would break the yoke and return all the articles from the temple within two years. Jeremiah said he hoped that would happen but the truth was people only want to hear prophecies of peace. Hananiah broke Jeremiah's yoke and God said he would replace that wood yoke for an iron one. Jeremiah predicted Hananiah's imminent death. Hananiah died that year.

JEREMIAH 29

After the first exile, Jeremiah wrote a letter to the exiles saying marry, plant and build in Babylon. For God knew the plans he had for them, plans to prosper them and give them hope. After seventy years God would return them to Jerusalem. Those left in Jerusalem now faced horrors since they did not listen to the prophets. Jeremiah promised punishment for a rebellious letter writer named Shemaiah who gave people false hope.

JEREMIAH 30

God told Jeremiah to write down about the days when God would bring his people out of captivity and back to Israel. God was with them and would save them.

JEREMIAH 31

God promised to be the God of all families of Israel as he built them back up again. Sing, rejoice and hear the word of the Lord. Israel would return to be the great city it once was. God declared that he would establish a new covenant, not like he did with the ancestors, but this one written on people's hearts. Everyone will know God.

JEREMIAH 32

During the tenth year of the reign of Zedekiah, while Babylon besieged Jerusalem, Jeremiah was imprisoned by the king. God told Jeremiah that his cousin would come and sell him a piece of land, which he did. This was a sign to Jeremiah that God, who had given this land of milk and honey to the Israelites, would certainly give the land back to them after these tragic events (all caused by Israel's sin).

JEREMIAH 33

God came to Jeremiah a second time while confined by the guard. God told him people would soon die, but he promised to bring health and healing. Though it would be desolate, God would restore it. He would raise up a righteous branch from David's line who will sit on the throne forever.

JEREMIAH 34

Jeremiah told Zedekiah that he would see the King of Babylon with his own eyes and he would die peacefully. Zedekiah had all the Hebrew slaves set free, then the people all changed their minds and enslaved them again. God did not like this, saying they were disobedient to break their own promise. Now God declared he was bringing the enemy back against the city to burn it down.

JEREMIAH 35

God had Jeremiah invite the Rekabite family to the house of the Lord and offered them wine. They refused it saying they had sworn never to drink wine or plant vineyards. God was pleased by the Rekabites and wanted all of Judah to see their obedience. While disaster was coming to Judah, God promised that the Rekabite family would always have someone serving God.

JEREMIAH 36

During the reign of Jehoiakim, the Lord told Jeremiah some words in hopes that the people would turn from their wicked ways. Jeremiah had Baruch write them on a scroll and read them in the temple. When Jehoiakim heard the words, he cut the scroll in pieces and tossed them into the fire. God pronounced that no one from his lineage would sit on the throne, his body would lay outside and his children would be punished. Jeremiah dictated another scroll to Baruch.

JEREMIAH 37

During the reign of Zedekiah, put into power by Nebuchadnezzar, Pharaoh's army marched out of Egypt so the Babylonians stopped their siege on Jerusalem. The Lord told the people not to get their hopes up. Jeremiah took the opportunity to visit a piece of land in the territory of Benjamin but the guards thought he was deserting. Jonathan the secretary had Jeremiah beaten. Zedekiah sent for Jeremiah and Jeremiah pleaded not to return to Jonathan's house, so he remained in the guard's courtyard.

JEREMIAH 38

Jeremiah was lowered into a muddy cistern by the officials because of his prophecies. Ebed-Melek, a Cushite, pleaded with the king to free Jeremiah. The king granted him the wish and Ebed-Melek pulled Jeremiah out. Zedekiah again questioned Jeremiah who told the king that if he surrendered to Babylon, everyone would be spared. Zedekiah didn't want anyone to know about this conversation.

JEREMIAH 39

In the ninth year of Zedekiah's reign, Nebuchadnezzar laid siege on Jerusalem. Zedekiah fled but the Babylonians captured him and Nebuchadnezzar had Zedekiah's boys killed in front of him and his eyes gouged out. The royal palace and the houses were burned down and the walls of Jerusalem destroyed. Nebuzaradan the commander of the Babylonian army took away the exiles to Babylon and left behind the poor people. Nebuchadnezzar told the commander not to harm Jeremiah but to do whatever he said. They freed Jeremiah from the courtyard and he returned home. God told Jeremiah that Ebed-Melek would be protected because of his faithfulness.

JEREMIAH 40

The Babylonian commander Nebuzaradan told Jeremiah that he did not have to go into exile. He was free to go wherever he wanted. Jeremiah chose to return to Jerusalem where Gedaliah, the king of Babylon's appointed governor, ruled. Gedaliah told the people not to be afraid of the Babylonians and to freely harvest wine and summer fruit. However, some wanted Gedaliah killed.

JEREMIAH 41

A man named Ishmael came with ten men at assassinated Gedaliah while he ate. Then he went after eighty men who came presenting gifts for the house of the Lord. Ishmael killed them (except for a few that begged for their lives and offered food) and threw their bodies in a cistern. Johanan went to fight Ishmael but Ishmael fled to the Ammonites. Johanan and his group headed to Bethlehem, then to Egypt because they were afraid of Babylonian retaliation.

JERMIAH 42

Johanan and his remnant went to Jeremiah for guidance and prayer. Jeremiah returned after a few days of praying and said to stay put in Judah, where the Babylonians would protect them. If they go to Egypt, God told Jeremiah, they would be cursed.

JEREMIAH 43

However, they did not like what Jeremiah said, so they disobeyed God's command to stay. They took their group and fled to Egypt, taking Jeremiah and Baruch with them. God told Jeremiah that Nebuchadnezzar would come to Egypt, burn it down and pick it clean.

JEREMIAH 44

God told Jeremiah how angry he was at the remnant of Jews, especially since they went to Egypt, burned incense to gods and never repented. They would all die by the sword or famine. The people didn't care. They wanted to burn incense, pour out drink offerings and bake cakes to the Queen of Heaven. They felt since they stopped doing that, their lives got worse. God told them to go ahead, but they would pay the price. He would deliver Hophra king of Egypt over to his enemies.

JEREMIAH 45

After Baruch wrote down Jeremiah's words, Jeremiah gave Baruch a personal message from God. He heard Baruch's painful cry, but God said he would uproot what he planted and allow Baruch to escape with his life.

JEREMIAH 46

Jeremiah relayed a message to Egypt, saying that no matter how well they prepared for battle, they would be shamed. God was going to use Nebuchadnezzar to bring them down. The people of Jacob would be protected.

JEREMIAH 47

Jeremiah communicated a message to the Philistines before Pharaoh attacked Gaza saying they would be destroyed.

JEREMIAH 48

God spoke about the complete devastation of Moab. It would be shattered and ruined. They mocked Israel with their own pride and arrogance, now they would wallow in their own vomit.

JEREMIAH 49

God prophesized against the Ammonites, the Edomites, those living in Damascus, Kedar, the kingdoms of Hazor which Nebuchadnezzar attacked and Elam. All of them would be severely devastated, if not completely wiped out.

JEREMIAH 50

Jeremiah proclaimed a prophecy against Babylon, saying an alliance of nations from the north would attack her and plunder her. The enemy would punish her as God punished Assyria. Israel though, the lost sheep, would return to her pasture. Babylon would never be inhabited again.

JEREMIAH 51

The Lord pronounced judgment on Babylon. She would be completely devastated. God once used her as a war club, shattering kingdoms, but now it would be reduced to a haunt for jackals. God judged Babylon for destroying the temple and worshipping idols. Jeremiah had this message read to Seraiah, a staff officer, then told him to tie the scroll to a stone and throw it in the Euphrates. In the same way, Babylon would sink because of the disaster coming upon her.

JEREMIAH 52

A brief overview of the fall of Jerusalem, starting with the rebellion of King Zedekiah from Babylon. Nebuchadnezzar marched into the city and everyone fled, including Zedekiah, whose children were killed in front of him and his eyes gouged out. Nebuzaradan the commander of the army had the temple and palace burned down and all the temple articles removed and taken to Babylon. 4,600 Jews were taken into captivity. In the 37th year of Jehoiachin's imprisonment, Awel-Marduk became king of Babylon and released Jehoiachin from prison. He allowed the former king of Judah to dine at his table for the rest of his life.

LAMENTATIONS

Number of Chapters: *5*
Most likely author: *Jeremiah*
Approximately written: *586 BC (After the fall of Jerusalem)*

LAMENTATIONS 1

The writer mourned the deserted city of Jerusalem, who was once a queen but now a slave. Her foes now rule as the children were taken into exile. Jerusalem's enemies just laughed and took all her treasures. The city was distressed and no one comforted her.

LAMENTATIONS 2

Like an enemy, the Lord swallowed up Israel, laying waste to her palaces, temple, altar, sanctuary, the walls and gates. The people were left in torment, weeping. Young and old laid in the streets, slain by the sword.

LAMENTATIONS 3

The writer had seen affliction because of God's wrath. God had made him grow old, broken his bones, walled him in, shut out his prayers and made his paths crooked. He had been attacked and mocked by his enemies. But, the Lord is good to those who hope in him. Great is his faithfulness. We must examine our hearts and return to him. Tears flowed unceasingly from the writer's eyes, yet he called out to God and God saved him from his enemies.

LAMENTATIONS 4

The punishment of the people was greater than those in Sodom, who were overthrown in a moment. Everybody had been broken – princes, women and children. The world could not believe what happened. All this devastation because of the sins of the prophets and priests. But, the punishment would end and the exile would not be forever. However, God had to punish their sins.

LAMENTATIONS 5

The inheritance of the city had been given to enemies. Water, wood and bread must be bought for a price. Women have been violated. Princes hung by their hands. The elders were gone. Music had stopped. God reigns forever but why have you forsaken your people? Renew our days.

EZEKIEL

Number of Chapters: *48*
The Author: *Ezekiel*
Approximate time span: 592-570 BC (To the Jews in exile at
                                      Babylon)

EZEKIEL 1
       While with the exiles, Ezekiel, a priest had a vision by the river Kebar. In his vision he saw a windstorm with, at its center, glowing metal and four living creatures. They looked like humans with four faces (human, lion, ox, eagle) and four wings. Fire and lightning flashed between them. Beside each creature were wheels, sparkling and full of eyes. Then a man appeared on a throne who looked like fire, radiating like a rainbow.

EZEKIEL 2
       The man in the vision called Ezekiel "son of man" then sent him to speak to the Israelites, a stubborn and obstinate people. A hand stretched out a scroll to him to eat. The words on the scroll were of mourning and woe.

EZEKIEL 3
       Ezekiel ate the scroll which tasted sweet. The man promised to make Ezekiel as tough as the people he was going to speak to. The Spirit lifted Ezekiel up and sent him to the exiles. After seven days of recovery, the Lord came to Ezekiel and told him he must repeat what God told him or he would be held accountable.

EZEKIEL 4
       God told Ezekiel to take a block of clay and draw Jerusalem on it. Then Ezekiel built a siege around it, with ramps, camps and battering rams. He had Ezekiel lay on his side facing it for 390 days, the number of years Israel sinned. Then, Ezekiel had to lay on his other side for 40 days, the number of years Judah sinned. God gave Ezekiel a recipe for bread that he must eat, baking it over human excrement. After Ezekiel

protested, God changed the fire's fuel to cow dung. This was all a sign for the Israelites since God was about to cut off the food supply to Jerusalem.

EZEKIEL 5

God told Ezekiel to shave his head and beard, then, during the siege, to burn a third of the hair in the city, strike a third of it with a sword, throw a third of it into the wind, then tuck a few in his garment. This sign predicted how God would punish those in Jerusalem – fire, sword and scattered. The people of Jerusalem worshipped idols and defiled God's sanctuary. God was angry.

EZEKIEL 6

God threatened the altars (high places) the Israelites had erected in the mountains, promising to lay dead bodies in front of their idols.

EZEKIEL 7

Israel, the time was coming for unheard of disaster, full of doom, panic, violence and death. Nothing could save the Israelites, not their gold, silver or fine jewelry. God was about to give all that wealth to foreigners. After all this, the people would know who the real God was.

EZEKIEL 8

One day, Ezekiel sat in his house when the glowing figure of a man appeared and the Spirit took Ezekiel by the hair and deposited him in Jerusalem, where he toured all the idol worship going on in the city. God wanted him to see what made him so angry.

EZEKIEL 9

Ezekiel then saw six men coming towards the city with deadly weapons in their hands. With them, a man clothed in linen and a writing kit in his hands. God directed the man to put a mark on the forehead of all those who grieved over the state of the city. The rest of the remnant in Jerusalem were to be slaughtered. Ezekiel pleaded for mercy but God would show no pity.

EZEKIEL 10

Ezekiel looked and saw a throne. The glory of the Lord filled the temple. Ezekiel saw four cherubs, with faces and wings, their entire bodies covered with eyes—the same living creatures he saw before by the Kebar River. The glory of the Lord then departed the temple.

EZEKIEL 11

The Spirit took Ezekiel to the gate of the temple where twenty-five men were plotting evil. The Lord called the city a pot and the dead bodies were meat. Ezekiel prophesied against them and one man died. The feeling in the city was that the exiles were far away and the city was theirs now, but God promised to bring his people back, cleansing the city of detestable idols. The Spirit carried Ezekiel back to the exiles in Babylonia.

EZEKIEL 12

God told Ezekiel to pack this things and dig through the wall as the people watched. The prophecy concerned the prince of Jerusalem and all the Israelites living there. They too would become exiles one day. The prince would try to escape through the wall, but would be captured and taken to Babylonia. He would never see the city though. The Lord told Ezekiel that despite popular opinion, God would not take a long time to make these prophecies happen. It would occur very soon.

EZEKIEL 13

God told Ezekiel to prophesy against the false prophets who claimed there would be peace. They have built up a wall and whitewashed it, but God would tear it down with his wrath. The women sewed magic charms on their wrists and veils for their heads. God vowed to tear all of this apart so people would know who the true Lord was.

EZEKIEL 14

The elders sat down before Ezekiel and the word of the Lord came to him saying these men had set up idols in their hearts. He told them to repent. God had set his face against them. The whole country was on notice by God's four judgments: sword, famine, wild beasts and plague. Even Noah, Daniel and Job, if they were tried, could not save them. God promised only some survivors.

EZEKIEL 15

God talked about how useless a vine was for building, especially after it had been burned. God compared this useless vine to Jerusalem, consumed by fire and left desolate.

EZEKIEL 16

God talked about raising Jerusalem like a small child, through puberty and tough times. God clothed and fed her with only the best until she became a queen. Then, trusting her own beauty, she turned to prostitution and built places of idol worship on every street corner. She sacrificed her own children. But, unlike a prostitute, she didn't receive gifts or accept payment. God would tear this all apart. Sodom and Samaria were not as sinful as Jerusalem. Eventually, God would remember his covenant with them when he made atonement for them.

EZEKIEL 17

God told a parable of an eagle carrying away a seedling from a cedar and planting a vine that grew. Then another great eagle showed up and the vine stretched out toward him. The imagery represented Israel, first uprooted by Samaria, then drawn to Babylon. God promised to stop Babylon and prevent Egypt from being a factor. God would take a shoot from the top of a cedar and replant it to make it flourish, saying Jerusalem would be the mighty force it once was.

EZEKIEL 18

God wanted to make clear that children would not die for the sins of their parents. If a man follows God's decrees, that man is righteous. If a man is unrighteous and his son righteous, the son would live, not sharing his father's guilt. The same holds true for the parent if the son is unrighteous. A righteous person who turns away from the Lord will be guilty. But an unrighteous person who turns to the Lord will not have their sins held against them.

EZEKIEL 19

God lamented over the princes of Israel who were raised to be great lions, kings of the beasts, but were captured in a net by the King of Babylon and thrown into prison. They were like a strong, fruitful vine, now uprooted, stripped and burned.

EZEKIEL 20

A group of elders sat down before Ezekiel to inquire of God. God outlined how he brought them out of Egypt and gave them rules to follow. The people did not obey and decided to worship idols. God would love to lead them and protect them, if they would only reject their idols. A time would come when the people would turn back to God and he would bring them back to the land.

EZEKIEL 21

Babylon would be God's sword of judgment on Israel and Jerusalem. The nation was ready to go and begin its slaughter. The King of Babylon would reach a crossroads and use divination to decide whether to attack the Ammonites or the Israelites. The answer would fall on the Israelites.

EZEKIEL 22

God detailed Jerusalem's sins, including idol worship, government mistreatment, sexual sins, bribes and profaning the commandments. God vowed to melt the people like a metal in a furnace. God tried to find someone to stand in the gap, but there was no one.

EZEKIEL 23

God told a story of two sister prostitutes. They were named Oholah and Oholibah, which represented the two nations of Israel whose capitals were Samaria and Jerusalem. Samaria prostituted itself with Assyria and Jerusalem with Babylon. Both of them were punished for their lust in a humiliating fashion.

EZEKIEL 24

While the king of Babylon laid siege on Jerusalem, God told Ezekiel to put some meat in a cooking pot, cook it really well, then cauterize the pot in the fire to represent the burning away of impurities from Israel. This all represented what God would do to them. Then, God warned Ezekiel that his wife would die, then emphasized he was not to mourn or follow any of the procedures for mourning. This too was a sign to the people of Jerusalem that God is in control.

EZEKIEL 25

God spoke prophecies against the nations of Ammon, Moab, Edom and Philistia. God would inflict punishment and carry out great vengeance against them.

EZEKIEL 26

Since Tyre gloated over Jerusalem's destruction, God opposed this city. He promised that he would use Nebuchadnezzar to siege the city, demolish its towers and loot their merchandise. Tyre would be no more.

EZEKIEL 27

God told Ezekiel to take up a lament over the passing of Tyre, the gateway to the sea, a merchant's port. Tyre called itself beautiful, constructed with the finest materials. Every nation that did business in Tyre was listed along with the goods they traded.

EZEKIEL 28

God had Ezekiel speak to the King of Tyre, a man who called himself a god because of his status, wealth and perceived wisdom. But God would bring him way down and show him he was a mere mortal. God compared the King of Tyre to Satan, whose was created beautifully and once blameless, then corruption and sin crept in, reducing him to a horrible end in fire. Then God spoke to Ezekiel about Sidon to whom God would send a plague. God promised to gather his scattered people so they could rebuild in Israel.

EZEKIEL 29

God pronounced judgment on Egypt, who claimed ownership over the Nile. Egypt would be desolate for forty years, then the people would gather again, weaker than before. Nebuchadnezzar struggled hard against Tyre to no avail, so God decided to give Egypt to Nebuchadnezzar.

EZEKIEL 30

God had Ezekiel lament over the coming destruction of Egypt. Nebuchadnezzar's ruthless army would destroy the land. Every city would cry out. God promised to break both arms of Pharaoh while strengthening the arms of the king of Babylon. They would know he is God.

EZEKIEL 31

God told Ezekiel to speak to Pharaoh and say Assyria was once a mighty power, like a beautiful cedar, which all the birds and animals nested in. However, because of its great height and pride, it was brought down. The same fate awaited Egypt.

EZEKIEL 32

God had Ezekiel lament over the imminent destruction of Pharaoh. God said he was once a great lion but he and his people would be thrown down into the pit of darkness. God promised to shatter the pride of Egypt and strip its land. Egypt would join other once proud nations like Assyria, Elam, Meskek, Tubal and Edom in the realm of the dead.

EZEKIEL 33

God told Ezekiel that any watchman had to warn the people when they saw danger coming. In the same way, Ezekiel as a prophet watched over the people and needed to communicate everything he heard from God. If not, God would hold him responsible.   A righteous person who turned to wickedness would face condemnation. A wicked person who turned to righteousness would be forgiven. Israelites may not have liked that, but that's the way it is. During the twelfth year of their exile, a man came to Ezekiel and said "the city has fallen." God explained to Ezekiel why this happened to Jerusalem – they ate meat with blood still in it, worshipped idols, trusted the sword (and not God) and defiled their neighbor's wives. God warned Ezekiel that people were listening to his words but not putting them into practice.

EZEKIEL 34

The shepherds of Israel (the leaders) had failed to take care of the flock, so God would remove them and rescue the flock himself. He would search for the scattered sheep and bring them back. God would place one shepherd over them – David – and make a covenant of peace with them, sending down showers of blessing and renewing the land.

EZEKIEL 35

God prophesied against Mount Seir, also known as Edom, saying he would turn the cities desolate because of their ancient hostility towards the Israelites. As a result, they would know the true God.

EZEKIEL 36

God offered assurance to the Mountains of Israel, that suffered the scorn of nations, but God would once again make them fruitful. As for the people in all of Israel, their conduct was like a woman's uncleanness and yet God said he would restore the land—not for their sake, but for God's holy name. He would do this by removing their hearts of stone and replacing them with hearts of flesh.

EZEKIEL 37

In a vision, Ezekiel saw a valley full of dry bones. Those bones began to come together and grow tendons and skin, becoming a vast army. God said these are the people Israel, whose graves he would open up and bring them together. Then God had Ezekiel take two sticks and write "Belonging to Judah and the Israelites" and "Belonging to Joseph" (Israel/Ephraim).

Ezekiel put them together which God said represented the reuniting of these two nations. At that time, they would have one shepherd, one law and their dwelling place would be with God.

EZEKIEL 38

God pronounced judgment on Gog, the leader of Magog, who one day would gather their troops and begin to attack unsuspecting villages and then set their sights on Israel. But, God promised to unleash all his fiery wrath on them so they would all know He was God.

EZEKIEL 39

God prophesied against Gog and said they would fall in the mountains of Israel and become food for birds and animals. The towns of Israel would not need to collect fire wood because they could burn all of Gog's weapons. God wanted to display his glory so his people would know he is God. He did not want to hide his face from them again.

EZEKIEL 40

After twenty-five years in exile, Ezekiel saw a man in a vision carrying a linen cord and a measuring rod. The man measured some buildings that looked like a city, including the gates, the inner and outer courts, the rooms for sacrifices and priests and the temple.

EZEKIEL 41

The man measured the main hall, inner sanctuary, the most holy place, the walls, the side rooms and the portico and inventoried the contents.

EZEKIEL 42

The man measured the rooms for priests and the walls around the temple.

EZEKIEL 43

Ezekiel watched as the glory of the Lord entered the temple through the east gate. God destroyed the temple because of Israel's sin, but he wanted Ezekiel to tell the people the measurements of the new temple so they could consider its perfection. The great altar was measured and the rules were given for it to be restored.

EZEKIEL 44

The man told Ezekiel that Israel needed to end their rebellious practices of allowing uncircumcised foreigners into the sanctuary. The Levites had strayed and could not serve in the more holy areas, only those priests who were the descendants of Zadok. The man gave instructions for those priests – their clothing, their consumption, their defilement and their wives plus their jobs as judges and keepers of the festivals. They were to have no possessions, since their only possession was God.

EZEKIEL 45

Ezekiel was given measurements for the land needed to build the temple and the sacred area. The princes of Israel were given a portion of land and told not to oppress the people any longer, like they did in the past, or use inaccurate scales. God gave more rules for the offering, including the procedure for Passover.

EZEKIEL 46

Ezekiel received more details regarding the Sabbath and various festivals, in terms of the sacrifices and the locations where the sacrifices were cooked.

EZEKIEL 47

The man measured a stream of water flowing from the temple. It eventually became a river flowing into the Dead Sea. The water turned the salt water fresh, where fish could now live and fruit trees grew on the banks, providing healing. The Lord then described the boundaries of the land to be divided up.

EZEKIEL 48

The tribes each received a portion of the land. The temple got its measurements along with areas for the city, houses, pasturelands and areas for the prince. Finally, the gates' measurements were given. The gates were to be named after the tribes and the city from then on would then be called "The Lord is There."

DANIEL

Number of Chapters: *12*
The Author: *Daniel*
Approximate time span: 605-536 BC (To the exiles in Babylon
                                  and then Persia)

DANIEL 1
       After Nebuchadnezzar besieged Jerusalem, he removed some of the temple articles and put them into the treasure house of his god. He also brought young Israelite men from royal families into the palace to teach them Babylonian language and literature. Among them were Daniel and his three friends, renamed Shadrach, Meshach and Abednego. They didn't want to defile themselves with the king's food, so they asked to eat only vegetables. The guard reluctantly agreed then ten days later saw how healthy they were. When in the presence of Nebuchadnezzar, the king found no other young men as wise as they were. Daniel remained in service until King Cyrus.

DANIEL 2
       Nebuchadnezzar had a dream that troubled him so he asked the magicians, enchanters, sorcerers and astrologers what it meant without telling them the dream. If nobody could tell the dream and its interpretation, the king was going to kill all the wise men. Daniel prayed and God showed him the dream and the meaning. He told Nebuchadnezzar that he saw a giant statue made of four metals: gold, silver, bronze, iron/clay. The head represented Babylon and successive kingdoms. The last kingdom God would set up could never be destroyed, crushing all the others. Nebuchadnezzar fell before Daniel, recognizing his God as the God of all gods. Daniel got a promotion and he made his friends administrators.

DANIEL 3
       Nebuchadnezzar made a ninety foot image of gold and summoned all his leaders to the dedication, telling them every time they hear the music play, they must all fall down and worship the image. If not, they would be thrown into a hot

181

furnace. Some astrologers told the king that Shadrach, Meshach and Abednego did not worship the image, so Nebuchadnezzar had them thrown into the furnace, which was made seven times hotter for them. However, they were not killed, but the soldiers who threw them in were. In fact, the king thought he saw a fourth man – a son of the gods – walking around with them. They were removed and not even their clothes smelled of smoke. Nebuchadnezzar made a decree that no one could speak against their God.

DANIEL 4

Nebuchadnezzar recounted, in a letter, about the time Daniel interpreted his statute dream, then about another dream of a large, beautiful tree that was cut down and stripped bare. A messenger said he would be drenched in dew and live with the animals. Daniel interpreted the dream saying the tree was the king, who would be driven away from the people, living like an animal and eating grass. Then one day, after Nebuchadnezzar praised himself for Babylon, his mind snapped and he lived in the wilderness, drenched in dew, eating grass and growing out his hair and nails. Finally, he praised God and his sanity was restored.

DANIEL 5

King Belshazzar, Nebuchadnezzar's son, had the gold and silver goblets, that were taken from the temple in Jerusalem, brought out during a party. The king, his nobles, his wives and his concubines all drank wine from them and praised other gods. Suddenly the fingers of a human hand appeared and began writing on the wall. The king told the wise men to interpret the meaning but they could not. The queen reminded the king of Daniel who had the spirit of the gods. Daniel was brought in and told Belshazzar that his father humbled himself before God, yet Belshazzar had not, drinking from the sacred goblets. Therefore, the writing on the wall – Mene, Mene, Tekel, Parsin – meant Belshazzar's days were numbered, he was weighed and came up short and his kingdom would be divided and given to the Medes and Persians. That night, the king was slain and Darius the Mede took over the kingdom.

DANIEL 6

Darius appointed 120 leaders (satraps) in positions around the kingdom and three administrators, one of them Daniel. The other leaders were jealous and tried to come up with a plan to bring Daniel down, however they could not find anything wrong with him. So they told the king to issue an irrevocable edict for thirty days that people must only pray to him. Daniel responded by praying three times a day to God with the windows open. The satraps brought Daniel in before Darius who reluctantly had Daniel thrown into a lion's den. The next morning, the king ran to the den and was pleased to see that Daniel was alive. Daniel said an angel shut the mouths of the lions. In response, Darius had the accusers thrown into the den with their wives and children. Darius told everyone to worship the God of Daniel

DANIEL 7

During the reign of King Belshazzar of Babylon, Daniel had a dream of four great beasts rising out of the sea – a lion with wings, a bear, a leopard with wings and a beast with iron teeth and ten horns. Then he saw God taking his seat, thousands attending to him and the books of the court opened. Then Daniel saw one like a son of man approaching God and given authority, glory and power. Everyone worshipped him. His kingdom would never pass away. Daniel asked the interpretation of the dream and was told the four great beasts represented the four great kingdoms that would rise. The fourth beast was the fourth kingdom and the ten horns represented ten kings who would rise in power from it. Another king (the small horn) would rise and subdue three other kings. This king would speak against God and oppress his holy people for a short time. Then his power would be stripped and all power would be handed over to the holy people of the Most High. Daniel was troubled by this but kept the matter to himself.

DANIEL 8

In the third year of Belshazzar's reign, Daniel had a vision of a powerful ram with two horns (one longer than the other) go up against a goat with one powerful horn. The goat shattered the ram's horns and trampled the ram. When the goat's horn broke, four horns grew in its place. A smaller horn came from one of the horns and grew to the heavens. This one would cause a rebellion that lead to desolation. Gabriel told Daniel the meaning of the vision. The ram with two horns was Media and Persia. The goat was Greece and the four horns were the four kingdoms that would emerge from the one. One king would rise to power, devastate, deceive and destroy. He would think he was superior.

DANIEL 9

During the reign of Darius, the first Persian king who defeated the Babylonian, Daniel said he understood Jeremiah's prophecy of seventy years of desolation for Jerusalem. So he confessed the sins of his nations and asked for forgiveness, pleading that God's wrath would turn away from Jerusalem. Then Gabriel arrived, saying they heard his request as soon as he began to pray. Gabriel told him "seventy sevens" (a time frame) were decreed for the people and the holy city to put an end to sin and anoint the Most Holy Place. During that time frame, Jerusalem would be rebuilt, the Anointed One put to death and the city destroyed by a ruler. This ruler would put an end to sacrifice and offering and he would set up an abomination that causes desolation in the temple.

DANIEL 10

During the reign of Cyrus king of Persia, Daniel stood on the banks of the Tigris when he saw a man dressed in linen, his face like lightning, his eyes like torches, his body like bronze and his voice like the multitudes. Daniel was frightened. The man was detained because of prince of Persia resisted him but Michael came to rescue him. The man said he was going to go fight the prince of Persia and the prince of Greece would come too.

DANIEL 11

The man told Daniel that four kings would rise in Persia, but the fourth would stir people up in Greece. He would rise and his empire would eventually be divided amongst four kings. The king of South would grow stronger and be at war with the king of the North, a conflict that would go on and on. Eventually the king of the North would desecrate the temple and abolish the daily sacrifices, setting up an abomination that caused desolation but God's people would resist him. This king would magnify himself above every god. The king of the South would engage the king of the North in battle once again. Many countries would fall including Egypt. The king of the North would set out to destroy and annihilate many, yet no one would come to help him.

DANIEL 12

Then the great prince Michael would arise. Everyone whose name was written in the book of life would be saved. Many would awaken to everlasting life or everlasting contempt. Daniel then saw two other men, one who told Daniel that it would take a time, times and a half a time for this all to be fulfilled. From the time the daily sacrifices end to the abomination that caused desolation, 1,290 days would pass. Daniel was told to go on his way, rest and receive his inheritance in the end.

HOSEA

Number of Chapters: *14*
The Author: *Hosea*
Approximately written: *753-715 BC (To the people of Israel)*

HOSEA 1
God came to Hosea and he told him to marry a promiscuous woman and have children with her, just like Israel was unfaithful to God. Hosea married Gomer and they had three children – Jezreel, Lo-Ruhamah (not loved), Lo-Ammi (not my people). All three names signified why God would punish Israel.

HOSEA 2
God promised to not show love to his people nor their children because they were born out of adultery. He would block all their efforts. Then, God said he would call her back and give Israel all they had before. They would be betrothed in righteousness and justice, love and compassion. God would say to those who were "not his people" that "You are my people."

HOSEA 3
The Lord told Hosea to buy back his adulteress wife and he did with silver and barley. He told her not to prostitute herself again. In the same way, God said, the Israelites would return and seek the Lord.

HOSEA 4
God could not find any faithfulness or love in Israel, only cursing, lying and murder. Just as the people ignored his priests and the law, he would ignore their children. God promised punishment on them and future generations because they prostituted themselves with idols.

HOSEA 5
God called out Ephraim whose deeds and prostitution to idols did not permit them to return to God. They would be laid to waste. God would become like a lion and tear them to pieces.

HOSEA 6

Israel was encouraged to return to the Lord. God injured them yet he would bind their wounds. But Ephraim, what to do about them? The words of the prophets kill them. Ephraim turned to prostitution and Israel was defiled.

HOSEA 7

Ephraim was deceitful, practicing wickedness, burning with passion for adultery. They tried to mix with other nations but the foreigners sucked them dry. They turned to Egypt then to Assyria like a senseless dove. God promised to throw a net over them. God wanted to redeem them yet they slashed themselves, calling out to their gods. Their leaders would fall.

HOSEA 8

Israel had disobeyed by rejecting what was good, setting up kings without God's approval and making idols, especially that calf-idol in Samaria. God promised to break it into pieces. Israel would be swallowed up because they turned to Assyria and Ephraim turned to other lovers, building altars for sin.

HOSEA 9

Hosea told Israel not to rejoice, because they had been unfaithful. No matter what they do, Egypt would gather them up and bury them. God won't forget their sins. Because of their sin, he won't love them. They would not produce another generation.

HOSEA 10

The Lord would demolish their altars and sacred stones. The calf-idol would be carried away to Assyria and Samaria's king destroyed. Ephraim was a threshing heifer that God promised to yoke.

HOSEA 11

When Israel was a child, God called his son from Egypt. He taught them to walk and led them with cords of kindness. God bent down to the feed them. Yet the people were determined to turn from God. But God cannot give up on them.

187

He cannot carry out his fierce anger even though they lied to him.

HOSEA 12

Ephraim pursued nothing but wind, yet Israel had always struggled with God. Ephraim boasted of its wealth and goodness, but God would make them live in tents again.

HOSEA 13

Ephraim sinned more and more, making cleverly fashioned images. They would disappear like the morning mist. God cared for them and fed them, now he would be like a lion, leopard and bear, attacking and ripping them open. God promised to deliver the people from the power of the grave, which has no power to plague or destroy.

HOSEA 14

God wanted Israel to return, asking for forgiveness and admitting that Assyria cannot save them. Once again they would flourish like a cedar, a lily, an olive tree and a juniper. Ephraim must end its attraction to idols. If they were wise, they would understand what they needed to do.

JOEL

Number of Chapters: *3*
The Author: *Joel*
Approximately written: *835-796 BC (To the people of Judah)*

JOEL 1

The word of the Lord came to Joel who spoke to the elders about a great locust devastation, much like the devastation of a mighty army that will come to ruin the land. Joel called the drunkards to wake up and the priests to mourn for the day of the Lord was near.

JOEL 2

The trumpet needed to sound from Zion preparing people for the day of the Lord. Fire, devastation and armies were coming. God pleaded for the people to return their hearts to him. Fast, assemble and minister all God's people! Then God took pity on the people and promised food and protection, driving the army away from Judah. God said he would repay them for the years the locusts had eaten. The people would know that God had returned to Israel. He would pour out his spirit on all people causing them to prophesize, dream and see visions once again. The great and dreadful day of the Lord was still coming but everyone who called on the name of the Lord would be saved.

JOEL 3

God would restore the fortunes of Judah and Jerusalem and put all the other nations on trial for what they did to his people. They would all gather in the valley of decision for judgment by God. Jerusalem would once again drip with wine, milk and water, while Egypt and Edom would be turned to waste. The Lord will dwell in Zion forever.

AMOS

Number of Chapters: *9*
The Author: *Amos*
Approximately written: *760-750 BC (To the people of Israel)*

AMOS 1

God spoke to Amos, a shepherd from Tekoa saying he would punish the nations of Damascus, Gaza, Tyre, Edom and Ammon.

AMOS 2

God continued to pronounce judgment on Moab, Judah and Israel for their sins. Israel trampled the poor and oppressed, worshipped at every altar, quieted the prophets and made the Nazirites drink wine. No soldier would be able to stand up against what God was bringing.

AMOS 3

God always revealed his plan to the prophets to destroy Israel. An enemy would overrun their land but only a part of them would survive. God would tear down the altars in Bethel.

AMOS 4

God said to those in Samaria that he had caused starvation and drought, blight and locusts, plagues and enemies, yet they never returned to God. Because of that, prepare to meet God!

AMOS 5

God took up a lament for Israel, once so strong now reduced to nothing. Seek God and live, Israel! Israel hated justice, incurred heavy taxes and took bribes. But the day of the Lord was coming – a dark day. God hated their religious festivals and burnt offerings. A stench! God wanted to send them into exile.

AMOS 6

Woe to the complacent, God said, who put off the day of disaster, lying in beds, eating choice foods, strumming on harps, getting drunk. They would be the first to go into exile. God would stir up nations against Israel.

AMOS 7

Amos saw a swarm of locusts stripping the land clean. Amos cried out for Israel's mercy and God relented. Then Amos saw judgment by fire and cried out. The Lord relented. Then he saw a man with a plumb line by the wall. The high places and sanctuaries of Israel would be ruined. Amaziah the priest sent a message to King Jeroboam complaining about Amos' message, telling Amos to go back to Judah. Amos said he was a simple shepherd when God came to him to prophesy to Israel. And the message was that many would die and others would go into exile.

AMOS 8

Amos saw a basket of ripe fruit and the Lord said the time was ripe. They would not be spared. Bodies would be laying everywhere. Darkness would come early to the land. Their religious festivals would be times of mourning. There would be a famine coming, not of food and water, but of hearing the word of the Lord.

AMOS 9

No matter how well they hid, no one would escape God's wrath. He wanted to destroy this sinful kingdom, especially all those who scoffed at disaster. However, one day, God would restore the altar, the walls and the vineyards. God promised to plant Israel again and never uproot it.

OBADIAH

Number of Chapters: *1*
The Author: *Obadiah*
Approximately written: *855-840 BC (To the people of Judah regarding the Edomites)*

OBADIAH

Obadiah had a vision against Edom who became prideful high up in the rocks, yet God would bring them down to the ground. Edom would be completely ransacked, like they stood by while their "brother" Jacob was invaded and picked clean. Since they rejoiced over what happened in Jerusalem and Judah, that same punishment was coming to them. There would be no survivors in Edom and their neighbors would occupy their land.

JONAH

Number of Chapters: *4*
The Author: *Jonah*
Approximately written: *760 BC (During the time of Jeroboam II*
                           of Israel, 780-753 BC)

JONAH 1

God came to Jonah and told him to go preach in the great city of Nineveh because of its wickedness, but Jonah ran towards Tarshish, catching a ship in Joppa to get there. Then a great storm hit the ship and the sailors were scared. They cast lots and realized the storm was Jonah's fault, so he suggested that they throw him in the sea. They did and the storm calmed. God provided a great fish to swallow Jonah, holding him for three days and three nights.

JONAH 2

From inside the fish Jonah prayed to God, thanking him for hearing his prayer. Though the waters threatened to engulf him, God brought him out of the pit. Salvation only comes from the Lord.

JONAH 3

God told Jonah to go to Nineveh and give it a forty day warning before the city would be overthrown. Jonah obeyed and the Ninevites believed in God, the king declaring a fast hoping God would relent.

JONAH 4

This felt wrong to Jonah and he became angry. Jonah said this was exactly why he ran away in the first place. He knew God was gracious and compassionate and would relent. Jonah wanted to die. Jonah took a seat to watch what would happen to the city. God provided a leafy plant to give Jonah shade in the hot sun. Then God had a worm eat the plant up. Jonah complained. God told Jonah he was concerned about a little plant...shouldn't God be concerned about a big city?

193

MICAH

Number of Chapters: 7
The Author: *Micah*
Approximately written: *735-710 BC (To the people of Judah and*
                                   Israel)

MICAH 1

God spoke to Micah concerning Samaria and Jerusalem saying he would come down from his dwelling place because of the sins of the people. He wanted to make Samaria a heap of rubble. The devastation would reach all the cities, even to Jerusalem. Weep and wail, people!

MICAH 2

God planned a disaster from which the proud could not be saved. False prophets rose up and don't want to hear bad news. In the future, God would gather the people and bring them together, like a shepherd tending his flock.

MICAH 3

God said the sin of the leaders of Israel was like tearing off the skin of the people and eating their flesh. The prophets would receive no visions. God promised to turn Jerusalem and the temple into a heap of rubble.

MICAH 4

In those last days, the mountain of the Lord's temple would become the highest of mountains, drawing many to it for knowledge and wisdom. In that day, God wanted to assemble the exiles and rule over them. They needed to go to Babylon first for protection then God could rescue them.

MICAH 5

From Bethlehem, this smallest of clans in Judah, would come a ruler over Israel, whose origin was from ancient times. He would shepherd his flock in the strength and majesty of the Lord. His greatness would reach to the ends of the earth. The remnant of Jacob would be triumphant over its enemies. In that

194

day, God promised to destroy the enemy cities and their idolatry, taking vengeance on them for not obeying.

MICAH 6

God questioned the people he brought up out of Egypt and saved from slavery, asking "What did I do to you?" Thousands of sacrifices won't satisfy him. Acting justly, loving mercy and walking humbly will satisfy God. Israel was full of wicked people who stole and lied. They would not ever be satisfied or prosperous.

MICAH 7

Micah mourned his job to tell Israel that the Lord was on his way in judgment. He warned them not to trust their neighbors or their own families. Micah told his enemies not to gloat over Israel's coming destruction. Their day was coming. God forgives and shows mercy. He would be faithful to Jacob as he pledged long ago.

NAHUM

Number of Chapters: *3*
The Author: *Nahum*
Approximately written: *663-612 BC (To the people of Judah regarding Nineveh and the Assyrians before Nineveh fell in 612 BC)*

NAHUM 1

This prophecy was aimed against Nineveh. The Lord is jealous and avenging. He is slow to anger but vents his wrath against his enemies. He can rebuke the sea and make mountains quake. Nobody can stand up to him…not even Nineveh. God vowed to bring them to an end so they would not afflict Judah any longer. Good news was coming. Judah could celebrate their festivals once again.

NAHUM 2

God warned Nineveh against its attackers. There would be a bloody war and the city would be pillaged, plundered and stripped. They would be exiled and carried away. God was against them.

NAHUM 3

More woes about Nineveh regarding the devastating war and the piles of dead, all because the city prostituted itself and enslaved other nations with her witchcraft. God wanted to pelt them with filth, shame them and make a spectacle out of them. Nineveh was not better than any other city that thought it could protect itself. The merchants, the guards, the officials, the nobles and the king were not prepared for what was coming. Nothing could heal them.

HABAKKUK

Number of Chapters: *3*
The Author: *Habakkuk*
Approximately written: *612-605 BC (To the people of Judah*
                              during the threat of the Babylonians)

HABAKKUK 1

Habakkuk wondered how long the people had to cry out for help before God could save them. God answered by saying he would do something they could not believe. He was raising up the Babylonians who would do great violence and sweep across the nation. Habakkuk asked God how a righteous God could tolerate such unrighteousness. The people were like fish and the enemy would just pluck them up.

HABAKKUK 2

Habakkuk waited for an answer then God replied. God said the enemy was arrogant but the righteous live by faith. God communicated many woes, especially for those who stole, plundered, shed blood and worshipped lifeless idols. God's glory will be spread throughout the world. He is in his holy temple. The world should be silent before him.

HABAKKUK 3

Habakkuk prayed (in a song) saying he knew of God's fame, his glory, splendor and power. God could shake the earth when he declared war on it. When Habakkuk heard the news, he trembled, yet he waited patiently for the day of calamity to come on the nation invading them. Even though the trees won't produce fruit and the fields fail, Habakkuk would rejoice. The Lord was his strength.

ZEPHANIAH

Number of Chapters: *3*
The Author: *Zephaniah*
Approximately written: 640-612 BC (To the people of Judah
during the time of King Josiah)

ZEPHANIAH 1

During the reign of Josiah, God told Zephaniah that he was going to wipe out Judah and Jerusalem. He wanted to destroy all the idol worship of Baal and Molek. That day was coming when he targeted the government officials, the merchants and the rich. Their riches won't save them.

ZEPHANIAH 2

He implored Judah and Jerusalem to seek the Lord and be humble. God promised to devastate Philistia and its cities of Gaza, Ashkelon, Ashdod and Ekron. He heard the insults coming from Moab and the Ammonites against his people so they too would be plundered. Cush would not escape and neither would Assyria, especially Nineveh which would be reduced to rubble.

ZEPHANIAH 3

God focused on the city of oppressors, whose officials, rulers, prophets and priests were disobedient. God thought that by destroying all these nations that Jerusalem would repent. God would remove the arrogant boasters and leave the meek and humble (a remnant). Jerusalem should rejoice as God gathered them back together in their homes and restore their fortunes.

HAGGAI

Number of Chapters: 2
The Author: *Haggai*
Approximately written: *520 BC (To the exiles who returned to Jerusalem)*

HAGGAI 1

During the second year of the reign of Darius king of Persia, the word of the Lord came to Haggai, Zerubbabel the governor and Joshua the high priest condemning them for building their own houses and planting vineyards while God's house remained in ruin. The people tried to prosper, but God would not let them. This is why nothing worked out. So Zerubbabel, Joshua and the whole remnant of people began to work.

HAGGAI 2

Over the span of two months, three more prophecies came to Haggai encouraging the leaders in Jerusalem to rebuild God's house. God pointed out that he was going to shake up the nations and he wanted them to make a house greater than the former house. He said what they were doing now defiled the nation and God withheld his blessing. Now, he promised a blessing on their fruit trees and fields.

ZECHARIAH

Number of Chapters: 14
The Author: Zechariah
Approximately written: 520-518 BC and 480-470 BC (During
                        and after the building of the temple)

ZECHARIAH 1

During the reign of Darius, the Lord came to the prophet Zechariah and said he was very angry with his ancestors who took too long to repent. Later, Zechariah had a vision of a man on a red horse among myrtle trees with other horses. They represented the ones God sent throughout the earth and found the world at peace. God promised to return to Jerusalem. Zechariah saw four horns, which scattered Judah, Israel and Jerusalem, but the craftsmen have come to throw down these horns.

ZECHARIAH 2

Zechariah saw a man with a measuring line going to measure Jerusalem. God promised to be a wall of fire around the city, protecting it and living among his people.

ZECHARIAH 3

Zechariah saw Joshua the high priest dressed in filthy rags and being accused by Satan. The angel dressed him in clean clothes and put a clean turban on his head. The Lord said he would bring the Branch and remove sin from this land in a single day.

ZECHARIAH 4

Zechariah saw a solid gold lampstand with two olive trees. These represented the word of the Lord to Zerubbabel who laid the foundation of the temple. The seven eyes of the Lord were watching everything that was happening. The angel told Zechariah that the two olive trees represented the two anointed ones who serve the Lord.

ZECHARIAH 5

Zechariah saw a flying scroll which was a curse going out over the whole land, especially for the thieves and those who swear falsely by God's name. Then he saw a basket with a woman in it. This stood for the sin and wickedness of the people. Two other women, like angels, took the basket away to Babylonia.

ZECHARIAH 6

Zechariah saw four chariots being pulled by four horses (red, black, white, dappled). They were the four spirits of heaven heading off throughout the earth. A silver and gold crown was to be made for Joshua, the high priest. His name was to be Branch, for he would branch out from his place and build the temple of the Lord. The Branch will be clothed with majesty and rule on his throne. He will also be priest. Many from far off nations would come to build the temple.

ZECHARIAH 7

In the fourth year of King Darius, the priests asked if they should mourn and fast during the fifth month like they did before. The Lord spoke to Zechariah and said when they mourned and fasted on the fifth and seventh month, did they really do it for God? When they ate, didn't they just feast for themselves? He told them to show justice, mercy and compassion. Don't oppress the fatherless, foreigner or poor. But the people just turn their backs and cover their ears. They don't listen.

ZECHARIAH 8

God promised to return to Zion and dwell in Jerusalem. The streets would be filled with young and old. Businesses would grow and so would the crops. The people must speak truth and not plot evil against one another. No more sad fasts. It's time for happy festivals. Many from other nations would be drawn to Jerusalem to seek him because they heard God was there.

ZECHARIAH 9

The word of Lord came against Hadrak, Damascus, Hamath, Tyre, Sidon, Ashkelon, Gaza and the Philistines. All would be destroyed. Zion should rejoice because her king would come riding on a donkey, a colt, the foal of a donkey. He would proclaim peace on the nations. His rule would extend to the end of the earth. God promised to appear and save them.

ZECHARIAH 10

God's anger burned against the shepherds and leaders, but God would take care of the people of Judah. From Judah would come the cornerstone. God would strengthen Judah and save the tribes of Joseph. He promised to bring back the people scattered into distant lands.

ZECHARIAH 11

God asked Zechariah to shepherd the flock marked for slaughter, while corrupt shepherds were all around. Zechariah shepherded the flock with two staffs called Favor and Union. The flock detested him and Zechariah gave up, breaking the staff called Favor, thus revoking the covenant he made with all the nations. Zechariah asked the oppressed to pay him so they gave him thirty pieces of silver. God told him to throw the money at the potter. He broke the second staff called Union, breaking the bond between Judah and Israel. God promised to raise another shepherd over the land who would not care for the lost.

ZECHARIAH 12

The God who made the universe prophesied that he would protect Jerusalem against all the nations. No one would be able to move it. Anyone who attacked it would be destroyed. He would pour the spirit of grace out and they would mourn for the one they have pierced and grieve bitterly for him as one grieved a firstborn son. All the people would weep.

ZECHARIAH 13

A day was coming when a fountain from the house of David would cleanse the people from sin and impurity. Idols would be banished. Prophets ashamed to prophesize. The shepherd would be struck and the sheep would scatter. Two thirds of the population would perish while one third refined in fire. They would be God's people.

ZECHARIAH 14

The day of the Lord was coming. All the nations would attack Jerusalem, ransacking and raping, sending half the city into exile. The Lord would fight, his feet on the Mount of Olives, splitting the nation, living water flowing out from it. The Lord will be king over the whole earth. Plagues would strike those other nations, rotting their flesh, eyes and tongues. The survivors who attacked Jerusalem would go there year after year to worship the Lord, nations like Egypt. The city would be holy, down to the horse bells and cooking pots.

MALACHI

Number of Chapters: *4*
The Author: *Malachi*
Approximately written: *430 BC (To the Jews living in Judah
                         after the exile to Babylon)*

MALACHI 1

The Lord said to the prophet Malachi that he loved Jacob, but hated Esau. He crushed Edom and reduced it to ruins. God then spoke against the priests who offered lame and diseased sacrifices to him. Shut the temple doors! God is a great king to be feared by the nations! You can't treat him this way.

MALACHI 2

God promised to send a curse to the priests for dishonoring his name. God established this covenant with them because Levi revered God and spoke truth, walking in peace and uprightness. A priest's lips should preserve knowledge, but since they have turned away, God humiliated them. Judah had been unfaithful, marrying foreign women. The people flood the altar with tears yet were unfaithful to their wives. God hates divorce. The people weary God with their words.

MALACHI 3

God promised to send a messenger, who, like a refiner's fire or a launderer's soap, would refine and purify the people. The people who defrauded, practiced sorcery, adulterers and perjurers would be put on trial. God asked everyone to return to him. The people want to know what they did wrong. God replied that they stole from his tithes and offerings. God told them to test him to see if they brought the whole tithe to him and see whether God would bless them. God said he would remember the righteous.

MALACHI 4

The day was coming when the arrogant and evildoer would be reduced to stubble and the righteous will rise and frolic. Remember the laws of Moses. God would send the prophet Elijah before the great and dreadful day of the Lord comes. He would turns the hearts of parents to children and children to their parents or strike the land with total destruction.

THE NEW TESTAMENT

MATTHEW

Number of Chapters: *28*
The Author: *Matthew*
Time span: *4 BC – 33 AD*

MATTHEW 1

The genealogy of Jesus from Abraham to Mary, divided up into three groups of fourteen. Mary was engaged to be married to Joseph but she became pregnant by the Holy Spirit. Joseph, her fiancé, wanted to break off the engagement then was told in a dream that this was from God. The angel told Joseph this fulfilled Isaiah 7:14 and the boy's name would be Jesus, because he would save the people from their sins.

MATTHEW 2

Jesus was born in Bethlehem during the reign of King Herod. Wise men from the east saw the star and came to Israel to worship him. Herod was disturbed to hear about another king being born and tried to get information from the wise man about this king's whereabouts. The wise men ignored Herod and found Mary and the Christ child. They worshipped him, giving gifts of gold, frankincense and myrrh. Herod, furious the wise men outwitted him, commanded that all children two years and younger be killed. But God warned Joseph in a dream to go to Egypt and wait until things cooled down. When Herod died, God told Joseph in another dream to return to Nazareth.

MATTHEW 3

John the Baptist preached in the Judean wilderness, calling for people to repent, for the kingdom of God was near. He baptized people in the Jordan River as they confessed their sins. John attacked the Pharisees and Sadducees, calling them snakes. Jesus arrived and asked to be baptized. When he was, the heavens opened up, God spoke and the Holy Spirit descended on Jesus.

MATTHEW 4

Jesus fasted in the desert for forty days, tempted by Satan three times. Jesus countered those temptations with scripture. After that, Jesus walked the Sea of Galilee and asked Peter, Andrew, James and John to follow him and become fishers of men. Jesus began his ministry, teaching in synagogues and healing people of all kinds of diseases from all over the region.

MATTHEW 5

Jesus began the sermon on the mountain. He spoke about the Beatitudes and those who are truly blessed. He encouraged his followers to be salt and light. Jesus said he came to fulfill the law of Moses, not tear it down. Jesus defined what murder was (hateful thoughts) and adultery (lustful thoughts). He discouraged divorce and making vows, telling people to stand by their word. Instead of taking revenge on evil people, give them more and go the extra mile. Jesus wanted his followers to love their enemies. These things will make them perfect as their heavenly father is perfect.

MATTHEW 6

Jesus warned against giving and practicing your good deeds publicly, just to be admired. He extended this warning to public prayer and fasting, all for the sake of being noticed for our spirituality. Jesus gave the model prayer as a simple example of the types of prayers we should be doing. He warned against making money a priority since no one can serve two masters. Jesus told his people not to worry about their provisions, but to seek God and his righteousness at all times.

MATTHEW 7

Jesus wrapped up the Sermon on the mountain telling his disciples not to judge the specks in other people's eyes when they have planks in their own eyes. He encouraged them to ask, pray and knock so the doors would be opened. Jesus told them to do to others as they wanted done for them. He warned against false prophets, wolves dressed like sheep, who claimed to be doing all kinds of religious things in God's name, but he didn't know them. Anyone who built their house on a solid rock won't be destroyed when the storms of life come.

MATTHEW 8

Jesus healed a man with leprosy and the servant of a Roman centurion who showed great faith by saying Jesus didn't even need to come to his house to heal the man – just say the word. Jesus healed Peter's mother-in-law. While traveling across the lake, Jesus calmed the storm, then arrived in Gadarenes to remove the demons from two men and cast them into a herd of pigs. The town greeted Jesus and told him to leave.

MATTHEW 9

Jesus stirred up the religious leaders when he forgave the paralyzed man's sins first, then allowed him to walk. He called Matthew to follow him, then ate with his sinful friends. The Pharisees didn't like that, but the unhealthy people were the people Jesus came to help. Jesus healed a bleeding woman who touched his cloak and raised a synagogue leader's daughter from death. Jesus also healed two blind men and a mute. He then told his followers that the harvest was huge, but they needed more workers.

MATTHEW 10

Jesus sent out the twelve apostles, giving them instructions to go only to the Jews, not take anything with them on the journey and to move on from any city if they were rejected. He told them to be shrewd and innocent and to speak boldly. Jesus warned them about betrayal, even from their own family, and not to be afraid of death. God knew their situation and they were valuable to him. Jesus did not come to bring peace, but carried a sword that caused division. They could not love anyone more than him.

MATTHEW 11

John the Baptist, now in prison, had his followers ask Jesus if he was the one they have been waiting on. Jesus affirmed his status as Messiah by saying the blind saw, the lame walked, the lepers were cured and the Good News was being preached. He told the people John the Baptist was one of the greatest because he was more than just a prophet – John the Baptist was the fulfillment of Elijah. Jesus denounced Korazin, Bethsaida and Capernaum for rejecting his message. He pleaded with all those who were burdened to come to him and find rest, for his yoke was easy.

MATTHEW 12

The Pharisees got upset when Jesus' followers picked wheat. Jesus reminded them of David's men who ate bread from the temple, breaking the law. Jesus healed a man with a withered hand on the Sabbath and told the Pharisees they would pull a sheep out of a pit on the Sabbath, why not help a man? After Jesus healed a demon possessed man, the Pharisees said Jesus got his power from Satan. Jesus wondered how a kingdom divided against itself could stand. Jesus said a good heart produced good fruit and everyone will be held accountable on judgment day. The teachers wanted a sign but Jesus refused expect the sign of Jonah who spent three days in the fishes' belly, comparable to Jesus being in the grave for three days. Jesus' true family were not his mother, brothers and sisters, but those who did the will of God.

MATTHEW 13

Jesus told the parable of the four soils, about a person's heart receiving the message. He told the parable of the wheat and weeds and how on judgment day the good will be separated from the evil. He told the parable of the mustard seed, the parable of the yeast, the parable of the hidden treasure, the parable of the pearl of great price and the parable of the fishing net, all of them were about the kingdom of heaven and how valuable the kingdom was. After receiving a cold welcome in Nazareth, Jesus could not do many miracles there because a prophet was not honored in his hometown.

MATTHEW 14

Herod had arrested John the Baptist for disagreeing with Herod's marriage to Herodias, his brother's wife. When

Herodias' daughter danced for Herod, he offered her anything and she chose the head of John the Baptist on a platter. Herod reluctantly agreed. Jesus fed the 5,000 using only five loaves of bread and two fish. Later, Jesus walked on water, joining the disciples in a boat during a heavy wind storm. Peter joined Jesus on the water, briefly, but sank when he saw the winds and waves. Jesus healed many in the land of Gennesaret.

MATTHEW 15

Jesus called the religious leaders hypocrites for criticizing his disciples who don't wash their hands. He called them the blind leading the blind. What truly defiles a person is what comes out of their mouth, not what goes into it. Jesus cast a demon out of a Gentile girl when her mom showed great faith. Jesus healed a great number of people then fed the 4,000, with seven basketfuls left over.

MATTHEW 16

The Pharisees and Sadducees asked for a sign but Jesus called them an evil generation. He warned his followers against their teaching, which was like yeast. The disciples thought he wanted bread and Jesus wondered, after the feeding of the thousands, why would he be worried about bread? Jesus asked his disciples who people thought he was. They replied John the Baptist, Elijah, Jeremiah or one of the prophets. Only Peter got the right answer – The Christ, the Son of the Living God. Jesus replied that he would build his church on Peter's statement. When Jesus hinted at dying in Jerusalem, Peter rebuked him. Jesus told Satan to back off. Jesus then told the followers to take up their cross and follow him, for what did it profit a man to lose his soul but gain the whole world.

MATTHEW 17

Jesus transfigured on a mountain, standing there with Moses and Elijah. God spoke, telling them to listen to his son. Jesus told them the Elijah the scriptures pointed to was John the Baptist. Jesus healed a self-destructive demon-possessed boy and told the disciples they needed more faith, like a mustard seed, to heal this kind of thing. The collectors of the temple tax wonder if Jesus was going to pay the Temple Tax. Jesus told his disciples to catch a fish and the money would be in its mouth.

MATTHEW 18

Jesus told his followers to have faith like a little child. He sternly rebuked any that tried to cause someone to lose faith, for it would better for them to drown themselves in the sea. He said it was better to go through life without an eye, hand or foot, then to live with one of those body parts that caused you to sin. Jesus gave specific instructions for confronting someone in regards to sin, first personally, then bringing another person with them, then before the whole church. Jesus encouraged people to pray, for if one or more agree, God will agree too. He also encouraged forgiveness, not just seven times but seventy-seven times. In the Parable of the Unforgiving Debtor, Jesus told a man forgiven of a huge debt who choked others who owed him a debt. The man was forgiven, but didn't forgive, so he was locked up forever.

MATTHEW 19

Jesus taught them about marriage and said divorce was only permissible if there was marital unfaithfulness. He blessed the children then confronted the rich young ruler, telling him to sell everything. He warned that the rich will have a hard time getting into heaven. The disciples wondered who could be saved, especially those who gave up everything. Jesus encouraged them and said those who have given up homes and family will get a hundred times more in return.

MATTHEW 20

Jesus told the parable of the vineyard owner who paid his workers a full day salary no matter when they started working. He predicted his disciples' deaths as they headed to Jerusalem. The mother of James and John asked Jesus to put her sons on his right and left when he entered the kingdom. They others were miffed by this. Jesus reminded them that it's not about thrones, but being a servant and even he didn't come to be served, but to serve. The greatest among them would be a servant. Jesus healed two blind beggars who cried out to him.

MATTHEW 21

Jesus rode into Jerusalem on a donkey, with people shouting Hosanna. Jesus cleared the temple, calling the merchants thieves, then began to heal people. Jesus cursed the fig tree. He told the disciples if they had faith they could do greater miracles than that, like throwing mountains into the sea. The religious leaders challenged Jesus' authority. Jesus told the parable of the evil tenants who killed the landowner's men and finally his son who came to collect payment. The leaders understood that they were the tenants in the parable. Jesus said they will stumble over the stone rejected by the builders that had become the cornerstone.

MATTHEW 22

Jesus told the Parable of the Wedding Feast and the people rejecting the offer to dine with the king. The religious leaders questioned Jesus about paying taxes, but Jesus said let Caesar have what he wanted and God will have what he wanted. The Sadducees questioned Jesus on the resurrection and who a woman would be married to in heaven. Jesus said there is no marriage in heaven. The Pharisees asked about the greatest commandment. Jesus gave them the top two.

MATTHEW 23

Jesus ripped the religious leaders with seven woes saying they did everything for show and to draw attention to themselves. He called them hypocrites, blind guides, sons of hell, fools, greedy, selfish, unclean, whitewashed tombs and murderers of God's messengers. He pleaded for Jerusalem and wished they put themselves under God's wing.

MATTHEW 24

Jesus gave the Olivet Discourse, a warning for the abomination that causes desecration prophesied in Daniel. He spoke of the destruction of the temple and how terrible it would be in those days for nursing and pregnant mothers. He warned against false messiahs and prophets who would rise up. People will hear of wars and rumors of wars and feel earthquakes, but those would be like birth pains. He gave apocalyptic signs for the coming of the Son of Man in judgment. People will be enjoying themselves and then be hit with sudden destruction. So be warned and be ready.

MATTHEW 25

Jesus told the parable of the ten bridesmaids, five of them were wise because they were ready for the bridegroom when he arrived. Jesus then told the parable of the three servants given bags of money (ten, five and one) based on their ability. The two invested the money and pleased the master ("well done good and faithful servant") while the third buried the money. The third was thrown out into darkness because he did nothing. Jesus said if we took care of the hungry, thirsty, the naked, strangers and those in prison, we really took care of Jesus.

MATTHEW 26

As Passover approached, Jesus went to the house of Simon the Leper and a woman anointed him with perfume. The disciples thought the money could go to something better like feeding the poor. Jesus said they would always the poor with them. Judas agreed to betray Jesus to the religious leaders while the other disciples prepared the Passover meal. Jesus ate the last supper with his disciples, announcing the betrayal of Judas, the denial of Peter and the significance of this last meal. Jesus and the disciples retreated to Gethsemane to pray but the disciples could not stay awake. Judas arrived with the leaders and kissed Jesus. He was arrested and brought to Caiaphas. False accusations against Jesus were heard and the sentence of death announced. Meanwhile, the people outside recognized Peter, who denied three times any association with Jesus. A rooster crowed alerting Peter to his betrayal.

MATTHEW 27

Judas, feeling guilty, tried to return the money to the religious leaders but was denied. He threw the thirty coins into the temple and hung himself. The religious leaders bought a field and buried Judas in it. Jesus stood before Pilate while the crowd shouted "crucify him." They even wanted the notorious criminal Barabbas released instead of Jesus. Jesus was sent to be crucified, beaten and mocked along the way. He was taken to Golgotha. Darkness fell for three hours. When Jesus gave up his spirit, the temple curtain tore, an earthquake shook the land and godly people stepped out of their graves. Even the Roman Centurion said, "This was the Son of God." Joseph of Arimathea and some ladies wrapped Jesus in linen and put him in a new grave cut out of stone. Pilate posted guards in case the disciples showed up to steal Jesus' body.

MATTHEW 28

Mary Magdalene and the other Mary went to the tomb and found an angel who told them Jesus was not there. He had risen. The angel told the women to have everyone meet in Galilee. Jesus also met the disciples and told them to go to Galilee. The religious leaders bribed the guards to tell everyone that Jesus' disciples stole the body. The eleven disciples met Jesus on a mountain in Galilee. Jesus commissioned them to go into the whole world and make disciples of all men.

MARK

Number of Chapters: *16*
Most Likely Author: *John Mark*
Time span: *29 – 33 AD*

MARK 1

John the Baptist preached a message of baptism for the repentance of sins. People came to the Jordan to be baptized. He wore a camel hair coat, leather belt and ate locusts and honey. He proclaimed someone was coming who would baptize with the Holy Spirit and he wasn't worthy to untie his shoes. Jesus was baptized and the Holy Spirit descended like dove. Jesus called Simon, Andrew, James and John, asking them to drop their nets. Jesus quieted demons and cast them out. He healed Peter's mother-in-law and a man of leprosy.

MARK 2

Jesus forgave the sins of a paralyzed man lowered through the roof, then commanded him to stand and walk. The Pharisees never saw anything like that. Jesus called Matthew to follow him then ate with his sinner friends. Jesus told the Pharisees he came to call the sick since the unhealthy don't need a doctor. Jesus was questioned by the Pharisees as to why his disciples don't fast and instead pick grain on the Sabbath. Jesus replied that the Sabbath was made for man.

MARK 3

Jesus healed a man on the Sabbath with a shriveled hand, causing the Pharisees to plot his death. He appointed the twelve to preach and drive out demons. Many accused him of conspiring with demons, but Jesus wondered how a house divided against itself would stand. His family was waiting for him, but Jesus told people that his true family did the will of God.

MARK 4

Jesus told the Parable of the Sower, but the disciples didn't understand. He wanted his disciples to know that people receive the word of God, then all kinds of things keep it from growing in their hearts. He also told the Parable of the Seed and the Mustard Seed, to communicate how a small amount of effort can grow into a huge thing. After being woken from his nap, Jesus calmed the storm by rebuking the wind. His apostles couldn't believe the storm obeyed him.

MARK 5

Jesus crossed the lake and faced off with a demon possessed man who could not be contained with chains. The demons begged for Jesus not to destroy them. Jesus cast the legion of demons into the pigs, who threw themselves into the sea. The man, now sane, asked to go with Jesus, but Jesus told him to go home and tell everyone what God had done. Jairus, a synagogue ruler, asked Jesus to heal his daughter. As Jesus went to his house, a woman with a bleeding condition touched his cloak and was healed. Jesus arrived at Jairus' house after hearing his daughter had died. Jesus commanded her to get up and she did.

MARK 6

Jesus headed back to Nazareth but they took offense to him. Jesus felt a prophet had no honor in his hometown. He sent out the disciples in groups of two, telling them not to take very much. Many thought he was Elijah or John the Baptist had been raised from the dead. Herod had John the Baptist beheaded because he objected to Herod marrying his brother's wife. The daughter of Herodias danced and Herod asked what she wanted, which she responded to by asking for the head of John the Baptist on a platter. Jesus fed the five thousand with only five fish and two loaves. Jesus walked on water, meeting his disciplines during a storm at night.

MARK 7

The Pharisees were upset that the disciples ate food without washing hands. Jesus rebuked them for their traditional rules, saying it's not what goes into the mouth that defiled a person, but their words and actions that come out of the mouth. It's one's thought life that defiled them. He entered the house of a Syrophoenician woman and expelled a demon from her daughter. In the Decapolis, he healed a man born deaf and mute, by sticking his fingers in the man's ears and touching his tongue with his spit.

MARK 8

Jesus fed the four thousand with seven loaves and a few small fish. Jesus warned his disciples about the yeast from the Pharisees and Herod. Jesus healed a blind man in Bethsaida. In Caesarea Philippi, he asked his disciples "Who do people say that I am?" Peter rebuked Jesus for talking about death and Jesus rebuked him. Jesus told them whoever saved their life, lost it and whoever gained the whole world lost their soul.

MARK 9

Jesus took his disciples to a mountain and transfigured before them. Elijah and Moses appeared next to him. Jesus healed a man whose son threw himself in the fire, even when the disciples couldn't heal him. Jesus predicted his death again. He told people to welcome little children because it was like welcoming him. People who do miracles in God's name can't be stopped. For those who are not against the kingdom are for it. Don't cause little ones to stumble. Might as well tie a huge millstone around your neck and jump in the water. Why go through life with a sinful hand, eye and foot. Cut them off. You don't want to go to hell.

MARK 10

Jesus was questioned about divorce and he told them God never intended for there to be divorce. Moses allowed that because of their hard hearts. Jesus blessed the children. He confronted the rich man and told him to sell everything. The rich have a hard time entering heaven, much like getting a camel through the eye of a needle. Jesus reinforced total sacrifice to receive the kingdom of heaven, promising a hundred times more to those who gave up family, homes and fields for his sake. Jesus predicted his death prompting James and John to ask to sit on his right and left when the kingdom comes. He spoke about the importance of humility, the first being last. Blind Bartimaeus was healed because of his faith.

MARK 11

Jesus rode into Jerusalem on a colt, amongst shouts of Hosanna. Jesus cursed a fig tree, saying no one will eat from it again. He entered the temple courts and drove out the money changers and dove sellers. The next day the fig tree had withered. The religious authorities asked Jesus who gave him this authority. Jesus asked whose authority was John's baptism – by men or by God. Jesus refused to answer them when they refused to answer him.

MARK 12

Jesus told the parable of the tenants who killed the servants sent to collect debt. Eventually they killed the son. The Pharisees then looked for ways to arrest Jesus, knowing he said this parable to shame them. They tried to trap Jesus in questions about paying taxes and marriage at the resurrection. Jesus gave the people the two greatest commandments. Then he attacked the teachers of the law and applauded a poor widow who gave from her poverty, not her wealth.

MARK 13

Jesus spoke about the destruction of the temple. He warned them about false Messiahs and persecution. He told them not to panic when wars and earthquakes occurred. Jesus prophesied about the abomination that caused desolation which would soon come and how dreadful it will be. He cautioned them to be on guard for that day. Only God knew when it would happen.

MARK 14

Jesus was anointed by a woman with an alabaster jar. Those present in the house thought the money could be used to help the poor. Jesus told them to leave her alone, they will always have opportunities to help the poor, but they won't always have him around. Meanwhile, Judas agreed to betray Jesus. At the Last Supper, Jesus announced a betrayer. Jesus distributed the bread (his body) and the wine (his blood). Jesus predicted Peter's denial—the rooster would crow twice after Peter denied him three times. At Gethsemane, Jesus prayed in sorrow, but his disciples slept. Three times he had to wake them. Judas and the officials arrived to arrest Jesus. Judas indicated to the others who Jesus was by kissing him. The disciples scattered (as Jesus predicted). Peter followed and watched from a distance. Before the Sanhedrin, the leaders could not find any evidence against Jesus so they created false testimonies. Jesus confessed to them he was the Messiah. They beat him for blasphemy. Peter denied Christ three times and the rooster crowed just as Jesus said.

MARK 15

Jesus confirmed to Pilate that he was the king of the Jews, but refused to answer accusations from the chief priests. Pilate offered to free one man and the crowd, influenced by the chief priests, asked for Barabbas, a murderer. The crowd demanded crucifixion for Jesus. Jesus was flogged, mocked, dressed in a purple robe and a crown of thorns, struck on the head with a staff, and spat on. Simon from Cyrene helped Jesus carry the cross to Golgotha. Jesus was crucified between two rebels. Darkness fell. Jesus cried out and those around him believed he called out to Elijah. As he died, the temple curtain tore in two. The centurion, who saw how he died, believed him to be the son of God. As evening approached, Joseph of Arimathea asked Pilate for Jesus' body, wrapped him in linen and buried him in a tomb cut out of rock. The women saw where they put Jesus' body.

MARK 16

After the Sabbath, the women discovered the stone rolled away and Jesus gone. An angel told them that Jesus was not here because he had risen. He asked for everyone to meet him in Galilee. [Not found in the earliest discovered manuscripts] *Jesus appeared to Mary Magdalene and to those on the road. He rebuked his followers for their lack of faith. He said if they truly believed they could pick up snakes and drink deadly poison and nothing would happen to them. Then Jesus ascended and the disciples preached everywhere.*

LUKE

Number of Chapters:	*24*
The Author:	*Luke*
Time span:	*4 BC – 33 AD*

LUKE 1

Luke wrote his message to Theophilus after careful investigation. Zechariah, a priest, received a visit from Gabriel telling him that his wife Elizabeth would have a baby and his name would be John, fulfilling the prophecy of Elijah returning to turn the hearts of the fathers to their children (found in Malachi). Zechariah did not believe so he became mute. Elizabeth became pregnant. Gabriel then visited Mary in Nazareth and said she would carry the Son of the Most High. She wondered how since she was a virgin. Gabriel told her the Holy Spirit would allow it. A pregnant Mary met her pregnant cousin Elizabeth and rejoiced at what God had done. Mary sang a song. Elizabeth gave birth and Zechariah insisted the baby be named John. Zechariah's mouth opened and he sang a praise song to God. John grew, living in the desert until he went public.

LUKE 2

During the days of Caesar Augustus, a census was issued that required everyone to return to the city of their lineage. Joseph needed to go to Bethlehem and took a very pregnant Mary. While there, she gave birth in a manger, because no one had room for them. The shepherds were met by angels who told them to go look for a baby in a manger, wrapped in cloths. The shepherds found the baby and spread the word about what they had seen. Eight days later, Jesus was presented at the temple for circumcision. Later, during the purification rites and dedication of the firstborn, two people, Annas and Simeon, praised God when they saw the child. After this, Mary, Joseph and Jesus went to Nazareth. At the age of twelve, during Passover, Jesus got separated from his family. Three days later, they found him and Jesus told them, "didn't you know that I would be at my father's house?" Jesus grew in stature and wisdom and in favor with men.

LUKE 3

John the Baptist began his ministry in the wilderness, preaching a baptism of repentance, in accordance to Isaiah's prophecy. Many came out into the desert to hear him. John chastised the Pharisees and teachers of the law. He told them to wait expectantly for one more powerful than he, whose sandal thong he was unworthy to touch. John did not have a favorable position with Herod because he rebuked his relationship with Herodias, his brother's wife. Jesus at the age of 30 came to John to be baptized. The Holy Spirit descended and God spoke from heaven. The genealogy of Jesus from Joseph to God is laid out in detail.

LUKE 4

Jesus was led by the Holy Spirit to the wilderness, where the devil tempted him for forty days. The devil wanted him to turn stones to bread, to throw himself off the temple and to accept power over all the cities he could see. Jesus refused, quoting scripture back to Satan. Satan departed. Jesus traveled to Nazareth and read from the prophet Isaiah saying the prophecy about the promised one who would come to free them had been fulfilled and was standing before them. The people in his hometown wanted to throw him off a cliff. Jesus cast demons out of people, who screamed, "You are the son of God!" Jesus healed many in Capernaum, even Peter's mother-in-law.

LUKE 5

Jesus called his first disciples, fisherman, after showing them, despite the odds, that they could catch an abundance of fish. The miracle wowed Simon, James and John so much, they left everything to follow Jesus. Jesus healed a man with leprosy and told the man to present himself to the priests. After a crippled man was lowered through the roof, Jesus forgave his sins, causing a disturbance amongst the Pharisees and teachers. Then, to show that he had the authority to forgive, he healed the man, telling him to take up his mat and walk. Jesus called Levi, the tax collector, who responded by throwing a party for Jesus and inviting his friends. The Pharisees balked wondering how he could eat with sinners. Jesus said the sick need a doctor, not the healthy. Then the Pharisees asked why Jesus' disciples don't fast and Jesus told them the moment many have anticipated finally arrived.

LUKE 6

The Pharisees disagreed with Jesus when his disciples picked grain to eat and Jesus healed a man with a shriveled hand on the Sabbath. Jesus called his twelve apostles. He then began the Sermon on the Mount, talking about those who are blessed and who will receive their reward in heaven. He spoke woes against those who laugh and are well fed, seeking their comforts of life now. Jesus encouraged love for enemies, doing for them what you want them to do for you. We must love never expecting anything in return. He also told his followers not to judge. The blind can't lead the blind and we can't judge what's in someone's eye if we have something in ours. No good tree has bad fruit and no bad tree has good fruit. Be fruitful. He also asked them to build their house on a solid foundation, because the elements of this world pound and erode a foundation built on sand.

LUKE 7

A centurion, who loved Israel and helped to build a synagogue, had a sick servant whom he loved, so he asked for Jesus to come heal the man. As Jesus approached, the servant sent messengers telling Jesus he wasn't worthy to have Jesus come to his house and Jesus could just say the word and his servant would be healed. Jesus was impressed by this man's faith. The servant was healed. In Nain, Jesus passed by a funeral for a widow's son. He touched the coffin and the boy got up. John the Baptist's servants came to Jesus asking if he was the one they have been waiting for. Jesus said to look at all the things he had done – healing, proclaiming the good news – then proceeded to talk about how great John the Baptist was among all men. Jesus, like John the Baptist, was slandered because of his association with sinners. At the house of a Pharisee, Jesus was anointed by a sinful woman who poured an alabaster jar of perfume on his feet while wetting them with her tears. Jesus forgave the woman and sent her on her way.

LUKE 8

      Jesus traveled from town to town. Many followed him including women healed of demons. Jesus told the parable of the soils. He told people not to hide their faith, just like no one would hide their light under a jar. Jesus told the crowd that his real family were those that heard the word of God and obeyed it. Jesus calmed the sea while on a boat with his disciples. They met a demon possessed man on shore and cast his demons into a herd of pigs. The people of the town were afraid and told Jesus to leave. Jesus told the healed man to go to town and tell everyone what Jesus had done. A synagogue leader named Jairus had a daughter who got very ill so he sent for Jesus. As Jesus was going, a bleeding woman touched the hem of his cloak and was healed. By the time Jesus got to Jairus' house, the girl was dead and the people were mourning. Jesus went up into her room with Peter, James and John and revived her.

LUKE 9

      Jesus sent out the twelve apostles telling them not to take anything with them and to shake off the dust of any town that rejected them. Jesus fed the 5,000 with only five loaves and two fishes. With the all rumors swirling around about Jesus' identity, Peter confessed that Jesus was the Messiah, the son of God. Jesus told them to take their cross and follow him, to not worry about gaining the whole world and losing their soul, and to not be ashamed about Him. Up on a mountain, he transfigured with Moses and Elijah by his side. God called him "My son." Jesus healed a boy with an evil spirit. The apostles argued who was the greatest. Jesus said following him means giving up everything, even your home. Many came up with excuses like burying their father or saying goodbye and Jesus said they weren't fit for service.

LUKE 10

      Jesus sent out seventy-two disciples saying the harvest was ready but the workers were few. Jesus told them to heal the sick and kick the dust off their feet if they weren't welcomed in a town. He warned cities like Korazin, Bethsaida and Capernaum who didn't receive his disciples well. Jesus said many throughout history wanted to see what they were seeing. An expert in the law wanted to know what to do to inherit eternal life. Jesus asked what the law said, so the expert responded "Love the Lord your God and your neighbor." When Jesus applauded that answer, the expert asked, "Who is my neighbor?" Jesus told the story of the Good Samaritan to answer his question. Jesus ate at Mary and Martha's house. Mary listened to Jesus while Martha worked. Jesus told Martha she was upset about too many things.

LUKE 11

Jesus taught his disciples about prayer, giving them a model prayer. He told the parable of a persistent neighbor who asked for bread, saying that God will answer the same kind of persistent prayer. Very simply, Jesus said, you need to ask to receive. While Jesus drove out demons, the people said he drove out demons because he was the prince of demons. Jesus said no house could be divided against itself. He warned the people to protect themselves against demonic influences by making sure their eyes were good and their bodies not full of darkness. He warned the Pharisees with six harsh woes, attacking their intentions for being religious and blaming the death of all prophets on people like them.

LUKE 12

Jesus warned against the Pharisees and said not to be afraid of those that can kill the body, but to be afraid of those who can kill the soul and throw it into hell. Jesus spoke against trusting in possessions, telling the Parable of the Rich Fool who built more barns to store his grain. He implored his followers not to worry because God took care of the ravens, the lilies and the grass, so seek his kingdom first. Jesus then told them to watch and be ready, for if an owner of a house had known at what hour a thief would break in, he wouldn't have allowed it. The son of man was coming soon too. Jesus did not come to bring peace but division, even among families. Watch the signs of the times, he said.

LUKE 13

Jesus healed a woman on the Sabbath who was crippled. The Pharisee balked, but Jesus told them they untied their donkey to get it water on the Sabbath so why can't he heal a poor woman? This humiliated them. He compared the kingdom of God to a mustard seed. He warned people that only a few will be saved, like the owner of a house who closed the door and stranding some outside that he did not know. The Pharisees warned Jesus that Herod wanted to kill him, but Jesus called him a fox. He said he longed to gather Jerusalem close to him like a hen gathers his chicks.

LUKE 14

While at a Pharisee's house, Jesus healed a man of dropsy (or swelling). He told the people that they would rescue their son or an ox who fell into a well on the Sabbath, so why not heal? Jesus noticed how people scrambled for the best places to sit at the banquet and told them to be humble in order to be exalted. He said to invite the poor and the crippled to the feasts. Jesus told the story of the man whose invited guests gave excuses why they couldn't come to his feast, so he told his servants to invite those in the streets and alleys. The cost of being his disciple is great. One must pick up their cross and follow him. A builder of a tower and a king about to go to war first calculated the cost before they proceeded and Jesus asked them to do the same before they became his disciples.

LUKE 15

Jesus told three stories to the Pharisees who were upset because he hung out with tax collectors and sinners. The lost coin, the lost sheep and the lost son, all of them highlighting the rejoicing that occurred in heaven when something lost turns up again. In the parable of the lost son, the older brother got jealous over the no-good brother who had returned, much like the Pharisees who get upset over sinners repenting.

LUKE 16

Jesus told the Parable of the Shrewd Manager, who, afraid of losing his job, cut his master's debt bill down so they would like him and give him a job when he got fired. Jesus commended the shrewdness of the manager, saying Christians need to be shrewd working with the world. We cannot serve two masters. Jesus told the story of the Rich Man and Lazarus who both died. Lazarus, the poor beggar, went to heaven resting with Abraham and the Rich Man went to hell. The Rich Man talked to Abraham wishing that his brothers would receive an angel to convince them to live for God, but Abraham said they had Moses and the Prophets, why would the brothers listen to an angel?

LUKE 17

Jesus said it would be better for someone to drown themselves in the water with a millstone around their neck then to cause an innocent person to stumble. He told them to forgive over and over and to have faith as small as a mustard seed. Jesus healed ten lepers but only one, a Samaritan, came back and thanked him. Jesus warned the people about the days of the Son of Man that will come quickly, like the days of Noah (the flood) and Lot (Sodom). People will be partying then, boom, destruction. Two people will be working and one will live and the other die.

LUKE 18

Jesus told the Parable of the Persistent Widow to show that God desired justice and will respond to the requests of the people through persistent prayer. Jesus told the Parable of the Pharisees and the Tax Collector to show it's not obedience that saves you but your desire for mercy. Jesus allowed little children to come to him because we need to receive the kingdom of God like a child would. A rich ruler wanted to know what to do to earn eternal life, since he's kept all the commandments. Jesus told him to sell everything and give it to the poor. The ruler went away sad and Jesus said rich people have a hard time getting into heaven. Jesus predicted his death again. A blind beggar in Jericho yelled out for Jesus to have mercy. Jesus asked him what he wanted him to do for him. When he asked to see, Jesus granted his wish.

LUKE 19

Jesus met Zacchaeus who desperately tried to see Jesus as he entered Jericho. Jesus invited himself over to his house. Zacchaeus was moved by Jesus and offered to pay back all the people he cheated. Jesus told the Parable of the Ten Minas, about ten servants who invested the same amount of money and got a return, except one who hid his money. The master had that one killed. Jesus entered Jerusalem on a colt that had never been ridden. The people cried out in praise during his triumphal entry. Jesus cleared out the temple, complaining that it had become a den of robbers.

LUKE 20

The Pharisees questioned Jesus' authority but they would not answer by whose authority John's baptism was from. Jesus told the Parable of the Tenants where a man planted a vineyard and the tenants kept killing everyone the master sent to collect the fruit. Eventually they killed the son, the heir. Jesus said the stone the builders reject will indeed become the capstone. Everyone who stumbles on that stone will be crushed. The teachers of the law sent spies to him, trying to trap him on a question about paying taxes. Jesus had them look at the coin and to pay taxes to the person whose face was on that coin (Caesar) and to give to God what was rightfully his. Some Sadducees tried to trap him on a question about resurrection and marriage, using an example of a woman who married seven brothers, one after the other, and was passed down after each of them died. Jesus said there is no marriage in heaven because people are like the angels. Jesus told the teachers the law they were arrogant and like to show off.

LUKE 21

Jesus admired a poor widow's offering of two coins. He applauded her for giving from her poverty. While the disciples admired the temple, Jesus said not one stone will be left on top of the other. When asked when this will happen, Jesus told them that terrible things were coming – earthquakes, false prophets, famines, pestilence, signs from heaven and persecution. But not to worry for God will give them the words and the wisdom. Jerusalem would be surrounded, he said, causing great distress and scattering. This generation, he promised, would not pass away until they see this occur.

LUKE 22

Judas agreed to betray Jesus, looking for an opportunity when no crowd was around. Jesus asked his disciples to prepare the Passover then presented the bread and the wine to them at the table. The disciples argued who would be greatest and Jesus said the greatest among them would serve the others. Jesus warned Peter saying Satan asked to sift him like wheat, predicting Peter's denial. Jesus took them to the Mount of Olives to pray, but they kept falling asleep. Judas arrived with the guards and one of the disciples cut off the ear of the high priest's servant. Jesus restored it then was arrested. Peter denied Jesus three times as the guards beat Jesus and mocked him. The elders asked if he was the Son of God and Jesus said if he told them they wouldn't believe.

LUKE 23

The assembly accused Jesus of not paying taxes to Caesar and claiming to be the Christ. Hearing that Jesus was a Galilean, Pilate sent Jesus to Herod. Herod had wanted to see Jesus perform miracles, but got no response from him, so he sent Jesus back to Pilate. Pilate offered to release Jesus, but the people chose Barabbas instead. Pilate consented to their demands for crucifixion though he found nothing wrong with Jesus. Simon of Cyrene helped carry Jesus' cross to the Place of the Skull. Two criminals hung on both sides of Jesus—one insulted him while the other defended him. Jesus said he would see the one criminal in paradise. At the ninth hour/noon, darkness fell and the curtain tore in the temple. Jesus died. The centurion said this was truly a righteous man. Joseph of Arimathea took Jesus' body and buried him while the women followed and saw the place where they put him.

LUKE 24

The women went to the tomb and found the rock rolled away. They saw two men in gleaming clothes inside who asked "Why are you looking for the living among the dead. He is not here. He is risen!" They told the others what they saw. Their words sounded like nonsense but Peter ran to the tomb and verified it. Jesus visited two men on the road to Emmaus and talked to them about recent events. He then broke bread and they knew it was him. Later, Jesus appeared to the eleven. They thought he was a ghost until he ate with them and they saw his hands and feet. He opened their minds and they understood. Near Bethany, Jesus was taken up before them. The disciples worshipped God with great joy in the temple.

JOHN

Number of Chapters: *21*
The Author: *John*
Time span: *29 – 33 AD*

JOHN 1

John introduced Jesus as the Word, through whom all things were made. In him was life and that life was the light of men. Jesus was God in the flesh, dwelling among mankind. John the Baptist wanted to make sure that he was not confused to be the Messiah, but he called himself a proclaimer of the Messiah, preparing the way for him by baptizing people. When he saw Jesus he called him the Lamb of God who takes away the sin of the world. He told of a miraculous baptism that occurred with the Holy Spirit descending on Jesus. John told his disciples who Jesus was and Andrew, one of John's disciples, went and told his brother Peter. Jesus met Peter and called him Cephas. Jesus called Philip who found Nathanael saying the chosen one had come from Nazareth. Nathanael had a hard time believing that until he met Jesus and believed.

JOHN 2

Jesus and his disciples, along with Jesus' mother, went to a wedding in Cana. When the wine ran out, Mary told the servants to do whatever her son said to do. Jesus asked that six stone jars, holding twenty to thirty gallons each, be filled with water. When they drew from the jars, they realized the water had turned into an excellent wine. Jesus went to the temple, made a whip out of cords, then tore up the tables of the moneychangers and sellers of sacrifices say they had made a marketplace out of the temple. The Jews asked Jesus what kind of sign he could perform to show he had the authority to commit such an act. Jesus told them to destroy this temple and he would raise it up in three days. Confused, they said it took forty-six years to build this temple, but Jesus was talking about his body.

JOHN 3

Nicodemus, a Pharisee and member of the Jewish ruling council, visited Jesus at night believing Jesus was a man of God. Jesus told him to see the kingdom of God one must be born again. Nicodemus could not understand. Jesus told him God loved the word so much he sent his son to the world as a sacrifice that whoever believes in him would not perish but have eternal life. God didn't send his son to condemn the world but to save it. Later, Jesus and his disciples went to visit John the Baptist who was baptizing. John told the crowd "I am not the Christ." John said he must become less while Jesus becomes greater.

JOHN 4

The people heard Jesus was baptizing more people than John, but it was not Jesus who was baptizing but his disciples. Jesus traveled through Samaria and stopped at a well. While his disciples went to find something to eat, a Samaritan woman came by the well. Jesus told her he had water that would make her never thirst again. She wanted this water. Jesus told her he knew she had five husbands and the man she was with now was not her husband. The woman was shocked that he knew and it confirmed for her that he was a prophet. She knew that a Messiah was coming called Christ and Jesus told her, "I am he." The Samaritan woman went to town and told a bunch of people who came out to meet Jesus. Many believed. Jesus returned to Cana and was met by a royal official whose son had a bad fever. Jesus said he would be fine. The man returned and found his son had gotten well the exact moment Jesus said the word. His whole household believed in Jesus.

JOHN 5

Jesus went to the Pool of Bethesda and met a man who had been invalid for thirty-eight years. He had been waiting for the waters to stir and to lower himself in, but others got there first. Jesus told him to pick up his mat and walk. He did so and the Pharisees complained that he was carrying his mat on the Sabbath. Jesus made the leaders angry because he called God his father. Jesus told them that the Son does what the Father says and the Son has been given all judgment. He told them whoever believed in Jesus has eternal life, the dead will rise from their graves and those who did good will live. Jesus confirmed that the testimony about who he was did not come from him, but from John the Baptist, His Father, the scriptures and Moses.

JOHN 6

Jesus crossed on the far shore of Galilee and great crowds followed him because he performed miraculous signs. He asked Philip how they were going to feed them. Andrew brought up a boy with five barley loaves and two small fish. Jesus had them sit down and miraculously reproduced enough bread and fish to feed five thousand. Twelve baskets were left over. That night, his disciples were in a boat when a storm hit. Jesus walked out to them and the boat immediately appeared on shore. The people looked for Jesus and found him. Jesus told them he was the bread of life and people would never go hungry if they fed off him. He is the living bread that had come down from heaven. If people ate his flesh and drank his blood, he would raise them up on the last day. Many disciples deserted Jesus, but the twelve stayed.

JOHN 7

While the Feast of the Tabernacles was about to start, Jesus' brothers encouraged him to go and do his miracles, even though they themselves were not believers. Jesus went to the Feast where people were looking for him. Jesus taught at the festival telling people his teaching was not his own, but from the one who sent him. They accused him of being demon possessed. Jesus told them that streams of living water would flow from those that believe in him (he was talking about the Holy Spirit which had not come to believers yet). The Pharisees sent guards to arrest him, but even the guards were amazed by his teaching.

JOHN 8

Jesus defended a woman caught in adultery, challenging any accuser who was sinless to throw the first stone. Jesus called him the light of the world. Jesus then defended his own ministry saying that his Father can act as witness to Jesus' identity and authority. The Pharisees called Abraham their father. Jesus told them the devil was their father. He then stated that Abraham looked forward to the day when Jesus would arrive. Jesus claimed to know Abraham. The Pharisees wondered how he could do that, being not even fifty years old. Jesus said "Before Abraham was born, I am" meaning he was around before Abraham. The leaders wanted to stone him but Jesus got away.

JOHN 9

The disciples saw a man born blind and asked whose sin caused his situation – the man or his parents. Jesus replied neither, but this happened to reveal God's glory. Jesus spit in the ground and made mud, then applied it to the man's eyes. He told him to wash in the pool of Siloam. The man could see. The Pharisees were upset since it was the Sabbath, so they called the formerly blind man and his parents before the religious leaders asking for the identity of his healer, who obviously couldn't be from God. The once blind man replied, "All I know is once I was blind, but now I see." Jesus later found the man and revealed himself, saying he came to world so the blind would see and those that see would become blind. The Pharisees wondered if he was talking about them.

JOHN 10

Jesus used sheep imagery to describe his relationship with his followers. His flock know his voice and respond to him. When he calls, they come running. He said "I am the gate for the sheep" allowing them passage in and out. He said "I am the good shepherd" willing to lay down his life for his sheep. During the Feast of Dedication, the Jews demanded that he tell them plainly whether he was the Christ. Jesus replied that his miracles were the answer. He said that he and the Father were one in the same. They picked up stones in retribution for blasphemy. Jesus escaped their grasp and slipped away to a remote region where John the Baptist had been baptizing.

JOHN 11

When Lazarus got very sick, his sisters Mary and Martha sent for Jesus. Jesus was only a couple miles away, but he delayed coming so that God's glory could be witnessed. When Jesus finally arrived, Lazarus had been in the tomb for four days. Jesus comforted Mary and Martha saying he was the resurrection and life. They all needed to believe in him to live. Jesus wept, seeing their mourning. He went to the tomb and had the stone rolled away. Jesus called Lazarus to come out and Lazarus did, wrapped in his funeral linens. Many began to believe in Jesus. The Pharisees and others could not stand it any longer. They started looking for Jesus to take his life (and Lazarus too), ordering people to report any sight of him.

JOHN 12

Six days before Passover, Mary and Martha threw a party for Jesus. Mary anointed Jesus with perfume and washed his feet with her hair. Judas, the money keeper, felt the value of this perfume could go to better uses, like the poor. Jesus told him you'll have the poor with you, but he'll only be with them a short time. Jesus made a triumphal entry in Jerusalem on a donkey. The crowds cheered and the Jewish leaders jeered. Their efforts were getting them nowhere. Jesus predicted his death again, like a seed that needed to die when it hit the ground, then sprouted again. Jesus shouted to heaven, "Father, glorify your name!" A voice from heaven responded saying it was being glorified. The writer cannot believe after all the miracles Jesus did, people still did not believe in him. Jesus implored the crowd, saying he did not come to judge the world, but to save it.

JOHN 13

Just before the Passover feast, Jesus, knowing where he was going and that God had given him all power, stripped down, put on a towel and washed his disciples' feet. Peter balked, saying he needed more than just his hands washed. Jesus said he did this as an example, telling them to wash each other's feet. In God's eyes, no servant was greater than his master. Jesus announced that someone would betray him. He dipped a piece of bread and handed it to his betrayer—Judas. Satan entered him and Judas, in charge of the money, ran out. Jesus told the rest of them that he was going to be leaving soon and to love one another so all people will know that they are followers of Christ by their love. Peter promised not to leave Jesus. Jesus replied that Peter would deny him three times before the rooster crowed.

JOHN 14

Jesus offered comfort to his followers by saying he was going to his Father's house and preparing a place for them. Then, he promised to come back and take them there. Jesus declared that he was the way, the truth and the life and you can't get to the Father except through him. Philip asked to see the Father, but Jesus told him that as long as they saw Jesus, they saw the Father. His words and his miracles proved it. Jesus promised them the Holy Spirit, who would be a counselor and teacher. The world will reject him, but Jesus offered them peace, telling them not to worry.

JOHN 15

Jesus called himself the vine and God the gardener, cutting off the dead branches and pruning the fruitful ones. We are the branches and only by remaining connected to Jesus can we be fruitful. By acknowledging God's love we can have complete joy. The greatest love someone can show is by laying down their life for another person. Jesus called us his friends, but the world will hate us. Jesus said not to take it personally, because they really hate him. We will be treated as the world treated Jesus. They have no excuse to reject Jesus. They have seen the miracles and the Holy Spirit is testifying about Jesus.

JOHN 16

Jesus promised to send his disciples the Holy Spirit, a counselor who will also convict the world of sin, righteousness and judgment. This Holy Spirit will speak on his own. The disciples wondered what all this talk was about going away and they questioned him, asking to be told plainly. When Jesus did, the disciples understood. Jesus rejoiced that they finally believed. Now that they know, they would have peace because Jesus has overcome the world.

JOHN 17

Jesus prayed for himself, acknowledging that he had glorified God. He prayed for his disciples for he gave them God's word. He asked for their protection because they were being sent into the world. Jesus prayed for all believers in the future, that they may be united as the Father and Son are united.

JOHN 18

Judas led a detachment of soldiers and officials from the priests and Pharisees to the olive grove where Jesus and the disciples frequented. When asked if he was Jesus of Nazareth, Jesus said "I am he" and his words caused them all to fall down. Peter struck the ear of the high priest's servant named Malchus, but Jesus reattached it. Jesus was led to Annas and Caiaphas while Peter was questioned in the courtyard about his affiliation with Jesus. Peter denied it three times. The rooster crowed. Jesus then was led to Pilate who told the Jews to punish him themselves. They replied that they had no right to execute anyone. Pilate could find no charges and offered to set free one prisoner. The crowd wanted Barabbas, who was involved in a rebellion.

JOHN 19

Pilate had Jesus flogged. The soldiers put on Jesus a crown of thorns and a purple robe, mocking him and striking him in the face. Pilate tried to negotiate with the Jews but they wanted him dead for claiming to be the Son of God. Pilate presented a beaten Jesus, saying "Here is your king" but the Jews swore allegiance to Caesar, their king. The soldiers took Jesus to Golgotha and crucified him with two others, one on each side. Pilate hung a sign that read "Jesus of Nazareth, The King of the Jews." The Jews hated that sign saying he claimed to be the king of the Jews but Pilate let it stay. The soldiers divided up Jesus' garments and offered him a drink when he said "I am thirsty." Finally Jesus said "It is finished" and died. Since he was dead, the soldiers did not break his bones, but pierced his side instead, as blood and water spilled out. Joseph of Arimathea, a secret follower of Christ, asked Pilate for Jesus' body and, with Nicodemus, buried Jesus in a tomb.

JOHN 20

Mary Magdalene arrived at the tomb and saw the stone rolled away. She ran to Simon Peter and the other disciple and told them that someone had taken Jesus' body. The disciples arrived and saw only strips of linen. Mary then saw two angels in white then a man, who she thought was the gardener, but it was Jesus. Jesus later appeared in a locked room to his disciples, breathed on them to receive the Holy Spirit. Thomas, who was not there at the time, said he would only believe if he saw the nail scars with his own eyes. Jesus arrived, a week later, and showed him the scars. Thomas declared, "My lord and my God." Jesus proclaimed that his followers were blessed because they saw, but what about the blessing others will receive who didn't see yet believed.

JOHN 21

Simon Peter, Thomas, Nathanael and others were at the Sea of Tiberias and decided to go fishing. All night they caught nothing. Jesus appeared on the shore line and called out, asking if they caught anything. Not knowing it was Jesus, they said "no." Jesus told them to put their nets on the right side of the boat. They did and hauled in a net full. Peter knew it was Jesus and swam over to him. Jesus had prepared breakfast for them. This was the third time Jesus appeared to them. Jesus asked Peter three times to feed and take care of his sheep and lambs. Peter agreed, frustrated that Jesus asked so many times. The writer of the book testified to everything written in this book, but if he had written down everything Jesus had done, there would not be room in all the books.

ACTS

Number of Chapters: 28
The Author: *Luke*
Time span: *33-62 AD*

ACTS 1

Luke mentioned that he wrote to Theophilus previously about Jesus and all that he did (the Gospel of Luke). After his resurrection, Jesus appeared to his disciples for forty days, convincing the people he was alive. He told them to wait in Jerusalem for the Holy Spirit and that they would be his witnesses in Jerusalem, Judea, Samaria and to the ends of the earth. After that, Jesus ascended into heaven. An angel asked the disciples why they were standing around. Jesus would be back. So the apostles casted lots to replace Judas, who had died in a field, and Matthias was chosen.

ACTS 2

The apostles were all together at Pentecost when a sound like a violent wind filled the house they were in. It looked like tongues of fire appeared over their heads and they began to speak in languages not their own. The people around them thought they were drunk. Peter stood and said what was happening to them was prophesied by Joel when he said in the last days there would be prophecies, visions and dreams. Everyone who called on the name of the Lord would be saved. Peter explained to them that Jesus was crucified and resurrected and they were witnesses to that. Three thousand people were saved that day and the church began to care for each other by giving their own possessions and fellowshipping together.

ACTS 3

A crippled beggar by the temple gate called Beautiful asked Peter and John for money. Peter didn't have money but gave the man the ability to walk. The people were amazed and Peter asked why they were astonished by God's power. Peter directed them to Jesus who the leaders made suffer and killed. He asked the crowd to repent because God had been sending them a message since the time of Samuel that a servant would be raised up.

ACTS 4

Peter and John were seized by the rulers and teachers of the law and put in jail. The next day, Annas the high priest and Caiaphas questioned them. Peter, filled with the Holy Spirit, told them that Jesus, who they crucified, had been raised from the dead. The rulers saw the courage of these unschooled, ordinary men. They told Peter and John not to preach any longer. Peter and John asked how they could not speak about what they had seen and heard. They were released and the church responded with prayer. The place shook and they were all filled with the Holy Spirit. The believers all got together with one heart and one mind and shared their possessions with each other. God's grace was powerfully at work in them. Barnabas sold a field and laid the money at the apostles' feet.

ACTS 5

Ananias and Sapphira tried to cheat their contribution to the church, and they both died, causing great fear to break out in the church. The apostles performed miraculous signs and, as a result, many new believers were added. The high priests were jealous and had the apostles arrested, but an angel opened the jail cell and they went right back out and preached. They were brought before the Sanhedrin. The apostles accused them of killing Jesus, but he rose from the dead and now stood exalted at the right hand of God. The Sanhedrin wanted them put to death but a Pharisee named Gamaliel told them others have claimed to be something in the past and all those movements fizzled. This will too, if it's not from the Lord. The group agreed and had the apostles flogged. Yet the apostles left praising God and continued proclaiming the good news.

ACTS 6

As the number of followers increased, so did the demands. The Hellenistic Jews (Greek) complained that the widows of Jews got preferential treatment, putting pressure on the apostles to step it up. So they decided to choose seven men to serve these groups, one of them named Stephen. Stephen performed great signs, stirring up opposition by the Synagogue of the Freedmen who accused him of saying Jesus would destroy this place and to change the customs of Moses. He was brought before the Sanhedrin and those who looked at Stephen saw his face was like an angel.

ACTS 7

Stephen answered the charges against him. He detailed the history of Israel, telling the stories of Abraham, Isaac, Jacob, Joseph, Moses, Aaron, Joshua, David and Solomon. Then Stephen accused stiff-necked people like the Sanhedrin of always persecuting prophets. This set the Sanhedrin off. Stephen looked to the sky and saw the glory of God. The Sanhedrin dragged him outside the city and stoned him. They laid their coats at the feet of Saul. Stephen asked God to receive his spirit and he died.

ACTS 8

After the death of Stephen, Paul persecuted the church heavily. The apostles scattered to Judea and Samaria. Philip, in Samaria, performed all kinds of miracles and the city rejoiced. Simon the Sorcerer performed amazing signs and people followed him, but when he saw Philip's miracles, he began to follow him. Peter and John came to Samaria and they prayed that people would receive the Holy Spirit. Simon the Sorcerer wanted that ability and offered to buy it. Peter rebuked him. Philip was sent by an angel to a road from Jerusalem to Gaza where he met an Ethiopian eunuch reading Isaiah while sitting in a chariot. Philip explained it as a prophecy about Jesus. The eunuch understood and believed. Philip baptized him and was immediately transported in Azotus, preaching some more in neighboring towns.

ACTS 9

While Saul traveled to Damascus to persecute people of The Way, a light from heaven flashed around him. Jesus spoke and asked why Saul was persecuting him. Saul went blind for three days. In Damascus a man named Ananias heard from God in a vision saying go find Saul and lay his hands on him to restore his sight. Ananias did and scales fell from Saul's eyes. Saul preached in synagogues. The people were baffled and wanted to kill him. Barnabas took him to the apostles in Jerusalem. The church experienced peace during that time and increased in numbers. Peter visited Lydda and healed a paralyzed man named Aeneas and raised a faithful servant named Dorcas/Tabitha from the dead.

ACTS 10

A God-fearing centurion named Cornelius was visited by an angel who told him to send men to Joppa to bring Simon Peter to his house. Meanwhile, Peter had a vision about a sheet of animals. God told him to eat. Peter refused to eat anything unclean, but God said not to call anything impure that he had made clean. This vision repeated three times. Cornelius' men showed up and took Peter to his house. Peter spoke to them and said the vision taught him that he needed to open his heart to the Gentiles. He needed to stop seeing them as unclean. Peter preached to them, not showing favoritism. The Holy Spirit came upon them and they spoke in tongues.

ACTS 11

Circumcised believers confronted Peter about going to the house of uncircumcised men but he responded by telling them about the vision. They understood and agreed with Peter. The believers scattered to Phoenicia, Cyprus and Antioch because of Stephen's death. Barnabas went to Antioch to check out what was going on there and was encouraged, so he went to Tarsus to find Paul and took him there. The disciples were first called Christians in Antioch. Some prophets came to Antioch and one named Agabus predicted a great famine that occurred during the time of Claudius.

ACTS 12

King Herod had James, the brother of John, executed by sword, then had Peter arrested. An angel appeared to Peter and released him from prison. Peter arrived at the house of Mary, mother of John, and communicated what God did. The guards were executed. Herod made a speech and thought himself to be equal to God. An angel struck him with worms and he died.

ACTS 13

The church in Antioch heard from the Holy Spirit to send Paul and Barnabas on a mission trip. John Mark joined them. They went to Seleucia, sailed to Cyprus and preached in synagogues. A Jewish sorcerer Bar-Jesus opposed them and tried to turn the proconsul, Sergio Paulus, from them. Saul, now called Paul, told Elymas (Bar-Jesus) he would go blind. When the sorcerer did, the proconsul believed. They traveled from Paphos to Perga where John Mark left them. In Pisidian Antioch, Paul told the Jews in their synagogue Israel's history and God's hand on them from Egypt to David. He finished by testifying about the life and resurrection of Christ and how forgiveness was found only in him. The people invited them to speak the next Sabbath and the whole town gathered. The Jews, who were jealous, contradicted the message and abused Paul. Paul said since the Jews rejected the message, then they must take it to the Gentiles. The Jewish leaders had them expelled from the region.

ACTS 14

In Iconium, Paul and Barnabas spoke in the synagogues and divided the city. When they heard about a plot to kill them, they fled to Lystra and Derbe. In Lystra, Paul told a lame man to get up and walk. He did. The people thought Zeus and Hermes had come to earth, but the Paul rebuked them, saying they were only men. Some Jews from Iconium stirred up the crowd, stoned Paul and dragged him outside the city. Paul got up and went back in. They returned to Lystra, Iconium and then to Antioch, encouraging the disciples with their report about opening the door to the Gentiles.

ACTS 15

Certain people were teaching that Gentiles needed to be circumcised to be saved. Paul and Barnabas debated with them. The church sent them to Jerusalem to meet with other apostles and elders. They told how Gentiles were being saved. James spoke up and said they should not make it difficult for Gentiles to turn to God. Instead, to focus on abstaining from food polluted by idols, sexual immorality and meat of strangled animals and blood. The council wrote a letter to the Gentiles in Antioch, Syria and Cilicia. Paul and Barnabas decided to return to the places where they visited before. Barnabas wanted to take John Mark but Paul disagreed since he abandoned them earlier. They parted ways – Barnabas with Mark and Paul with Silas – and they all strengthened the churches.

ACTS 16

Timothy joined Paul and Silas. The Spirit of Jesus prevented them from entering Bithynia but a vision led Paul to Macedonia. There Lydia was converted. Paul called a demon out of a girl who made money fortune telling so her owners had Paul and Silas arrested. While in prison, singing praises, an earthquake opened the doors and loosened the chains. The jailer thought he was a dead man until Paul and Silas said they were still inside. The jailer threw himself at their feet and asked how to be saved. He took Paul and Silas to his house and everyone there was baptized. The magistrates finally released Paul and Silas and they went to Lydia's house.

ACTS 17

Paul came to Thessalonica to preach about Christ, but the Jews formed mobs and started riots. He moved to Berea where they were much more open and curious. But the Jews in Thessalonica came to Berea and stirred up trouble there. Paul moved on to Athens where he debated with Epicurean and Stoic philosophers. Paul stood up at the Aeropagus and saw an altar to an unknown God. He proceeded to tell them who this God was, that he created all people and raised Jesus from the dead. Some rejected this message but others believed.

ACTS 18

Paul left Athens and set sail for Corinth where he met Aquila and Priscilla. He made tents and reasoned in the synagogues. Silas and Timothy joined him from Macedonia. Most Jews rejected the message but through a vision God told

Paul to stay. He did, for a year and a half. He traveled next to Ephesus, Caesarea, Jerusalem and then to Antioch. Paul encouraged the churches in Galatia and Phrygia. Aquila and Priscilla, who stayed in Ephesus, explained the gospel more clearly to Apollos who became a strong debater of the Scriptures.

ACTS 19

Paul entered Ephesus and found disciples who knew of the baptism of John, but not the Holy Spirit. Paul prayed and the Holy Spirit came upon them. They spoke in tongues. Paul argued in the synagogue for three months, then moved the discussion to a lecture hall for two years. All the Jews and Greeks heard the word. God did miracles through Paul, so that even his handkerchiefs and aprons healed people. Seven sons of Sceva, a Jewish priest, tried to cast out a demon, but the demon knew Jesus and Paul—not these guys. The sons ran away, naked and bleeding. A number of sorcerers burned their scrolls when they came to Christ. A silversmith named Demetrius saw that his profits in making idols for Artemis were dropping so he stirred up a riot against this new teaching in town. Paul wanted to appear but his disciples held him back. A city clerk dismissed the assembly and said for them to take it up in court.

ACTS 20

Paul went to Macedonia, Greece then back to Macedonia and off to Philippi. A young man named Eutychus, while listening to Paul speak, fell asleep then fell three stories to his death. Paul raised him back. Eventually Paul made his way to Ephesus where he told them he would never see them again. They were very sad.

ACTS 21

While setting sail, Paul was warned not to go to Jerusalem. A prophet named Agabus tied Paul's belt around his hands and feet and said this would happen to him in Jerusalem. Paul went anyway, prepared for whatever God brought. Paul arrived in Jerusalem and was greeted warmly by the church, including James. Paul told them how Gentiles were coming to

God. Some Jews saw Paul in the temple and began to riot. The Roman guards saved him, carrying him away. Paul asked to address the crowd.

ACTS 22

Paul told the crowd about his background as a zealous Jew who persecuted the Way and led many believers to their death, including Stephen. He told about his conversion experience on the road to Damascus. The crowd still wanted him killed, so the Roman guards took him away and flogged him to find out why they wanted him dead. Paul told them he was a Roman citizen and the torture stopped and he was released. The commander had Paul stand face-to-face with his Sanhedrin accusers.

ACTS 23

Paul spoke to the Sanhedrin about the resurrection from the dead and caused an argument between the Pharisees and Sadducees. It got so heated the commander had Paul taken away. The Lord encouraged Paul that night and told him he would eventually testify in Rome. Forty men made a vow not to eat or drink until Paul was dead. Paul's nephew heard about this plot and warned the guards. The commander had Paul transferred, under tight security, to Governor Felix in Caesarea.

ACTS 24

The high priest Ananias took a lawyer named Tertullus to Caesarea to bring charges against Paul before the governor. The lawyer accused Paul of stirring up riots and trying to desecrate the temple. Paul spoke, denying all charges. He claimed his faith was the same as his accusers, both of them looking forward to the resurrection of the dead. Felix ordered Paul to be watched under guard. Felix's Jewish wife, Drusilla, wanted to hear Paul speak. As Paul talked about matters such as righteousness and self-control, Felix stopped him. Two years later, Porcius Festus succeeded Felix and left Paul in prison.

ACTS 25

King Festus went to Jerusalem to discuss Paul's matter with the chief priests and Jewish leaders. They wanted Paul transferred to Jerusalem. Festus didn't know this was a plot to kill Paul along the way. Festus returned with the Jews to face Paul. Paul appealed to Caesar and Festus granted him the privilege to face Caesar. Later, King Agrippa and his wife Bernice came to town and Festus discussed the perplexing case with them. King Agrippa and Bernice wanted to hear Paul so they were paraded in to meet him.

ACTS 26

King Agrippa allowed Paul to speak and Paul told them his testimony—about his own zeal to persecute the followers of Christ, putting them in prison and hunting them down. Then Paul said he heard from Jesus on the road to Damascus and it changed his life. Paul stayed obedient to that vision. Festus called Paul insane. Agrippa said Paul did nothing wrong and could have been released if he didn't appeal to Caesar.

ACTS 27

Paul and other prisoners set sail for Italy but a terrible wind and storm pounded the ship. Paul warned them about moving forward but the centurion did not listen. When all seemed lost, Paul told them that no one would perish if they followed his instructions. They ate, were encouraged and eventually ran the ship into the sandbar of an island. All 276 people were safe.

ACTS 28

The crew washed up on the island of Malta and the people there welcomed them. Paul gathered firewood and a viper bit him. The people expected him to die, as judgment for something he did wrong, but he did not. The chief official welcomed them into his home and Paul healed his father, sick from dysentery. Everyone on the island brought their sick to Paul. Three months later, they set sail for Rome where Paul lived in a rented house under guard. He met local Jewish leaders and proclaimed the Gospel for two years with boldness.

ROMANS

Number of Chapters: 16
The Author: Paul while in Corinth
Approximately written: 57 AD (to the church in Rome)

ROMANS 1

Paul stated that he was called to be an apostle to spread the Gospel to the Gentiles. He longed to visit Rome to encourage them with his spiritual gifts. He felt obligated to reach both the Greeks and non-Greeks without any shame of the Gospel. God has made himself known through his creation, so people have always known he was there. However, they have worshipped his created images instead of the Creator. God gave them over to their shameful lusts and their minds have become filled with all kinds of wrong.

ROMANS 2

You can't pass judgment on people when you are committing the same sins. That just stores up God's wrath against you. Hearing God's law does not make you righteous. Obeying God's law declares you righteous. Gentiles who do by their very nature the things of the law show that the law is written on their hearts. Being a Jew doesn't make you righteous unless you are following the law that you preach. It's not about appearances but your heart.

ROMANS 3

Some believed that their unrighteousness brought out God's righteousness and glory more powerfully. They do evil so good may come out of it? Let them be condemned. There is no one good or righteous. Everyone sins and no one has the fear of God in them. People can only be declared righteous through faith in Jesus Christ, not by their works. Jesus Christ demonstrated true righteousness. This truth is for the Gentiles and the Jews.

ROMANS 4

Was Abraham justified by works? Scripture said he believed God and was credited with righteousness. This happened before circumcision, so he was the father of all who believe and were not circumcised. Abraham did not receive the promise because of the law, but by faith. He was an old man and his wife barren, yet he believed God would produce offspring through him. We must have this same kind of belief that Jesus Christ died for our sins and was raised to life for our justification.

ROMANS 5

We have peace with God, justified by our faith in Jesus Christ, who died for the ungodly. God showed his love for us by allowing Christ to die for sinners. We have been reconciled to God. Sin entered the world through one man, causing death. If unrighteousness entered through one man, then righteousness also entered the world through one man. The law increased sin, but grace increased all the more.

ROMANS 6

We cannot go on sinning to see more grace. We have died to sin. We were raised to live a new life. Our old self was crucified and done away with. Now we live with Christ. He died for sin once for all. Death has no mastery over him and sin should not have a hold on us. We have been set free from our slavery to sin and now we are slaves to God. The wages of sin is death but the gift of God is eternal life through Christ Jesus our Lord.

ROMANS 7

Like a widow no longer bound to her husband by the contract of marriage, so are people no longer bound to the sinful passion of their old life. They now belong to Christ. The law is not sinful. The law points out sin. Once sin is recognized, sin springs to life. So the law leads to our deaths. The law is holy and spiritual and we are not. We do things which we have no idea why we do them. We love the law, but sin wages war against us and takes us prisoner. Thank God he rescues us!

ROMANS 8

There is no condemnation for those who are in Christ Jesus because the law of the spirit sets us free from the law of sin and death. We do not live according to the flesh which is hostile to God. We have the spirit of Christ who raised Jesus from the dead and now lives in us. This makes us children of God, co-heirs with Christ. Our present circumstances do not compare to the glory that will be revealed in us. All of creation hopes for this future adoption. In the meantime, the Spirit helps us, praying and interceding for us. God works this all out for good. He put this plan into place that we would be adopted as brothers and sisters of Christ. God is for us. No one can condemn us. We are more than conquerors. Nothing can separate us from the love of God.

ROMANS 9

Paul wished he could be cut off for his people. God wanted them to be adopted through an ancestry that began with Abraham. However, adoption into God's family is really not by physical descent. God raised the Jews up to proclaim his name. He showed mercy on who he wanted to show mercy and nobody could really complain. All throughout the Old Testament, God preferred these people over those and wiped out people groups. So why can't the Gentiles obtain righteousness if God wants them to? The Israelites had it yet stumbled.

ROMANS 10

Paul wanted his Israelites to be saved. They were zealous for God but it was not a zeal based on knowledge. People must declare with their mouth that Jesus is Lord and know in their hearts that God raised them from the dead to be saved. Everyone who calls on the name of the Lord can be saved. People have to hear this message and we must bring it to them. Throughout the Old Testament, God brought his message to those who were obstinate and did not seek Him.

ROMANS 11

God had not rejected Israel, but raised up a remnant, like in the days of Elijah, to carry on the faith. The Gentiles were like branches grafted into the root. They were not superior in any way, but brought in through God's kindness. God could graft back in the other branches from Israel at any time. God had hardened the hearts of the Israelites so that the Gentiles could come in. They all could receive God's mercy according to his master plan.

ROMANS 12

People must offer their bodies as living sacrifices, never thinking more highly of themselves than they should. A body has many members, all working toward the same function. Use your gifts, doing it diligently, with mercy and cheer. Love must be sincere, even blessing those who persecute you, rejoicing with those who rejoice and mourning with those who mourn. You must associate with people of lower status. Do not repay evil for evil.

ROMANS 13

We must be subject to the governing authorities – paying taxes and obeying them – for they are there because God put them there. We owe each other a debt of love, fulfilling the commandments which are summed up in the command of loving our neighbor as ourselves. Wake up. The time is soon coming. Don't sin, thinking about how to gratify the flesh.

ROMANS 14

We must accept those people who have weak faith. One can eat anything, while another is weak, eating only vegetables. Why judge them? Some treat certain days more holy than others. We all must live or die for the Lord. At one point every knee will bow and every tongue will confess Jesus is Lord, so stop judging and putting stumbling blocks in people's way. God's kingdom is not about matters of eating and drinking

ROMANS 15

Paul felt people's focus should be on those weaker and not just on pleasing themselves. Everything written in the past was to teach us and give us endurance and hope. Paul felt his call to be a servant to the Gentiles, to spread the Gospel in places where it had not reached. Paul hoped to make it to Rome on his way to Spain. At the time of the letter, he was heading to Jerusalem since Macedonia and Achaia made contributions for the poor in that city. It showed the Gentiles blessing the Jews for their blessing of faith. Paul asked for prayers of protection.

ROMANS 16
Paul asked that a number of people be greeted at the church in Rome, including Priscilla and Aquila, who risked their lives. He also warned against those who caused division. Paul then passed on greetings from people on his end (including Timothy) and closed hoping all Gentiles come to faith through Jesus Christ.

1 CORINTHIANS

Number of Chapters: 16
The Author: Paul while in Ephesus
Approximately written: 53-55 AD (to the church in Corinth)

1 CORINTHIANS 1

Paul thanked God for the church in Corinth, urging them not to lack any spiritual gift as they wait for Jesus Christ. He appealed for no divisions, segregating themselves over who they were following – Paul, Apollos, Cephas, Christ. The message of the cross, Paul said, was foolishness to the dying and the foolish things of God were still wiser than anything humans could come up with. That was the wisdom they could boast about.

1 CORINTHIANS 2

Paul claimed he did not come to them with eloquent or persuasive speech, but only the message of Christ crucified. The Spirit of God had revealed these things to them. This was true wisdom, not from humans but a spiritual reality.

1 CORINTHIANS 3

What was all this jealousy and quarreling amongst them, Paul wondered. Paul planted the seeds, Apollos watered and God made them grow. Paul laid a foundation which was Jesus Christ. Others may try to build their foundation on worldly things, but that would be tested with fire and destroyed. We are God's temple and God's spirit resides in us. Don't be deceived.

1 CORINTHIANS 4

As apostles, Paul said they needed to be faithful to the message. They have been put on display, a spectacle to the whole universe, fools for Christ. They went hungry and homeless, persecuted and slandered – the scum of the earth. Paul asked that the people imitate him so he sent Timothy to them to teach and remind them. Don't become arrogant, as some have become. Paul didn't want to have to come and visit them personally. It was their choice – should he come with a rod of discipline or a gentle spirit?

1 CORINTHIANS 5

Paul cannot believe he heard that there was a man from their church that was sleeping with his father's wife. And the congregation was proud? Paul insisted that they remove this person from their midst. A little yeast can infect the whole batch. They cannot associate with brothers or sisters who commit these kinds of sexually immoral sins.

1 CORINTHIANS 6

Paul told the church to settle their own internal matters and not to drag each other into court in front of unbelievers. Why cheat and do wrong against each other? The body was not meant for sexual immorality, but for the Lord. If you unite with a prostitute, you become one with her body and you unite Christ with a prostitute. Flee from these sexual sins. Your bodies are temples of the Holy Spirit. You were bought with a price so honor God with your body.

1 CORINTHIANS 7

Paul said it was good for a man not to have sexual relations with a woman, except for married couples. A married couple do not have authority over their own bodies and must come together so they won't be tempted. If unmarried people were tempted, they should marry. Married couples should not separate, except for a time leading to reconciliation. Divorce was out of the question. Those married to an unbeliever must remain married, for they could introduce their unbelieving spouse to salvation. But if people were unmarried, Paul thought it best for them to remain so. Married people are concerned about pleasing their spouse and the things of this world. Unmarried can focus on the Lord.

1 CORINTHIANS 8

Regarding food sacrificed to idols, we all know idols don't exist and there's only one God, but some who are weaker in faith don't know that. We may have the right to eat food sacrificed to idols, yet it would better that we don't so a weaker brother or sister does not fall into sin.

1 CORINTHIANS 9

Paul made a case that he had the same rights as other apostles, especially to be paid for preaching. He felt he should reap the benefits of his job, even if it were in some way materially (just like those who serve in the temple). However, he would do it for free and could not imagine not preaching the Gospel. He became weak for the weak and all things for all people to save some. All runners run but not all get the prize—a prize/crown that will not last forever. Paul did not want to be disqualified for that prize.

1 CORINTHIANS 10

Paul remembered their ancestors who God was displeased with because they were idolaters and tested God. Their stories were warnings to keep us from temptations that have always been common to man. God always provides a way out of those temptations. So flee from idolatry and do not eat the sacrifices of idols and arouse Lord's jealousy. We have the right to do anything, but in the process we could cause others to stumble. Seek the good of others, not just yourself.

1 CORINTHIANS 11

Paul detailed some rules about worship that were proper for each gender. These rules communicated tradition and authority since apparently people were blurring the lines. Also, while they ate the Lord's Supper, they treated it as a time to eat and get drunk, forgetting the focus of the practice – the crucifixion of Jesus Christ. Before they took communion, the people needed to evaluate themselves or face judgment.

1 CORINTHIANS 12

There are lots of gifts but the same Spirit distributes them all. All the gifts are for the common good – wisdom, knowledge, faith, healing, miracles, prophecy, discernment, tongues. The body has many parts and no part is greater than the other. They all need each other – eyes don't reject hands and the head can't reject the feet. So there can't be division over gifts. All of us are a part of the body of Christ.

1 CORINTHIANS 13

Speaking in tongues, prophesizing and giving mean nothing if they aren't done with love. Love is patient, kind, not envious, not boastful, not proud, does not dishonor, not selfish, not angered, keeps no record of wrongs, does not delight in evil, protects, trusts, hopes, perseveres. It never fails. Prophecies, tongues and knowledge will all end one day, but not love. It's time to put our childish ways behind us, even though we only see and know God in part. One day we will see him fully. As for faith, hope and love, the greatest is love.

1 CORINTHIANS 14

Paul felt prophecy was a gift one should eagerly desire because it edifies the church. Speaking in tongues edifies only the person speaking unless there is an interpreter. The things said in church must be clear and intelligible, just like notes from a musical instrument. Paul would rather speak five intelligible words in church than 10,000 words in tongues. Everything must happen to build up the church and done in an orderly manner.

1 CORINTHIANS 15

Jesus Christ died for our sins, then was resurrected, appearing first to Cephas (Peter), the Twelve, over 500 brothers and sisters, then James, the apostles and then to Paul, who felt he didn't even deserve to be called an apostle because of his persecution of the church. Now Paul worked hard to preach that Christ rose from the dead. For if there was no resurrection, then their preaching was useless as was their faith. If Christ was not raised, we are still in our sins and we won't be resurrected either. Christ was the first resurrection of the dead and it all came from him, just as all death came from one man (Adam) so will death come from one man (Jesus). The last thing to be destroyed will be death. The dead will be sown perishable but raised imperishable, in a different body—spiritual and heavenly. Those who are not dead when Jesus returns will be changed instantly, in a flash and a twinkling of the eye. Death has no victory.

1 CORINTHIANS 16

Paul concluded by asking the church to make financial collections to send to Jerusalem before he arrived. He had a couple stops to make first then he promised to come to Corinth. In the meantime, Paul was sending Timothy and Apollos. The churches in Asia sent their greetings and Paul, with his own handwriting, concluded the letter.

2 CORINTHIANS

Number of Chapters: *13*
The Author: *Paul while in Macedonia*
Approximately written: *55-57 AD (to the church in Corinth)*

2 CORINTHIANS 1

Paul wrote to the church in Corinth, praising God who comforts us in our troubles. The church of Corinth shared in Paul's comfort and suffering. Paul told them about his troubles in the province of Asia, a death sentence, yet God delivered his team. Paul wanted to visit Corinth after Macedonia, but for their sake he did not come.

2 CORINTHIANS 2

Paul spoke about his last letter to them, which was not meant to cause them grief but to help them understand his great love for them. Paul then spoke about those who caused grief that they should be forgiven, so Satan does not outwit all of them. Paul said Christians needed to be a pleasing aroma of Christ among the saved and the perishing. Not for any profit, but out of sincerity.

2 CORINTHIANS 3

Paul called the church letters of testimony, read by everyone, not written with ink or on tablets of stone, but on human hearts. This was a letter of the Spirit. Those letters written on stone during the time of Moses brought glory to God. Shouldn't the Spirit's ministry be more glorious? The law brought condemnation and was still glorious. What about the ministry that brings righteousness? It can't compare. Just as Moses put a veil over his face after he was with God and saw the people, so also a veil goes over the hearts of men when they hear the law. When someone turns to God, the veil goes away and there is freedom to transform into God's image.

2 CORINTHIANS 4

Paul said that they don't use deceptive, secret or shameful ways to distort God's word. There is nothing hidden.

If anything is hidden, it's because the enemy blinds the minds of unbelievers. We have treasures in these fragile human bodies that are being hard pressed and persecuted so others may live. Our hope rests that the same spirit who raised Jesus from death will raise us. So don't lose heart. We may be wasting away, but we are achieving an eternal glory better than all this. We must not fix our eyes on what is seen, but what is unseen.

2 CORINTHIANS 5

Paul said that we live now in these earthly tents, but we groan, longing to live in our heavenly home, in the presence of the Lord. But first we will all have to appear before the judgment seat for the things we did in this body. If we are in Christ, we are a new creation – the old is gone, the new has come. This is all part of Christ's reconciliation of us to God. We are his ambassadors.

2 CORINTHIANS 6

Paul asked that the Corinthian church did not receive God's grace in vain. No stumbling block should be put in anyone's path, so they needed to show their selves in the way they endured great hardships, the way they talked, the way they reacted and the way they lived, whether rich or poor. Paul wanted them to be honest with him. He warned them against marrying unbelievers, which was like putting Christ with an idol or an idol in the temple. It doesn't work.

2 CORINTHIANS 7

Paul stated that he spoke to the Corinthians with great frankness but great pride. Titus told him about the church's longing for Paul, their great sorrow and concern, which encouraged Paul and brought joy. He knew his previous letter hurt them, but it led to godly sorrow, not worldly sorrow. Godly sorrow leads to repentance and salvation. Paul wrote that first letter so this would happen. Titus bragged about the church and that made Paul glad.

2 CORINTHIANS 8

Paul recognized the giving heart of the Macedonia churches who gave from their extreme poverty and exceeded Paul's expectations. Paul wanted the Corinthians to exceed in everything, including giving. Jesus, though he was rich, became poor so that others could be rich. So Titus was going to Corinth to receive the collection with two other men who were highly praised in the churches. Paul wanted the Corinthians to prove to these men their love.

2 CORINTHIANS 9

Paul commended the Corinthian church since their enthusiasm to give stirred the Macedonians into action. Paul wanted to make sure the Corinthians were giving so his confidence would not lead to his shame. If you sow sparingly, you reap sparingly. God loves cheerful givers. A gift supplies seed to sowers to enlarge a harvest of righteousness. And, because of the Corinthians' gift, it brought praise and thanks from others for their generosity.

2 CORINTHIANS 10

Paul said he was a timid guy when he was with them, but bold when he was away. He didn't want to be bold when he showed up. We all live in the world, but we don't fight like the world. We have weapons of divine power and we must take captive every thought, making them obedient to God. Paul didn't want to frighten them with his letters though some say his letters were more impressive then he himself in person. Paul did not want to boast about himself, but in the power of the Lord. It is God's commendation we seek, not other people's favor.

2 CORINTHIANS 11

Paul warned the church not to put up with doctrines about Jesus, the Spirit or the gospel that was different than what they know. Paul took support from other churches to come to them because he loved them. These other false teachers wanted to be equal to him and came as servants of righteousness, yet even Satan masquerades as an angel of light. Paul asked that they put up with him a little longer. He had worked so hard and endured so much persecution (flogged, beaten, stoned, shipwrecked, on the run, starving, cold and hungry). Paul was not boasting about himself, only his weakness. He was also captured in the city of Damascenes but was lowered over the wall in a basket to escape.

2 CORINTHIANS 12

Paul didn't want to go on boasting except regarding his weaknesses. God gave him a thorn in the flesh, a messenger of Satan, to torment him. Three times he prayed for it to go away, but God said his grace was sufficient. Because of this Paul delighted in weakness. Paul was ready to visit them a third time and he was afraid they would not be ready. He didn't want to find the church in a state of discord and was afraid that he would grieve over their sin.

2 CORINTHIANS 13

Paul wanted to visit a third time but will not put up with those who sinned earlier. The people needed to examine and test themselves. Paul wrote to them so they could clean up their act, then, when he arrived, he didn't have to use a harsh tone. He ended the letter telling them to strive for restoration and live in peace.

GALATIANS

Number of Chapters: 6
The Author: *Paul*
Approximately written: *49-50 AD (to the churches in Galatia)*

GALATIANS 1

Paul was astonished that the church in Galatia so quickly deserted the gospel of Christ. Anyone – person or angel – who preached a gospel other than the truth they previously heard from Paul, would be cursed. Paul never tried to win the approval of men. Paul received the gospel by a revelation from Jesus Christ. After persecuting the church and being called by God, Paul went to Arabia, Damascus then three years later to Jerusalem to get acquainted with Cephas/Peter and James, the Lord's brother. Then he visited churches in Syria and Cilicia.

GALATIANS 2

After fourteen years, Paul went to Jerusalem with Barnabas and Titus to meet with leaders about his message to the Gentiles. They were facing pressure on the issue of circumcision. Yet Paul felt compelled to preach to the uncircumcised. James, Cephas/Peter and John gave Paul their blessing. Later, Paul opposed Cephas/Peter saying he ate with the Gentiles yet pulled away when the circumcision group showed up. Paul said we are not justified by the law, but by faith in Jesus Christ. We died to the law to live for God. We have been crucified with Christ so we no longer live, but Christ lives in us.

GALATIANS 3

Paul wondered how they got bewitched by the law. Did they receive the Spirit by the law? Did they do miracles by the law? Abraham believed God and it was credited to him as righteousness. Before the law, God promised that all nations would be blessed (Gentiles too). Those who rely on faith were blessed with Abraham. If you rely on the law you are cursed because you don't have faith. The law pointed out transgressions until the promised one, Jesus Christ, would come to mediate the situation. The law guarded them until Christ came. Now all of us – Jew/Gentile, slave/free, male/female – are no longer under the law, but one in Christ according to his promise.

GALATIANS 4

Paul said God sent his Spirit into our hearts so we would know we are God's adopted sons. And since we are sons, we are heirs too. Why did the church in Galatia reject this message? Paul wished he could be with them because he was perplexed. It's like Hagar and Sarah. Hagar was a slave and had Abraham's son by the flesh. Sarah was a free woman and had Abraham's son because of a promise. These women represent the two covenants – the law makes you a slave and the promise makes you free. Slaves don't share in the inheritance. The free ones do.

GALATIANS 5

Christ set us free, so why return to slavery? If people return to the law of circumcision, then Christ becomes worthless. People must return to following the whole law and they have all fallen away from grace. It's not about circumcision! But faith expressing itself in love. The church ran a good race then someone cut them off. All it took was a little yeast to work its way into the whole dough. Live free, people! Serve one another humbly in love. Love your neighbor as yourself. Walk by the Spirit, not the law. The acts of flesh are obvious – immorality, impurity, hatred, jealousy, etc. People that do those things aren't getting into heaven. Live by the fruits of the Spirit – love, joy, peace, patience, kindness, goodness, faithfulness, gentleness and self-control. There's no law about that! Crucify the flesh and its passions and live by the spirit.

GALATIANS 6

Restore someone gently who has sinned. Carry each other's burdens. Don't take pride and compare yourself to others. Don't be deceived. Don't sow things in the flesh or you will reap destruction. Please the Spirit and do good. Don't boast about circumcision. Boast about the cross of Jesus Christ.

EPHESIANS

Number of Chapters: 6
The Author: *Paul while under arrest in Rome*
Approximately written: *60 AD (to the church in Ephesus)*

EPHESIANS 1

Paul wrote to the people in Ephesus praising God for choosing all them to be holy and blameless in his sight. God predestined us for adoption through Jesus Christ, who redeemed us by his blood. Now we know God's will until the time when everything in heaven and earth will be under Christ. We were chosen by God's plan then marked with a seal, guaranteeing our inheritance. This mark is the Holy Spirit. Paul was pleased to hear about the faith of love coming from the Ephesian church. Paul prayed that God would give them greater wisdom, revelation, hope and power. The kind of power God used to raise Jesus from the dead and which he now receives sitting at the right hand of God.

EPHESIANS 2

We were dead, gratifying the cravings of the flesh, but because of God's great love for us, he made us alive through Christ. We are saved by grace through faith, not works. We were created in Christ to do good works. Those who were Gentiles were separated by God, but now Christ reconciled the two groups into one, preaching peace to those near (Jews) and far away (Gentiles). The Gentiles are no longer foreigners, but part of God's holy building plan with Jesus as the chief cornerstone.

EPHESIANS 3

Paul, a prisoner of Christ for the Gentiles, wanted the church to understand the mystery of Christ that the Gentiles were co-heirs to the Gospel with Israel. Paul saw himself as a servant of this gospel by grace to make known this truth through the church. Through faith, now, we can approach God with freedom and confidence. Paul prayed that God would strengthen the Ephesians, dwell in their hearts and that they would understand just how huge was the love of Christ. God can do more than we ever could think or imagine.

EPHESIANS 4

Paul encouraged the church to be humble, gentle, patient, loving and keep the unity. There is only one body, one spirit, one hope, one Lord, one faith, one baptism, one God and Father of all. Christ gave himself to all the leaders of the church to equip the people for service, to achieve a unity of faith. We cannot be infants, tossed about by every deceitful teaching that comes around, but grow and build up the body in love. Christians cannot live like the Gentiles. They must put off the old self and put on the new, created to be like God in holiness. So speak the truth, don't get angry, don't steal, work hard and don't let unwholesome talk come from your mouth. This just grieves the Holy Spirit.

EPHESIANS 5

God's children must walk in love without the slightest hint of sexual immorality. They shouldn't even talk with any obscenity, foolishness or coarse talking. They must be children of light, not darkness, exposing dark deeds since it will all come to light. Make the most of every opportunity. Don't get drunk but get filled with the Spirit. Encourage one another and give thanks. Everyone must submit to one another. Wives to their husbands, just like the church submits to Christ. Husbands must love their wives, cleansing them and making them pure, giving them as much devotion as they show their own bodies. Husbands must love their wives and wives must respect their husbands.

EPHESIANS 6

Children must obey their parents, because it's the only commandment with a promise, so things may go well with you and you may enjoy a long life on earth. Fathers must not wear out their children, driving them to anger. Slaves must respect their masters and serve them wholeheartedly. Masters must treat their slaves without threats. Christians must put on the armor of God to protect themselves from Satan's attack. We're not fighting against earthly forces, but spiritual forces. So put on the belt of truth, the breastplate of righteousness, feet fitted to be ready, the shield of faith and the helmet of salvation. Paul asked for prayer so he could speak fearlessly as an ambassador in chains. He sent Tychicus to Ephesus to inform them of his situation and to encourage them.

PHILIPPIANS

Number of Chapters: *4*
The Author: *Paul while imprisoned in Rome*
Approximately written: 62 AD (to the Christians in Philippi)

PHILIPPIANS 1

Paul and Timothy wrote to the church in Philippi. Paul gave thanks for the church, knowing God would complete the good work in them that He started. He wanted the church to have more knowledge, depth of insight, discernment and fruits of righteousness. Though Paul was in chains, the palace guards and others knew he was there for Christ. Many preached the Gospel other ways, from envy, rivalry and goodwill, and Paul was glad to hear that whatever way it occurred, Christ was being preached. For Paul, to live was Christ and to die was gain. He'd rather be with the Lord, but he had work here to do. So stand firm, church, because there will be struggles.

PHILIPPIANS 2

Paul encouraged the church to be like-minded with Christ, who himself did nothing out of selfish ambition or vain conceit. Jesus did not use his Godhood as an advantage, putting it aside and taking the nature of a servant when he became a man and humbled himself to the cross. As a result, God exalted him to the highest place where every knee will bow and every tongue confess that he is Lord. In the meantime, everyone should do everything without grumbling, being blameless and shining like stars in the sky. Paul hoped to send Timothy to them some day. Epaphroditus was delivering this letter and Paul hoped they greeted him warmly since he almost died for the work of the Lord.

PHILIPPIANS 3

If anyone had reason to put confidence in the flesh, it was Paul—circumcised, from the tribe of Benjamin, a Pharisee, a persecutor of the church. Now he considers that all a loss for the sake of Christ. Paul didn't want a righteousness from the law, but through faith in Christ. He wanted to know Christ and the power of his resurrection. Paul pressed on, forgetting what was behind—the goal to win the prize which called him to heaven. Paul wanted the church to keep their eyes on him, as a model, and not to focus on the enemies of the cross. Their mind was set on earthly things. Christians are citizens of heaven, eagerly awaiting their Savior and resurrection.

PHILIPPIANS 4

Always rejoice. Don't be anxious about anything, but pray. Allow the peace of God that passes all understanding guard your hearts and minds. Think about the true, noble, pure, admirable things. Paul thanked them for their financial gift. He appreciated it even though he learned how to be content with a lot or little. Everybody sent their greeting to Philippi, even those in Caesar's household.

COLOSSIANS

Number of Chapters: *4*
The Author: *Paul while imprisoned in Rome*
Approximately written: *60 AD (to the church in Colosse)*

COLOSSIANS 1

Paul and Timothy wrote to the church in Colossae. They gave thanks for them because they heard about the church's faith and how the gospel bore fruit. They asked God to fill them with wisdom, to live a life worthy of the Lord, to bear fruit in every good work and to grow in knowledge. God had rescued them from darkness. Jesus is the image of the invisible God, the firstborn over all creation. Everything was created through him and he holds it all together. He is the head of the church and God was pleased to have his fullness dwell in him so that the world could be reconciled to God through Jesus' blood, shed on the cross. Once we were alienated from God, but now we are reconciled. Now Paul suffered for them for the sake of the church. He was a servant to reveal the mystery of the gospel to the Gentiles.

COLOSSIANS 2

Paul wanted them to have a full understanding of Christ so they wouldn't be deceived by fine-sounding arguments and hollow and deceptive philosophies. Christ fully exhibited God in bodily form. He is head over every power and authority. Our circumcision was done by Christ, who removed our old self, ruled by flesh. We were buried with him in baptism, raised with him through faith. God forgave all our sins, canceled our legal indebtedness, nailing them to the cross. We are free from all those human rules – eating and drinking, festivals and Sabbaths – all based on human commands and teachings. They look like wisdom, but they are all about false humility and lack any value.

COLOSSIANS 3

Paul encouraged the church to set their minds on the things above, since they had been raised with Christ. They needed to put to death all those earthly desires like sexual immorality, lust, greed, anger, slander, filthy talk, lying. These are all part of the old self and its practices. Put on the new self which is being renewed in the image of its Creator. Christ is in all so be clothed in compassion, kindness, patience, forgiveness and love. Everything should be done in the name of the Lord. Wives need to submit, husbands love, children obey and slaves serve. There is no favoritism. Whatever you do, do it with all your heart as if you're working for God not man.

COLOSSIANS 4

Paul wanted the Colossians to devote themselves to prayer so more doors could open for the Gospel. He told them to be wise and to make the most of every opportunity with outsiders. Paul sent Tychicus to give them an update on their situation as well as Onesimus. Aristarchus, Mark, Justus, Epaphras and Luke all sent their greetings. Paul sent his greetings to the church at Laodicea and wanted the letter read to them. Paul signed off with his own hand and told them to remember his chains.

1 THESSALONIANS

Number of Chapters: *5*
The Author: *Paul while in Corinth*
Approximately written: 51 AD (to the churches in Thessalonica)

1 THESSALONIANS 1

Paul, Silas and Timothy wrote to the church in Thessalonica, applauding them for being imitators of them and the Lord. The power of the Holy Spirit really came upon them. They became a model to Macedonia and Achaia, then everywhere. They turned from idols to serving the living God.

1 THESSALONIANS 2

Paul looked back at their visit and the results that came of it. They listened to their challenge, which did not come from impure motives, trickery or flattery. Paul was not looking for praise from people. He genuinely cared for the people and was delighted to share the Gospel. He treated them as his own children, encouraging, comforting and urging them to live lives worthy of God. The church received God's word and, like the other churches in Judea, suffered from the Jews because they reached out to the Gentiles. Paul looked forward to seeing them again, but Satan always got in the way.

1 THESSALONIANS 3

Paul had sent Timothy to find out how the church in Thessalonica was doing. He brought back great news of the experience and it encouraged Paul and the others. He looked forward to visiting them again.

1 THESSALONIANS 4

Paul told them to avoid sexual immorality, control their bodies and live holy. They should lead a quiet life, mind their own business, work hard and don't be dependent on anybody. As for those who sleep in death, Paul wanted them to be informed because believers don't grieve without hope. Jesus died and rose again so, when he returns, he will raise those who had died in Christ first. At the voice of the archangel and the trumpet call of God, those who are alive when Jesus comes will be caught up in the air with the dead in Christ. They will all be with the Lord forever.

1 THESSALONIANS 5

The day of the Lord will come like a thief in the night. Many will say things were okay, but they will not escape. The church should not be like people of the darkness, but people of the light. Stay awake! In the meantime, work hard, encourage the disheartened, help the weak, rejoice, pray, give thanks and don't quench the spirit.

2 THESSALONIANS

Number of Chapters: *3*
The Author: *Paul while in Corinth*
Approximately written: *51-52 AD (to the church in*
                           Thessalonica)

2 THESSALONIANS 1

Paul, Silas and Timothy wrote another letter to the church of the Thessalonians. They gave thanks for them and their growth. Paul and the others boasted about them to other churches, especially about how they suffer for the kingdom. But God will pay the persecutors back. On that day, Jesus will be revealed from heaven and punish them with an everlasting destruction and come into eternal glory. They prayed for the church that their desires would come to fruition.

2 THESSALONIANS 2

Paul wanted to make sure they knew that Christ had not come. A man of lawlessness needed to come first. He will oppose and exalt himself above everything that was godly and proclaim himself as God. The lawless one will appear but Jesus will overthrow him with just his breath. The lawless one will deceive with lies and false miracles. God sent a delusion to see who will believe a lie.

2 THESSALONIANS 3

Paul asked for prayer to spread the message of the Lord. He warned against believers who were idle and disruptive. If they don't work, they shouldn't be allowed to eat. Many have become busybodies and people should not associate with them.

1 TIMOTHY

Number of Chapters: *6*
The Author: *Paul*
Approximately written: *64 AD (to Timothy, the pastor at Ephesus)*

1 TIMOTHY 1

Paul wrote to Timothy in Ephesus and told him to stop people from teaching false doctrines, myths and endless genealogies. These cause meaningless controversies. These people wanted to be teachers of the law, but the law is for the unrighteous. Paul himself was once a persecutor and a violent man, but God's grace poured out on him abundantly and Jesus came to save sinners, which Paul said he was the worst of all. He told Timothy to keep fighting the battles against those who have shipwrecked their faith, especially Hymenaeus and Alexander.

1 TIMOTHY 2

Paul asked that people pray for their leaders. God wanted all people to be saved and to come to a knowledge of the truth. There is one God and one mediator between God and man, Jesus Christ. Men should pray and women should dress modestly. Women should also learn quietness and submission. A woman cannot have authority over a man. She was deceived first, not Adam. Women are saved through childbearing if they continue to have faith, love and holiness.

1 TIMOTHY 3

Paul gave qualifications for an overseer – above reproach, faithful to his wife, temperate, self-controlled, respectable, hospitable, teachable, not a drunkard, not violent, not quarrelsome and not greedy. He must manage his family well and cannot be a recent convert. Deacons must be worthy of respect, not heavy drinkers, not pursuers of dishonest gain, faithful to his wife and manage his household well. The women should be worthy of respect, not malicious talkers, temperate and trustworthy.

1 TIMOTHY 4

Paul warned Timothy that in the later times people would abandon their faith, follow deceiving spirits and hypocritical liars. Timothy must point these things out! He cannot follow godless myths and old wives' tales, but command and teach the truth. Timothy must not let people look down on him because he was young, but set an example. He could not neglect his gift, given to him by prophecy and the laying on of hands. Timothy must watch his life closely.

1 TIMOTHY 5

Paul told Timothy not to rebuke an older man harshly and to treat them like fathers, older women like mothers and the younger ones like brothers and sisters. Widows must be cared for, but only those sixty or older who have a good reputation and took care of their family. People should take care of their own families or they are acting worse than an unbeliever. Younger widows should not be on the list because many want to remarry. Besides, some of them become busybodies. The church must be able to help those who really needed it. Elders who oversee the church deserve honor and any accusations against them must include two or more witnesses. Don't show favoritism.

1 TIMOTHY 6

Slaves should show their masters respect, especially if those masters are believers. As for false teachers, they have an unhealthy interest in controversies and quarrels about words. People must be godly and content with simple food and clothing. The rich fall into traps of temptation, plunging people into ruin. The love of money is the root of all kinds of evil. Many wander from the faith. Pursue righteousness. Fight the good fight of faith. The rich must not be arrogant and do good deeds instead. Don't put your hope in riches, but in God.

2 TIMOTHY

Number of Chapters: *4*
The Author: *Paul while imprisoned in Rome*
Approximately written: *67 AD (to Timothy, the pastor at Ephesus)*

2 TIMOTHY 1

Paul wrote to Timothy, saying he constantly prayed for him and remembered his sincere faith which he first saw in his grandmother Lois and mother Eunice. Paul encouraged Timothy to keep using his gifts. The spirit of God does not make us timid, but gives us power, love and self-discipline. There is no reason to be ashamed. God will guard us. Everyone had deserted Paul in Asia while people like Onesiphorus searched hard for Paul in Rome until he found him.

2 TIMOTHY 2

Paul told Timothy to pass on the things he learned to reliable people who could teach others. But there were those out there who loved to quarrel about simple words. Just godless chatter! Some said the resurrection had already taken place. God knew who those people were. So pursue righteousness, faith, love and peace. Stay out of arguments. Gently instruct opponents with the hope that they will come to their senses.

2 TIMOTHY 3

Paul warned that in these final days people will become lovers of self, lovers of money, boastful, unholy, brutal, treacherous, lovers of pleasure. They will work their ways into people's homes and control gullible women. They will have depraved minds. Paul was persecuted and remained patient, full of love and preserved. He urged Timothy to do the same as things got worse. Stay in the Scriptures. It's from God and useful for teaching, rebuking, correcting and training in righteousness, to equip all servants for good works.

2 TIMOTHY 4

Paul encouraged Timothy to preach the word, in season and out of season. The time will come when people will not tolerate sound doctrine and so, to suit their own desires, will turn to teachers who say what their itching ears want to hear. They will turn to myths. Continue to do the work of an evangelist! Paul was being poured out. His departure was near. He had fought the good fight, finished the race and kept the faith. A crown of righteousness awaited him. He greeted many as the letter closed. Only Luke was with him and he hoped Mark could join them soon. Alexander, a metalworker, did a great deal of harm to Paul, but the Lord gave Paul strength and the message was proclaimed.

TITUS

Number of Chapters: *3*
The Author: *Paul*
Approximately written: *64 AD (to Titus, the overseer of*
                                    churches in Crete)

TITUS 1

Paul wrote to Titus and told him he left him in Crete to complete the unfinished work and find elders in every town. They must be blameless, faithful to their wife, with believing children. As for the overseer, they too must be blameless, not quick-tempered, not a drunkard, not violent, but hospitable, self-controlled, upright and hold firm to the message. There were rebellious people around, especially from the circumcision group. They must be silenced. Many claimed to know God but their actions deny it.

TITUS 2

Paul told Titus to teach the older men to be temperate, respectable, self-controlled and sound in their faith. He told Titus to teach the older women to be reverent, not slanderers or addicted to much wine. The older women could then teach the younger women to be self-controlled and pure, busy at home and subject to their husbands. The younger men had to be encouraged and self-controlled. Slaves needed to be subject to their masters, not to talk back or steal from them. Grace offers salvation to all people, teaching them to say "no" to ungodliness and worldly passions. Jesus will appear, who gave himself to redeem us from all wickedness. Encourage and rebuke with authority, Titus!

TITUS 3

The people must be subject to rulers, obedient, without slander, peaceable and considerate. One time we were all disobedient fools, but when we encountered the kindness and love of God our Savior, things changed. Through mercy we were washed by the Holy Spirit, poured out generously through Jesus Christ, saving us and justifying us by his grace. We are heirs with hope of eternal life. No more foolish controversies, genealogies, arguments and quarrels about the law can be tolerated. Warn a divisive person once then twice, then have nothing to do with them. Paul wanted Titus to meet him in Nicopolis where he wanted to winter. Everyone must devote themselves to what is good!

PHILEMON

Number of Chapters: 1
The Author: *Paul while under arrest in Rome*
Approximately written: *60 AD (to Philemon, a member of the Colossian church)*

PHILEMON

Paul, a prisoner, and Timothy wrote to Philemon (and Apphia and Archippus) saying he heard of his love for God's people and his faith in Jesus. Paul could be bold and order him to do something, yet he preferred to appeal in love for Onesimus, Philemon's runaway slave, who became a son to Paul while in prison. He had become very useful to Paul and he wanted to keep him around, but not without Philemon's consent. Paul sent Onesimus back, hoping Philemon would see that maybe he ran away as a slave, only to return as a brother. Paul wanted to pay for any wrongs Onesimus did and he reminded Philemon that he owed him his very life. Paul told Philemon to prepare a room for him. Epaphras, Mark, Aristarchus, Demas and Luke all sent their greetings.

HEBREWS

Number of Chapters: *13*
Author Unknown: *Possibly Paul, Apollos, Barnabas, Luke,*
                         Philip
Approximately written: 64-68 AD (to Jewish Christians)

HEBREWS 1

God spoke through prophets at many times and in many ways, but in these last days, he spoke through Jesus Christ, the heir of all things, the creator, the radiance of his glory, the exact representation of his being. He is superior to the angels and the angels worship him. Angels serve and minister to those inheriting salvation.

HEBREWS 2

God announced salvation and confirmed it through signs, wonders, miracles and gifts of the Holy Spirit. Jesus was made a little lower than angels for a time, now is crowned with all glory and honor. He brought many sons and daughters to glory and now that they are holy, he calls them brothers and sisters. Since the people are flesh and blood, he too shared in their humanity so his death could break the power of death and free those held in slavery and fear. Jesus was made like them to be a faithful high priest and to make atonement for the sins of the people. He suffered and was tempted to help those being tempted.

HEBREWS 3

All thoughts must be fixed on Jesus. He was faithful as the Son over God's house and found worthy of a greater honor than Moses. Don't harden your heart. God was angry at their ancestors in the wilderness because their hearts went astray. Encourage each other daily so no one is hardened by sin's deceitfulness.

HEBREWS 4

Believers enter into true Sabbath rest, where they rest from their works, as God rested from his. We must make every effort to enter that rest. The word of God is alive and active, sharp and penetrating. Nothing is hidden from God. Everything is uncovered. Jesus is our great high priest, who can empathize with us, was tempted yet did not sin. We can approach God's throne with confidence.

HEBREWS 5

A high priest was selected from the people and appointed to represent the people, offering gifts and sacrifices for sins. He offered sacrifices for his own sins. He became a high priest when called by God. Christ did not take on the job of a high priest. He was God's son and had been a priest forever like Melchizedek. While on Earth, Christ prayed for the people, learned obedience through suffering and was a perfect sacrifice as a source of eternal salvation. He was designated to be a high priest like Melchizedek. This is a hard concept to understand. Many need milk like an infant before they have the solid food, consumed by the mature.

HEBREWS 6

The writer wanted to move to more mature topics, leaving behind the elementary discussions. It's impossible for those who once shared the Holy Spirit and tasted the goodness of God's word then have fallen to ever be brought back to repentance. They can't keep crucifying Christ. God will not forget our good works. We cannot become lazy, but must stay faithful and patient to inherit what was promised. When God promises, he swears by himself, like he did with Abraham. We all swear by something greater than ourselves. When God makes an oath, it will happen because by his nature he cannot lie. That encourages us with a hope like an anchor.

HEBREWS 7

Melchizedek, king of Salem and priest of God, met Abraham after the defeat of the kings and Abraham gave him a tenth of everything. Melchizedek, whose name means "king of righteousness" and Salem which means "king of peace" was without father/mother, genealogy, beginning or end, just like the Son of God. He represents a forever priest. Abraham even gave him a tenth, just like one would give a Levite, but Levi was still an ancestor in Abraham's body. Melchizedek blessed Abraham too and the lesser is always blessed by the greater. The Levitical priesthood could not attain perfection, so a priest like a Melchizedek needed to come, not based on ancestry, but based on the power of an indestructible life. Jesus lives forever and represents the permanent priesthood, saving people completely, interceding for them, holy, blameless, pure, set apart, exalted in the heavens. He does not have to offer sacrifices day after day, first for his own sins, then for the people. He sacrificed once for all when he offered himself.

HEBREWS 8

We have a high priest in heaven who serves in the true sanctuary made by the Lord. Every high priest on earth served in a sanctuary that was a copy of what is in heaven. Jesus is superior and so the covenant is superior because it is established on better promises. The new covenant puts the law in their minds and on their hearts. This new covenant makes the first one obsolete.

HEBREWS 9

The writer created a picture of inside the temple – the lampstand, the bread, the curtains, the Most Holy Place and the ark. The priest entered that inner room only once a year, carrying blood, for the sins the people had committed in ignorance. People only carried various laws, such as food, drink and ceremonial washings, until the time came for a new plan. Christ entered the Most Holy Place not with the blood of goats and calves. He offered himself completely unblemished and became the mediator of a new covenant. A will/covenant cannot work unless the person dies and forgiveness cannot happen without the shedding of blood. Christ does not have to offer himself again and again. He died once for all, to take away all sin and he will appear again to bring salvation to those who are waiting for him.

HEBREWS 10

The law and sacrifices can never make people perfect or they would have stopped long ago. They were a reminder of sin. The blood of bulls and goat cannot take away sin. We are made holy by the sacrifice of Jesus, made one time for all time. We can draw near to God with assurance and faith. We must also draw closer to each other, encouraging one another as we meet together, especially as that final day draws near. Don't deliberately sin and trample on the blood of Christ. You don't want to fall into the hands of the living God. The writer told his readers to persevere under so much persecution. Be confident. You will be rewarded.

HEBREWS 11

Faith is confidence in what we hope for and assurance about what we don't see. Our ancestors had faith. People like Abel, Enoch, Noah, Abraham, Isaac, Jacob, Sarah and Joseph. They all believed God existed and rewarded those who sought him. They longed for a better country—a heavenly one. Others had faith such as Moses, the Israelites, Rahab, Gideon, Barak, Samson, Jephthah, David and Samuel. Many faced sword, fire, armies, jeers, flogging, chains, imprisonment and stoning. They were poor and persecuted, wandering in caves. All of them commended for their faith though they never experienced what was promised, only saw it from a distance.

HEBREWS 12

Inspired by those faithful witnesses, we throw off everything that entangles us and run with perseverance the race marked out for us. We must fix our eyes on Jesus. He endured the cross and opposition. We should endure hardship as discipline, for God disciplines us, his children, for our good, even though we don't like it at the time. Make every effort to live at peace with everyone. Don't allow any bitter root to defile others. We are approaching the city of the living God, the church of the firstborn, with thousands of angels. Jesus has mediated a new covenant with his blood. We are receiving a kingdom that cannot be shaken.

HEBREWS 13

Keep loving each other. Show hospitality to strangers for they may be angels. Remember those in prison. Keep the marriage bed pure. Be free of the love of money. Jesus Christ is always the same—yesterday, today and tomorrow—so don't be carried away by the latest, strange teachings. Offer God the sacrifice of praise. Have confidence in the leaders. May the God of peace equip you for every good work. Timothy had been released and the writer wanted to visit them with him.

JAMES

Number of Chapters: 5
The Author: *James the half-brother of Jesus*
Approximately written: *46-49 AD (to Jewish Christians)*

JAMES 1

James wrote to the twelve tribes (the Jews) among all the nations telling them to consider it joy when they face trials. These trials produce perseverance, maturity, completeness, wisdom and faith. Those who ask of God for wisdom should believe and not doubt. When tempted, don't blame God. They've allowed desire to give birth to sin, then sin leads to death. Be quick to listen, slow to speak and be angry. Get rid of all moral filth. Don't just listen to the word, do what it says and don't forget it. Pure religion looks after orphans and widows.

JAMES 2

Don't show favoritism to the rich. The poor are rich in faith while the rich exploit people and drag them to court. If you say you keep the whole law, yet stumble on one point, you break the whole law. Show mercy in your judgment. Your faith must be accompanied by deeds. You can't have one or the other. Even the demons believe and they shudder. Abraham had faith and offered his sons as a sacrifice. Rahab had faith and hid the spies. Faith without deeds is dead.

JAMES 3

Not many should be teachers because teachers are held up to a higher standard. Everyone must watch what they say. A small bit can make a horse obey. A small rudder can steer a whole ship. A small spark can set a forest on fire. A small tongue can do a lot of damage. It's untamable. A poison. We can't curse and praise from the same mouth. A spring can't produce salt and fresh water. Likewise you can't harbor bitter envy and selfish ambition. That's earthly and demonic. Sow in peace and produce a harvest of righteousness.

JAMES 4

All the fights and quarrels occur in this world because of selfish desires and wrong motives. People want to be friends with the world and, in the process, they become enemies with God. So submit to God and resist the devil. Don't slander each other. There is only one judge who is able to save and destroy. Who are you to judge? Don't make your plans. Your life is but a mist. You should say, "If it's the Lord's will..."

JAMES 5

James warned the rich. Their wealth had rotted and their corruption obvious. As for others, be patient until the Lord comes. Don't grumble. The judge is coming. Persevere like Job. Don't swear by heaven, just let your yes be yes and your no be no. If you're sick, let the elders anoint you with oil and make you well. Confess your sins and pray for each other. The prayer of a righteous person is powerful and effective. If anyone wanders from the truth, bring them back. You will save them from death and a multitude of sins.

1 PETER

Number of Chapters: 5
The Author: Peter
Approximately written: 60-64 AD (to Jewish and Gentile believers in Asia Minor during severe persecution by Nero)

1 PETER 1

Peter wrote to the chosen elect scattered throughout Asia. He praised God for his great mercy in sending Jesus Christ who gave us an inheritance that can never spoil. Trials have come to prove the genuineness of our faith, refined by fire. Though we do not see God, we love him and believe in him. The early prophets pointed to this time. So therefore, set your hope on Jesus Christ's coming. Don't conform to evil desires. Be holy. We are foreigners to this world. We are not saved with perishable things like silver and gold but the precious blood of Jesus.

1 PETER 2

The people need to get rid of all malice, envy and slander. They must crave spiritual milk to grow up in our salvation. Jesus is the living stone, rejected by the builders, who causes many to stumble. We too are stones being built up into a spiritual house. As believers, we were chosen, a royal priesthood, a holy nation, God's special possession. So live good lives so the pagans cannot accuse us of wrong. Submit to human authorities, emperors and governors. Live as free people who are slaves. Slaves should submit to their masters, the good and the harsh. It's commendable to be beaten for doing good. Christ was insulted and never retaliated. He bore our sins on the cross so we might die to sins. By his wounds we were healed.

1 PETER 3

Wives must submit to their unbelieving husbands and win them over with the purity and beauty of their lives, not with outward adornment. The inner spirit of gentleness is of great worth to God. Husbands must be considerate to wives and treat them with respect as a weaker partner. Be sympathetic, compassionate, humble and don't repay evil with evil. Always be prepared to give an answer for the hope that is inside you. Suffer for doing good, not evil. Christ suffered for doing good then was made alive, proclaiming victory to the spirits of Noah's time. In that day, eight people were saved through water which symbolizes baptism as the removal of shame and sin from your life.

1 PETER 4

Do not live for evil human desires. The world can't understand why a Christian refuses to engage in those things. Love each other because love covers a multitude of sins. Be hospitable. Don't grumble. Serve with God's strength. Don't be surprised by the insults and persecution you endure. Suffering as a Christian should cause no shame, because it's not like suffering as a criminal. Commit yourselves to God and do good.

1 PETER 5

To the elders, be shepherds of your flock and serve because you are willing, not pursuing dishonest gain. When the Chief Shepherd appears, you will receive a crown of glory. The younger must submit themselves to the older. Humble yourselves. Cast all anxiety on him. Be alert. Don't let the devil, who is prowling around like a lion, devour you. Resist him. God will restore you after your suffering. Silas helped Peter write this letter. Mark sent his greetings too.

2 PETER

Number of Chapters: 3
The Author: *Peter (possibly from Rome)*
Approximately written: *65-68 AD (to Christians in Asia Minor)*

2 PETER 1

Peter told believers that God had given them great promises to participate in the divine and escape evil. So make every effort in your faith to pursue goodness, knowledge, self-control, perseverance, godliness, mutual affection and love. These will make you productive for Christ. If you skip them, you are blind and forgetting that Christ forgave you. Confirm your calling. Peter not did follow cleverly devised stories about Christ. Peter witnessed it himself. He heard God speak on that sacred mountain about Jesus. The apostles had a reliable message, so pay attention to it. No prophecy was spoken according to human will, but through the Holy Spirit who spoke through humans.

2 PETER 2

There were false prophets and false teachers among the people, introducing destructive heresies. They engaged in depraved conduct and exploited followers with fabricated stories. God did not spare angels when they sinned, protected Noah, condemned Sodom and Gomorrah, rescued Lot – so God knows how to punish the lawless and protect the righteous. These unrighteous heaped abuse on celestial beings, were nothing but unreasoning animals, full of adultery and experts in greed. They were springs without water, blackest darkness, and have empty mouths. They promised freedom while they were slaves of depravity.

2 PETER 3

Peter acknowledged that this was his second letter to encourage wholesome thinking in a world that followed their own desires. The world scoffed at Jesus' coming, but don't forget, with the Lord a day is like a thousand years. He's not slow in keeping his promise. He's patient, not wanting any to perish. That day will come like a thief and everything will be gone. In light of that destruction, the people should live holy and godly lives. Make every effort to be found spotless, blameless and at peace with God. Paul wrote about these things in his letters which people distorted like other Scripture. Grow in grace and knowledge of Jesus Christ.

1 JOHN

Number of Chapters: 5
Most likely author: John
Approximately written: 85-90 AD (to the churches around
                        Rome)

1 JOHN 1

The writer testified that he heard, saw and touched the Word of life firsthand. He wrote this to make his joy complete. God is light and there's no darkness in him at all. You can't have fellowship with him and walk in darkness. You must walk in the light. If you say you don't sin, you're a liar. Confess your sins and God is faithful and just to forgive your sins and cleanse you of all unrighteousness.

1 JOHN 2

The writer wrote this so his "children" would not sin, but, if they do, they have an advocate with the Father, Jesus Christ. If you know him you would not sin. If you obey him, the love of God is truly in you. This is not a new command. You can't walk in the light and hate your brother in darkness. Don't love the world or you don't really love the Father. The lust of the flesh, the lust of the eyes and the pride of life all come from the world. Time is running out and many antichrists have arrived. Antichrists deny the Father and Son. Remain in the Son and the Father and you will have eternal life. Don't be led astray!

1 JOHN 3

We are children of God and God is our father. Christ appeared to take our sins away so we can be like the Father. Don't be led astray by the devil who has sinned since the beginning. The Son of God appeared to destroy the devil's work. You can't go on sinning. Love one another. If you hate your brother (like Cain), you're a murderer and eternal life is not in you. Love is what Jesus did when he laid down his life for us. We should do the same for others. Don't love with words, but action. In you know the truth, your heart should be at peace. So believe in Jesus Christ and love one another.

1 JOHN 4

Don't believe every spirit, but test them and see if they are from God. Here's the test: every spirit that acknowledges Jesus came in the flesh is from God. Any that deny Jesus are not from God. That's the spirit of the antichrist. Children of God have overcome these false teachers because they have something greater than the world offers. So love one another since love comes from God. There's no fear in love, because perfect love drives out fear. Fear has to do with punishment. We love because God first loved us and if you love God then you will love your brother and sister.

1 JOHN 5

Everyone who believes that Jesus is the Christ born of God is a child of God. Love is also keeping God's commands and overcoming the world. Jesus came by water and blood and these two with the Spirit testify that he's true. The testimony is that God gives us eternal life and this life is in his Son. No son...no life. John wrote this so the readers would have confidence in eternal life so everyone can be confident approaching God. If we ask anything according to his will, he hears us. Pray for those brothers and sisters committing sin that God will give them life. Anyone born of God does not sin. They know the truth – this world is controlled by the evil one and Jesus Christ is the true God, the giver of eternal life.

2 JOHN

Number of Chapters: *1*
Most likely author: *John from Ephesus*
Approximately written: *90 AD*

2 JOHN

       The elder wrote to the lady and her children who knew the truth. The elder rejoiced that many walked in the truth, but wanted to write to them about an old command – love one another. Love is walking in obedience to his commands. He said this because many deceivers among them do not acknowledge Jesus Christ came in the flesh. That kind of person is an antichrist. Don't allow them into homes or welcome them. The elder had more to say, but not with paper and ink. He hoped to visit them soon.

3 JOHN

Number of Chapters: *1*
Most likely author: *John while in Ephesus*
Approximately written: *90 AD (to Gaius a leader in a church*
                                 found in Asia Minor)

3 JOHN

      The elder wrote to Gaius saying he was glad to hear from believers how faithful he was. The elder was proud to hear good news about his child. Many of those brothers and sisters were going out into the world telling the news. The writer wrote to them before but Diotrephes, who always wants to be in charge, did not welcome them, spreading malicious nonsense instead. He refused to welcome other believers and kicked people out of the church. On the other hand Demetrius was well spoken of by everyone and the writer confirmed that. There was more to say, but not with pen and ink. Hopefully face to face.

JUDE

Number of Chapters: *1*
The Author: *Jude a brother of Jesus and James*
Approximately written: *65-80 AD*

JUDE

      Jude identified himself as a brother of James and warned those who have been called to protect the faith from individuals who have slipped in and perverted the grace of God. This had been going on since the unbelievers in the time of Moses, the angels who abandoned their dwelling place (who are now locked in chains) and the immoral people of Sodom and Gomorrah. They polluted their own bodies, rejected authority and slandered whatever they didn't understand. Irrational animals! Woe to them! They are self-serving shepherds, clouds without rain, trees without fruit. Grumblers and faultfinders. Jude told believers to build themselves up, pray to the Holy Spirit, stay in God's love as they waited for eternal life. Be merciful. Save people from the fire. Glory, majesty, power and authority to God through Jesus Christ our savior.

REVELATION

Number of Chapters: 22
The Author: *John while on the island of Patmos*
Approximately written: *95 AD (to the seven churches in Asia*
                                   Minor)

REVELATION 1

John received a vision on the island of Patmos, where he was sent because of his testimony of Christ. The vision came via an angel and was directed to the seven church in Asia. Jesus was coming in the clouds and every eye would see him, even those who pierced him. John heard a trumpet call, turned and saw seven golden lampstands. Walking among them was someone like the son of man, dressed in a robe, holding seven stars with a doubled edged sword coming from his mouth. John fell at his feet and was told to write these things down. The man was dead, but now alive and held in his hands the keys of death and Hades. The stars in his hand represented the angels/messengers of the seven churches which were the seven lampstands.

REVELATION 2

Jesus knew of the hard work and perseverance of the church in Ephesus, that they endured hardships and did not tolerate wicked people. Yet, they had forgotten their first love and needed to repent. To the church in Smyrna, Jesus said he knew their afflictions and poverty, yet they were rich. He warned them of a coming persecution and encouraged them to stay faithful. To the church in Pergamum, Jesus said he knew that Satan lived in their region and yet they remained true to God. However, some in their church held to the teachings of Balaam and the Nicolatians, so they needed to repent. To the church in Thyatira, Jesus acknowledged that they were doing more than ever before, however they tolerated a self-proclaimed prophetess named Jezebel who led some into sexual immorality and eating the food of idols. She would be punished and those that followed her. To the rest of the church, hold on until Jesus comes!

REVELATION 3

Jesus told the church in Sardis that they had a reputation for being alive, but they were dead. They needed to repent. Some had not soiled their righteousness and were worthy to be written in the book of life. To the church in Philadelphia, Jesus complimented them on holding fast despite the opposition from a synagogue of Satan. He told them he was coming soon and when he did, the victorious ones would be pillars of the temple in the New Jerusalem. As for Laodicea, they were neither hot nor cold, but lukewarm and Jesus wanted to spit them out of his mouth. They said there were rich and didn't need anything. Jesus said they were pitiful, poor, blind and naked. He stood at the door and knocked. If they would only answer and let him in.

REVELATION 4

A door opened up before John in heaven. A voice invited him up. Suddenly he was in the Spirit and saw a throne in heaven, with someone sitting on it. Around the throne were twenty-four thrones with twenty-four elders sitting on them. In front of the throne were seven lamps or the seven spirits of God. Around the throne were four living creatures with the appearance of a lion, an ox, a man and a flying eagle. They each had six wings and were covered with eyes. They kept saying "Holy, Holy, Holy is the Lord God Almighty, who was, and is and is to come."

REVELATION 5

An angel asked who was worthy to take the scroll with seven seals. John wept because no was worthy. An elder told him that the Lion of Judah, the Root of David had triumphed and could open the seal. The Lamb, who looked like he had been slain, took the scroll from the one on the throne. Then the four living creatures and the twenty-four elders fell down and worshipped, singing a new song. Tens of thousands of angels joined in and praised the Lamb. Then every creature on heaven and earth joined in.

REVELATION 6

The first seal was opened and a white horse appeared with a rider bent on conquering. The second seal was opened and a fiery red horse appeared with a rider given power to take away peace on earth. The third seal was opened and a black horse appeared with a rider holding scales. The fourth seal was opened and a pale horse of death rode out and given power to kill, wiping out a fourth of the earth. The fifth seal was opened and the souls of those martyred for their faith cried out for justice. They were given white robes and told to wait. The sixth seal was opened and there was a great earthquake. The sun turned black and the moon red. The stars fell from the sky. The kings, princes, the slaves and free all ran to caves and hid in the rocks, pleading for death. Nobody could withstand this day.

REVELATION 7

Before four angels could harm the land and sea, another angel stopped them until a seal could be put on the foreheads of the servants of God. 144,000 were sealed, 12,000 from each tribe. Then a great multitude from every nation, tribe, people and language stood before the throne wearing white robes and carrying palm branches, praising God. The angels, elders and living creatures fell down too and joined them. This great multitude were those who came through the great tribulation. They will not hunger, thirst or cry any more.

REVELATION 8

When the seventh seal was opened, seven angels were given seven trumpets. An angel with a golden censer, filled with fire from the altar, hurled it at earth causing thunder, rumblings, lightning and an earthquake. When the first angel blew the first trumpet, hail and fire hit the earth, burning up half the earth. At the second trumpet, something like a huge mountain hurled into the sea, turning the water into blood and killing a third of the creatures. At the third trumpet sound, a great blazing star named Wormwood fell into the rivers and springs and turned a third of the water bitter. At the fourth trumpet, a third of the sun, moon and stars turned dark. An eagle flew overhead and said "Woe to the people of the earth because three more trumpet blasts are coming!"

REVELATION 9

At the sound of the fifth trumpet, a star fell from the sky to earth and was given the key to the Abyss. When he opened the Abyss, locusts flew out and, like scorpions, stung those who did not have the seal on their forehead for five months. These locusts looked like horses, with something like gold crowns on their heads, human faces, women's hair, lion's teeth, breastplates and wings. The king over them, an angel, was named Abaddon (Apollyon in Greek). One woe down – two to go. The sixth angel sounded his trumpet and four angels were released from the Euphrates. Mounted troops in the thousands emerged and out of the horses' mouths came fire, smoke and sulfur. These killed a third of mankind. The rest of mankind still worshipped demons and idols and did not repent.

REVELATION 10

A mighty angel came down holding a little scroll. Seven thunders spoke and John was about to write down what they said, but the angel stopped him. There would be no more delay. The voice told John to take the scroll from the angel and eat it. It tasted sweet and turned his stomach sour. John was told to prophesy about many peoples, nations and languages.

REVELATION 11

John was given a measuring rod to measure the city. God told him he would appoint two witnesses who would prophesy for 1,260 days. If anyone tried to harm them, fire would come from their mouths. They had the power to turn the waters to blood and strike the earth with plagues. The beast would kill them and their bodies would lie in the streets. Everyone around the world would celebrate. Then three and half days later they would come back to life. A great earthquake would strike and destroy one tenth of the city. The second woe would pass. The seventh trumpet would sound and the twenty four elders fell to their faces and praised God. The temple opened and inside was the Ark of the Covenant.

REVELATION 12

John saw a great sign in heaven – a woman clothed with the sun, moon and stars all around her, giving birth to a son who would rule the nations. An enormous red dragon with seven heads, ten horns and seven crowns swept a third of the stars out of the sky and wanted to devour the child, but God protected him. A war broke out between Michael and his angels and the dragon and his angels. The dragon (the devil, Satan) was hurled down to earth. He pursued the woman but she was given wings like eagles to get away to the wilderness. The serpent tried to sweep her away with a torrent and the earth swallowed up the river. The dragon went to war against those who kept God's commands and held fast to their testimony about Jesus.

REVELATION 13

While the dragon stood on the shore, a beast with ten horns, seven heads and ten crowns rose out of the sea. It resembled a leopard, with feet like a bear and a mouth like a lion. The dragon gave the beast great authority. One of the heads appeared wounded, but the wound had been healed. People worshipped the beast, who uttered proud words and blasphemies for forty-two months. The beast waged war on God's people and was given authority over every tribe, people, language and nation. God's people needed endurance and faithfulness. A second beast came from the earth, exercising authority on behalf of the first beast and performing great signs, like making fire coming down from heaven. The second beast deceived the earth and ordered an image set up to honor the first beast. Anyone who refused to worship the image was killed. The second beast forced everyone to put a mark on their forehead and hand. Without it they could not buy or sell. The number of the beast, the number of a man, was 666.

REVELATION 14

The Lamb and the 144,000 stood on Mount Zion while harps played and they sang a new song. The 144,000 had not defiled themselves with women, remaining virgins. They followed the Lamb, never lied and were blameless. Then an angel flew in the air with the gospel to proclaim to every nation.

A second angel announced that Babylon the Great had fallen. A third angel proclaimed judgment on those who those who received the mark on their forehead and hand. Then a white cloud appeared and sitting on it was one like a son of man with a gold crown with sickle. An angel announced that it was harvest time and another angel swung his sickle, gathering the grapes and throwing them into the winepress. Blood flowed out of the press as high as the horses' bridles.

REVELATION 15

Seven angels with seven plagues appeared. One of the four living creatures gave the seven angels seven golden bowls filled with the wrath of God. The temple was filled with smoke of God's glory and power and no one could enter the temple until the seven plagues were complete.

REVELATION 16

When the first bowl of wrath was poured out, festering sores broke out on the people with the mark of the beast. The second angel poured the second bowl into the sea, turning it into blood. The third angel poured out the third bowl into the rivers and springs, turning them into blood. The fourth angel poured the fourth bowl onto the sun, allowing it to scorch the people of the earth. The fifth angel poured out the fifth bowl on the throne of the beast, plunging his kingdom into darkness. The sixth angel poured the sixth bowl into the river Euphrates, drying it up. Impure spirits, looking like frogs, came out of the mouths of the dragon, the beast and the false prophet. The kings of the world gathered at Armageddon. The seventh angel poured out the seventh bowl on the temple and the biggest earthquake ever occurred. The great city split into three parts. The cities of the nations collapsed. Every island fled. Mountains disappeared. Huge hailstones, nearly one hundred pounds in weight, fell on people. The people cursed God.

REVELATION 17

An angel showed John the great prostitute who sat by many waters. The kings of the earth committed adultery with her and she intoxicated them. The woman sat on a scarlet beast with seven heads and ten horns. On her forehead was written mysterious names: Babylon the Great / The Mother of Prostitutes / the Abominations of the Earth. She was drunk the blood of God's people. The seven heads and the ten horns represented kings from the past, present and future. They will wage war against the Lamb. The waters represented all nations and languages. The beast and the ten horns will hate the prostitute and bring her to ruin. The woman was the great city that ruled over the kings of the earth.

REVELATION 18
Another angel with great authority announced the fall of the great city called Babylon the Great. Demons, impure spirits and unclean animals dwelt there. Another voice cried for the people to get out of the city. The kings of the earth, the merchants and the ship captains mourned the city's destruction while God's people were told to rejoice. The great city was going down, never to be the place of revelry again.

REVELATION 19
Heaven sang hallelujah in praise of God's victory over the great prostitute. The twenty-four elders and four living creatures worshipped God. Blessed are those who are invited to the wedding supper of the Lamb. The rider on the white horse appeared, called Faithful and True and the word of God. The armies of heaven followed him. From his mouth, the sharp sword and in his hand an iron scepter. The beast, the kings of the earth and the armies waged war on the rider and his armies. The beast was captured with the false prophet and both were thrown into the lake of fire. The armies were killed by the sword coming out the rider's mouth.

REVELATION 20
An angel seizes the dragon (Satan/devil) and binds him with a chain for a thousand years. He is locked in the Abyss then set free. The souls of those beheaded (because of their testimony for Jesus and because they did not take the mark of the beast) came to life and reigned with Christ. This is the first resurrection. After the thousand years, Satan is released and

deceives the nations. They march against God but fire from heaven devours them. The devil is thrown into the lake of fire with the beast and the false prophet forever. At the great white throne, the books are opened and the dead judged. The sea and the grave give up their dead. Those not in the Book of Life are thrown into the lake of fire. This is the second death.

REVELATION 21

John saw a new heaven and new earth as the holy city came down out of heaven. Now God would dwell with his people. He will wipe away every tear from their eyes. No more mourning, crying or pain. Everything will be new. God will be the father and everyone else his children. The sinners who refuse God are sent to the lake of fire...the second death. The Holy City shone with twelve beautiful jewels, with twelve gates named after the tribes of Israel and twelve foundations named after the apostles. The angel measured the city—a square, as high as it was long. There was no temple, because God and the Lamb are the temple. There is no sun or moon because God is the light. The gates are never to be shut since nothing impure will ever enter it.

REVELATION 22

The angel showed John the river of life flowing from the throne of God and the Lamb. It goes down the center of the great city street, with the tree of life on both sides (12 crops of them), yielding fruit every month. The throne sits in the city and the servants serve God. We all see his face. There's no more night because God provides the light. Everyone reigns forever. Jesus is coming soon. Keep the words of the prophecy written here. John declared that he saw all these things. The angel said not to seal up these words because the time was near. Jesus promised to reward everyone according to what they have done. He is the Alpha and the Omega, the First and the Last, the Beginning and the End, Root and Offspring of David, the Bright Morning Star. Come, said the Spirit and the Bride. If you are thirsty, drink the free gift of the water of life. Don't add anything to these words or take anything away. Jesus is coming soon. Amen!

ABOUT THE AUTHOR

Troy Schmidt began writing animation in Los Angeles in 1985 (*Dennis the Menace, Heathcliff, Flintstone Kids*). In 1992, he moved to Orlando to write for *The Mickey Mouse Club*, for three seasons. He adapted a Max Lucado children's book *Hermie* into a video, then created and wrote all the future video installments and twenty Hermie books. Troy directed documentary footage in Israel for iLumina Gold, then returned in 2008 to host a documentary entitled "In His Shoes: The Life of Jesus" for GLO Bible software. Troy was also a producer for the GSN game show "The American Bible Challenge" starring Jeff Foxworthy and wrote the board game based on the show.

Troy is married to Barbie and they have three grown boys. He is a campus pastor at First Baptist Church Windermere, Florida.

PRAYING THROUGH THE BIBLE SERIES

Genesis   Exodus   Leviticus   Numbers   Deuteronomy
Joshua/Judges/Ruth   Psalms   Matthew   Mark   Luke
John   Acts   Romans   Galatians/Ephesians/Philippians/Colossians
1 & 2 Corinthians   Revelation   Praying Through the Law
Praying Through the Minor Prophets   Praying Through the Gospels

BOOKS

Bible Trivia, Jokes & Fun Facts for Kids (Bethany House)
The Extreme Old/New Testament Bible Trivia Challenge (Broadstreet)
The Best 100 Bible Verses About Prayer (Bethany House)
The Best 100 Bible Verses About Heaven (Bethany House)
The 100 Most Encouraging Verses of the Bible (Bethany House)
This Means War: A Prayer Journal (B&H Kids)
The American Bible Challenge Daily Reader: Volume 1 (Thomas Nelson)
Chapter by Chapter: An Easy to Use Summary of the Entire Bible (Amazon)
Reason for Hope: Answers to Your Bible Questions (Amazon)
Reason for Hope: MORE Answers to Your Bible Questions (Amazon)
Reason for Hope: Answers to Your Questions about Heaven (Amazon)
40 Days: A Daily Devotion for Spiritual Renewal (Amazon)
Saved: Answers That Can Save Your Life (Amazon)
Release: Why God Wants You to Let Go (Amazon)
In His Shoes: The Life of Jesus (Amazon)
Laughing Matters (Lillenas Publishing)
Foundations: A Study of God (Amazon)
Living the Real Life: 12 Studies for Building Biblical Community (Amazon)

THE EXTREME OLD TESTAMENT / NEW TESTAMENT BIBLE TRIVIA CHALLENGE

Over 6,000 questions, written in the order as they appear in the Bible – from Genesis to Revelation. One question appears from EVERY chapter in the Bible. Great to use for a personal or group fun, for long car trips or morning devotions. Get to know the Bible in a fun and challenging way.

THE 100 BEST BIBLE VERSES SERIES

The 100 verses that are highlighted include the well-known passages as well as hidden treasures. Each verse contains a brief devotional reading that will help you find comfort from the text, and in the process draw ever nearer to God. The book's length and focus make it perfect as a daily meditation or to read as a family. It also makes an ideal gift for those who love the Bible and seek the hope of God's promises.

IN HIS SHOES: THE LIFE OF JESUS

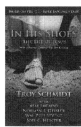

IN HIS SHOES: THE LIFE OF JESUS journeys to the all the places Jesus visited, from birth to death to resurrection and ascension. To help him along in his journey, Troy met up some of the greatest thinkers and writers from diverse perspectives to help him understand the experience (Max Lucado, Norman Geisler, William Paul Young, Joel Hunter and Avner Goren). The book includes a chapter-by-chapter Study Guide for Small Groups to use with the documentary which is available on the Glo Bible.

310

REASON FOR HOPE:
ANSWERS TO YOUR BIBLE QUESTIONS

With over 50 answers to your Bible questions in every book, this book series answers some of the toughest questions people ask about God, their faith and the Bible.

PRAYING THROUGH THE BIBLE SERIES

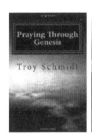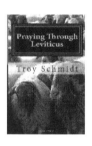

PRAYING THROUGH THE BIBLE SERIES takes the reader through written prayers, with additional prompts to help you continue a focused time for prayer based on the passages.

There is also space to record what God is saying to you during your time with Him. By the end of the book, you will have prayed through God's word and have a deeper understanding and appreciation for God's word.

Titles in the series include:

Genesis   Exodus   Leviticus   Numbers
Deuteronomy Joshua/Judges/Ruth   Psalms
Matthew   Mark   Luke   John   Acts
Romans   1 & 2 Corinthians
Galatians/Ephesians/Philippians/Colossians   Revelation
          Praying Through the Law (First 5 Books of the Bible)
                Praying Through the Minor Prophets
                Praying Through the Gospels

SAVED: ANSWERS THAT CAN SAVE YOUR LIFE

SAVED answers 25 questions that many ask before they find God—good questions, tough questions—that drown many in doubt and confusion before they find the answers. Questions such as: Do you have to know the Bible to be saved? Why was Jesus crucified? Is Christianity the only true faith? Don't we have to believe and do good works? Is the Trinity one God or three? How are those who never hear the Gospel saved? How am I saved?

RELEASE: WHY GOD WANTS YOU TO LET GO

Jesus focused on the concept of releasing. He told people to let go of things all the time. Why do we need to know that today? Our hands are so full that we can't receive God's blessing. Our grip is so tight that we can't grab on to what really matters. RELEASE explores this concept found throughout the Gospels – what was released and what the person received in return. From the characters in the parables to the real people in Jesus' life, we'll see that releasing our lives actually fills our lives.

40 DAYS: A DAILY DEVOTION FOR SPIRITUAL RENEWAL

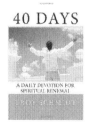

40 is a very significant number in the Bible, especially when it comes to 40 days. Some of most significant characters of the Old and New Testament had experiences that lasted 40 days—Noah, Moses, Joshua, David, Elijah, Ezekiel, Jonah, Jesus. What happened during that time and what did it take 40 days for them to experience? Renewal.
40 DAYS examines their life-changing encounters and draws from their lessons of transformation using 40 daily devotions you can use for your own renewal experience. It worked for them…why not you. After 40 days, you'll come back as good as new.

THIS MEANS WAR: A STRATEGIC PRAYER JOURNAL

The teen years can be tough; don't try to make it through without one of your most powerful weapons—prayer. A companion book to the movie *War Room,* this new kind of journal will get you ready for a new kind of prayer life, one that's strong, growing, and reflects just how powerful prayer is. Each short chapter tackles one of the biggest questions teens have about prayer. Just-right journaling prompts will then get you thinking—and praying—and reinforce the real power of fighting battles on your knees.

THE AMERICAN BIBLE CHALLENGE DAILY READER

In fall 2012, a new show premiered on the Game Show Network that quickly surprised Hollywood. Hosted by Jeff Foxworthy, *The American Bible Challenge* built up an audience of 2.3 million viewers in just nine weeks, making it the highest-rated show ever in GSN history. Now, the producer for the show, Troy Schmidt, with a foreword written by host Jeff Foxworthy, has released a daily reader based on *The American Bible Challenge* designed to take us deeper into the questions from the show and the life applications that they inspire.

CHAPTER BY CHAPTER: AN EASY TO USE SUMMARY OF THE ENTIRE BIBLE

The Bible is an intimidating book. It's easy to get lost in its pages. We all, sometimes, just need a little help to navigate through its pages. CHAPTER BY CHAPTER walks you through the Bible so that you understand all 929 chapters of the Old Testament and all 260 chapters of the New Testament. This book is not meant to replace your reading of God's word but it is useful as a reference guide to understand what you are reading or where to find passages and stories you know are in the Bible. It's time to begin your study of the entire Bible…chapter by chapter.

72063198R00177

Made in the USA
Columbia, SC
09 June 2017